THE FOUN⌐
CHRISTIA

THE FOUNDATION OF CHRISTIAN ETHICS

Michael Keeling

T&T CLARK
EDINBURGH

T&T CLARK LTD
59 GEORGE STREET
EDINBURGH EH2 2LQ
SCOTLAND

.First published 1990
Latest impression 1994

ISBN 0 567 29180 4

British Library Cataloguing-in-Publication Data
A catalogue record for this book is available
from the British Library

Typeset by Trinity Typesetting, Edinburgh
Printed and bound in Great Britain by The Cromwell Press, Wiltshire

CONTENTS

Acknowledgements

This book could not have been written without the help in discussion over many years of the students in St Mary's College in the University of St Andrews and of colleagues in the Faculty of Divinity and in particular my colleagues in the former Department of Practical Theology and Christian Ethics, Professor James Whyte, Douglas Trotter and Steven Mackie. Thanks are also due to those who have been responsible for the word-processing, Miss M. C. Blackwood and Miss Karen Sillence, and to Dr R. A. Piper for advice and practical help on formatting. The responsibility for all remaining errors and omissions is, of course, my own.

Copyright Permissions

Biblical quotations are taken from the Jerusalem Bible, published and copyright 1966, 1967 and 1968 by Darton, Longman and Todd Ltd and Doubleday & Co Inc, and are used by permission of the publishers.

The quotation from Matthew Arnold, 'Dover Beach', taken from ARNOLD: POETRY AND PROSE, 1939, Oxford University Press, is reprinted by permission of the publishers.

The quotations from Anna Akhmatova, REQUIEM AND POEM WITHOUT A HERO, 1976, translated by D. M. Thomas and published by Paul Elek, a division of Grafton Books, are reprinted by permission of John Johnson Ltd.

The quotations from St Augustine, CONFESSIONS, translated by R. S. Pine-Coffin, copyright © R. S. Pine-Coffin, 1961, are reprinted by permission of the publishers, Penguin Books Ltd.

The quotations from William Blake are taken from BLAKE: COMPLETE WORKS, 1974, edited by Geoffrey Keynes, and are reprinted by permission of the publishers, Oxford University Press.

The quotations from Jerome Bruner are reprinted by permission of the publishers from ACTUAL MINDS, POSSIBLE WORLDS by Jerome S. Bruner, Cambridge, Mass.: Harvard Uni-

SHOWINGS, translated by Edmund Colledge, O.S.A. and James Walsh, S.J., 1978, by permission of the publishers, Paulist Press and SPCK.

The quotations from Jurgen Moltmann, GOD IN CREATION, 1985, are reprinted by permission of SCM Press and Harper and Row Inc.

The quotations from George Steiner, LANGUAGE AND SILENCE, are reprinted by permission of Atheneum Publishers, an imprint of Macmillan Publishing Company, and Faber and Faber. Copyright © 1967 George Steiner.

The quotations from F. R. Tennant, THE ORIGIN AND PROPAGATION OF SIN, 1902, are reprinted by permission of Cambridge University Press.

The quotations from Thomas Traherne, CENTURIES, edited by Hilda Vaughn, published by The Faith Press, 1963, are reprinted by permission of Cassell Plc.

The quotations from MORALITY AND CHRISTIAN ETHICS, edited by Jan L. Womer, copyright © 1987 Fortress Press, are reprinted by permission of Augsburg Fortress.

1
Setting the Scene:
Christian Ethics in the Twentieth Century

In the twentieth century Christian ethics has become concentrated on the question of social justice. The radical potential of Christianity has been awakened by the realisation that social change is both possible and unavoidable if we are to survive on the planet earth. The search for relevant models to connect our understanding of God with our perception of human need has been long and confused, but it has been increasingly marked by the knowledge that there is no understanding of God that is valid except in the context of a stance on particular human needs. What has tied all the models together has been the belief that the Gospel is about changing the world, not only in some distant future but by joining in God's action in the present moment. The enormous productivity of contextual theology — the belief that the Gospel is about the liberation of all persons from all forms of oppression — has been one of the great revolutions in the history of Christian thought. How has this come about?

(i) The Social Gospel Movement

At the beginning of the twentieth century the problems of Christian ethics seemed largely to be solved. Confidence in prosperity and technological progress was unchecked until the First World War entered the period of the great slaughter of 1916 and 1917. Technical problems existed to be solved and industrial capacity existed to solve them. Social problems were either a part of the natural order or a small but necessary price to pay for a God-given liberty of production.

In the United States the strong bias against the intervention of federal or state power in the economic and social problems of families and individuals meant that the Christian emphasis was on voluntary societies to provide relief. The flood of immigrants from Europe in the second half of the nineteenth century put pressure on the rapidly growing industrial system and some church leaders began to see that personal religion and personal charity might not be enough to combat

1

the problem of unemployment.

The beginning of the Social Gospel movement may be traced back to the work of Washington Gladden who, in 1875 in Springfield, Massachusetts, addressed employers attending the North Church on the responsibility for actively providing jobs. Ronald White comments: 'The experience of Washington Gladden was repeated again and again in other settings; ministers and laypersons, nurtured in an evangelical religion that emphasized individual salvation, confronted with a new world born of the industrial revolution being forced to rethink their whole understanding of Christian faith and life' (1978:54).

The basic note was nevertheless one of confidence. Walter Rauschenbusch, the leading theologian of the movement, announced in his Taylor Lectures in April 1917 on *A Theology for the Social Gospel* : 'We have a social gospel. We need a systematic theology large enough to match it and vital enough to back it' (1918:1). Rauschenbusch extended the concept of sin from the personal to the collective, the 'supra-personal forces' of city councils, police forces, trade unions, industrial companies and national states. These collectivities had the potential to constitute either the Kingdom of Evil or the Kingdom of God. Personal salvation remained an important part of the gospel, but the test of true individual conversion was conversion to others. 'Complete salvation, therefore, would consist in an attitude of love in which he would freely co-ordinate his life with the life of his fellows in obedience to the loving impulses of the spirit of God, thus taking his part in a divine organism of mutual service' (1918:98). The salvation of the supra-personal forces would consist also in their learning to become co-operative and democratic.

Co-operation in business and democracy in government were Rauschenbusch's practical answers to the problem of the collectivities. The theology which was to back this remedy was the theology of the Kingdom of God, which for Rauschenbusch meant the assurance that Jesus was leading human history in the direction of ever greater co-operation. This Kingdom was the whole of humanity organized according to the will of God; both the personal salvation of individuals and the whole life of the Christian church were to be seen as part of this process of the progressive reign of love in human affairs.

In this perspective the importance of Jesus was not in the union of the divine nature with an individual human nature in the Incarnation, nor in the atoning power of a sacrificial death, but in the new experience of God not as judge but as the loving creator who forgave sins freely. It was this new understanding of God through Jesus that gave power to human beings to overcome evil in personal and social life. 'So we have in Jesus a perfect religious personality, a spiritual life completely filled by the realization of a God who is love' (1918:154). The question of the future hope still remained, because the Kingdom was seen clearly in Jesus but was not yet fulfilled on earth; but the process of fulfilment should be seen as one of development rather than one of waiting for a future catastrophe.

Rauschenbusch freely admitted that his theology owed a debt to Schleiermacher and to Ritschl, but claimed to have grounded the theology of the Kingdom more firmly in the present social reality and in the human personality of Jesus. There was an element of Christian spiritualism in his teaching, whether conscious or unconscious, which no doubt contributed to his universalism and his lack of interest in a doctrine of atonement. His achievement along with other Social Gospel theorists was that within the general social and economic optimism of the late nineteenth and early twentieth centuries he saw clearly that the evils of urban poverty could not be dissociated from the structures of industrial capitalism. The experience of his own years as a pastor in the New York district nicknamed 'Hell's Kitchen' gave him the practical basis for an attempt to reform theology and ethics. But in the end his answer lay in a personal conversion to co-operation by the parties involved in the collectivities, rather than in a detailed analysis of the nature of industrial production and the conflicts which arise in it.

(ii) Christian Realism

Rauschenbusch remarked of Ritschl that 'He was born too

early to get sociological ideas' (1918:139). So indeed was Rauschenbusch himself, but the next figure of importance on the American scene both understood the importance of social analysis and challenged some of the prescriptions for society that social science was by then putting forward. In *Moral Man and Immoral Society*, published in 1932, Reinhold Niebuhr accepted a basic contention of Marx and Engels, that the problem of society is the problem of conflicts of interest between social groups, rather than of the moral behaviour of the individual. The relationships of groups, said Niebuhr, were not ordered by the same morality as those of individual persons; persons could move in the order of love, but groups moved in the order of justice. The basis of love was sacrificial giving of the self, but the basis of justice was the distribution of power. The religious hope that love could order the relations of whole societies could only be an illusion, but an illusion that was none the less valuable and even essential because it created hope.

Niebuhr's argument here presented two separate problems, about the nature of power and the nature of love.

The first was the recognition of the reality of power. Dealing with social psychology, Niebuhr wrote that social scientists often aim at 'accommodation', a solution by the mutual moderating of demands. 'But will a disinherited group, such as the Negroes for instance, ever win full justice in society in this fashion?' he asked (1932:xvii). For what was being sought was a transfer of power and it would be impossible for any group being asked to give up power to regard that demand objectively. Niebuhr did not go all the way with the Marxist analysis of society; he recognised the dangers both of cynicism and of vengeance that are built into the class theory of society. But he emphasized that the attraction of Marxism for industrial workers derived from its rootedness in their day-to-day experience, and his own life as a pastor among the anxieties of the new mass production motor industry in Detroit gave credibility to the view that 'the full maturity of American capitalism will inevitably be followed by the emergence of the American Marxian proletarian' (1932:144). America in fact overcame the great economic depression of the 1930's, and its economic resilience remains today the main hope of the western world. But Niebuhr put the analysis of power relations as a basic element of industrial society permanently on the agenda of Christian ethics.

The second problem stemmed directly from this fact. The separation which Niebuhr made between personal relationships and social justice arose in part from his very high view of Christian faith. 'The religious ethic (the Christian ethic more particularly, though not solely) insists that the needs of the neighbour shall be met, without a careful computation of relative needs' (1932:57). The religious demand he saw as always being absolute, 'millenial', in the sense of always placing its hope beyond the possibilities of the present time. It was personal because its obligations were felt to be towards God who is symbolized as the fulfilment of what is personal. No loyalty to a group could be as great as the loyalty to a person. 'The holy will is a personal will' (1932:53). But in denying the operation of this holy will at the social level he cut God off from history in a way which is unacceptable to Christian faith.

In the Gifford Lectures for 1939, *The Nature and Destiny of Man*, Niebuhr gave a more dynamic account of the tension between the absolute love of God and the reality of present history. The struggle for justice he now saw as being in a dialectical relationship with the law of love. 'Love is both the fulfilment and the negation of all achievements of justice in history' (1943: 246). Love had now two aspects: 'mutual love', which was concern for others within the possibilities of history, and 'sacrificial love', the love of Jesus on the cross, which took place within history but which would be seen to be justified only when history was transcended in its own overcoming by the Kingdom of God. Mutual love provided the opportunity for grounding sacrificial love in history; but sacrificial love was the power which enabled mutual love to proceed without fear. The dialectic of the two loves existed fully only in Jesus; but the weakness both of religion and of politics was the continuing tendency to opt solely for one or the other.

This tension between transcendence and history, of which

5

Niebuhr's Gifford Lectures are one of the best expressions in the twentieth century, none the less leaves open a host of decisions on practical questions. Niebuhr practised what he called 'Christian realism', recognizing the necessities of power in the opposition to National Socialism in Germany and in the acceptance of the retention of atomic weapons after 1945. Some followers have suggested that with the same realism he might have opposed the later stages of the American involvement in Vietnam and the present form of the nuclear arms race. What is quite clear is that his magisterial analysis of the relationship of Christian faith and history was not meant to relieve anyone of the responsibility for decision; the whole point of the analysis was that no Christian decision could ignore either history or faith.

(iii) Dialectical Theology

The leisurely reflection available to the theologians of the USA was less available to the theologians of Europe, whose lives were being shaped by more brutal forces than economic depression. The experience of Karl Barth as a pastor at Safenwil in Switzerland from 1911 was rooted in the same problems of industrial life as Rauschenbusch and Niebuhr, giving him a life-long interest in socialism. But the most powerful theological protest of the twentieth century came from Barth's observation of the manner in which liberal Protestant theology was serving the propaganda interests of the competing powers in the war of 1914-1918 and of the horrors of that war itself. 'The Gospel is not a religious message to inform mankind of their divinity or to tell them how to become divine. The Gospel proclaims a God utterly distinct from men' (1933:28). These words, from the beginning of Barth's commentary on *The Epistle to the Romans*, first published in 1918, laid down the basic premise of dialectical theology, that God's word to the human being was always a declaration of human sin, of human inability to construct out of human resources anything that is good. 'Whether we attempt to build up some positive human thing or to demolish what others have erected, all our endeavours to justify ourselves are in one way or another shattered in pieces' (1933:490).

This applied above all to the possibility of human co-operation in the divine act of forgiveness. In his lectures on *Ethics*, given in 1928-1929 and published posthumously, Barth said 'Because forgiveness is forgiveness for Christ's sake, all human co-operation is sharply excluded from that which is given to us by forgiveness' (1981:287). The present time was a time of 'crisis', of judgment, for individuals and for societies. The only co-operation God allowed to human beings was the recognition of the necessity of that judgment.

The second stage of the dialectic was nevertheless the recognition that after God's 'No' there came God's 'Yes'. The human being who accepted the negative judgment became open to the free gift of God's love in Christ. The word 'obedience' changed from a connotation of fear to a connotation of freedom. Within obedience to the command of God came a gracious freedom of action limited only by the fact of being in one concrete situation rather than another. Only in the late essays 'The Gift of Freedom' and 'The Humanity of God' did Barth emphasize this fully. But it was always implicit in the notion of dialectic. So at the end of the lectures on ethics he said 'Christian freedom does not mean that we no longer stand under the command, that our conduct is no longer obedience. It means that we stand under the command that we ourselves affirm, that our obedience is our own will' (1981:502).

By 1953 he included both natural freedom and the freedom of eternal life in God's gift of freedom to human beings. 'To call a man free is to recognize that God has *given* him freedom. Human freedom is enacted within history, that history which leads to the ultimate salvation of man' (1960:75). The natural freedom of human beings could be understood only within the freedom of God, who was always a partisan for human beings. Human freedom was sharing in the freedom flowing from God. For this reason even Christian ethics could never take the form of a set of rules. 'Holy Scripture defies being forced into a set of rules; it is a mistake to use it as such' (1960:85). Human beings took the risk of making ethical demands on one another in concrete situations, but only with due humility before the freedom of the other, the freedom of the self, and the freedom of God.

This sharp call to obedience to the God who was always in opposition to human works, which was at the same time an assertion of the unlimited power of God to work both through and against human life, gave a theological basis to those Protestant Christians who opposed National Socialist policy in Germany. Barth himself, after professorships in Göttingen and Münster, was Professor of Systematic Theology in Bonn from 1930 and took part in the political opposition to the Nazis and in the formation of the 'Confessing Church' in opposition to the unified Protestant state church set up after Hitler assumed the Chancellorship in 1933. He lost his teaching post by refusing to take the new oath of loyalty to Hitler, and from 1935 taught theology in Basel. The very transcendence of the authority of God forced Christians in this moment of crisis into actions that were necessarily political. The God who was 'utterly distinct' from human beings was not in any sense remote from present human life.

The engagement of theology with political life was carried further by Dietrich Bonhoeffer. As a German citizen opposed to the Nazi government he faced the options of leaving the country, staying passive in the face of open evil, or taking part in direct political resistance. In 1933 he went to a pastorate in London, but in 1935 he returned to Germany to run an illegal training centre for ministers of the Confessing Church at Finkenwalde, on a model of community which he described in *Life Together*. In 1939 he was persuaded to move to the USA but soon returned to Germany in the knowledge that this meant a decision to resist the Nazi regime by any means possible. He was arrested in 1943 and executed in April 1945, just before the end of the war in Europe. Although Bonhoeffer was already a major theologian by 1939, the nature of his commitment to the struggle for the Christian faith in the last years of his life gave a particular value to the two fragmentary works he wrote during his imprisonment, which were published after the war, *Ethics* and *Letters and Papers from Prison.*

At New Year 1943 Bonhoeffer wrote a review of the effects of the past ten years on his own life and the lives of those around him, in which he asked of the future after the Nazis, 'Will our inward power of resistance be strong enough, and our honesty with ourselves remorseless enough, for us to find our way back to simplicity and straightforwardness?' (1971:17). For Bonhoeffer the question was always the practical question of the nature of human obedience. In 1937 in *The Cost of Discipleship* he had expressed the question in its sharpest form: 'The only man who has the right to say that he is justified by grace alone is the man who has left all to follow Christ' (1959:43). In the reflections at the beginning of 1943 he had come to see 'that personal suffering is a more effective key, a more rewarding principle for exploring the world in thought and action than personal good fortune' (1971:17).

It is the nature of this key which was explored in the *Ethics.* What seems to have happened is that in the midst of the great suffering brought upon a whole civilization Bonhoeffer's mind turned more to the general human condition of suffering and less to the absolute announcement of God's opposition to human sin. Precisely out of the destruction caused by demonic forces, Bonhoeffer was able to announce the taking-over of the whole world by Christ. Over and over again in the *Ethics* he stressed that the world was already reconciled to God in Christ — not the world as it shall be, but the world as it is in its present disorder. 'The world is not divided between Christ and the devil, but, whether it recognizes it or not, it is solely and entirely the world of Christ' (1963:176). This reconciliation, announced in the New Testament, was always and everywhere a source of joy.

The purpose of the existence of the world was that Jesus Christ was taking form in human beings. Because only a part of humanity recognized its redemption, those in whom Jesus was actually taking form constituted the church. 'The Church is nothing but a section of humanity in which Christ has really taken form' (1963:64). This church was clearly not co-terminous with any

9

existing ecclesiastical institution, though Bonhoeffer did not have time to explore this problem in detail. The church remained under judgment and its function in society was to be the place of the recognition of guilt; a society could not be justified by grace in the same way as an individual, but its practical justification consisted in the restoration of justice, order and peace. The church thus clearly had a role towards the political order, even if this was put first in negative terms, for the strength of the negation arose from the greatness of the hope for the world embodied in the church.

From his own human experience Bonhoeffer did not deny the existence of tension between the already-redeemed and the not-yet-redeemed. In the 'ultimate', the justified existence, there was no ethical debate or method. The method and rule was simply to receive forgiveness and to act in the fulness of the presence of Christ. But although this ultimate had form in the present, present history was also experienced as the 'penultimate', the time of struggle, defeat and hope. Bonhoeffer rejected both the radical solution of attempting to live only in the ultimate and the liberal solution of compromising by pushing the ultimate away into the distant future. The Christian had to live in a tension, both experiencing the ultimate within the penultimate and hoping for the victory of the ultimate over the penultimate. Such a life was possible because the tension was already resolved in Christ, who was Lord both of the ultimate and of the penultimate. 'In Christ the reality of God meets the reality of the world and allows us to share in this real encounter. Christian life is participation in the encounter of Christ with the world' (1963:110). The penultimate, the not-yet-redeemed, thus had its own validity as the preparation for the future of Christ the lord of all.

This complex and fragmentary discussion in the Ethics did not entirely solve the problem posed in *Letters and Papers from Prison* by Bonhoeffer's references to the world as 'come of age' (1971:327; 341). The argument seems to have combined three themes. The first was that the world had become secular; it saw no need of God, having reasonably effective answers to most of its practical problems and anticipating the finding of solutions to others at some time in the future. The second was the need for Christians to live simply in the world, making no claims to power or authority, living the life of the world as it was given and seeing in it not their own sufferings but the sufferings of God. The third was that this life of simplicity required both the individual and the church to live for others — not to worry about problems of doctrine and ecclesiastical order, but to join in Jesus' participation in human life. 'The church is the church only when it exists for others' (1971:382).

The question may be asked whether Bonhoeffer was moving towards a theology of the action of Christ in the world as being in the creative possibilities of human action in general rather than in the proclamation of the gospel directly? Certainly this was the direction in which his ideas were developed by others in the years after 1945.

What would he have made, for example, of that spiritual resistance to Hitler among Communists and atheists as well as Christians, so movingly recorded in the collection of letters from prisoners of the regime in *Dying We Live?* (Gollwitzer, 1958) The most that can be said now is that Bonhoeffer saw the proclamation of the gospel to lie as much in the sharing of the suffering of the poor and oppressed as in the preaching of the church — but never one without the other. A time had come for the church to put aside both worldly pretensions and obsession with its own activities, in order to serve God better in the world.

Hidden within this model of dialectical theology was another and more problematical ethical concept, that of situationality. The point can be observed most clearly in the contribution of Emil Brunner, the third of the great German-speaking theologians who remade European theology between the wars. In *The Divine Imperative,* first published in 1932, Brunner attempted to resolve the tension between the state of the world and the demands of the Gospel by defining two sets of moral imperatives. The first consisted of those commandments which arose from the common human nature given in creation — the 'orders of creation'. This common morality, largely to be found in the Old Testament, was sufficient for the day-to-day running of major institutions such as the family, government, industry and the church.

The other moral imperative came as a direct command to the individual in a moment of serious choice. Here salvation broke through into the creation in a new way. This pure divine command could not be specified in the form of lists of rules. 'Precisely on the borderline between the past and the present stands the *present moment*, the moment of decision' (1937:122). All the guidelines of the past, including the Biblical revelation, could contribute to the decision; so too could the promise of faith for the future. But the dynamic of Christian ethics was in the fact that the knowledge of the past and the hope for the future converged on the present moment. The decision taken now would be the right decision.

This situationality is the chief problem of the model of the pure transcendence of God. Brunner gave a very attractive picture of the nature of the divine command as a gift from God. 'God reveals His own Nature where He manifests Himself as the Giver of life, as the Creator of the Good, where at one and the same time He gives salvation and goodness, life and love' (1937:115). The divine command was a single command, to recognize the source of life in creative love. But when the command was recognized not only as a gift, but also as a demand, what was the content of the demand?

Brunner's attempt to solve this problem by retreating to the notion of the 'orders of creation' did not work. Jewish ethics had always considered that the world was given a fundamental moral structure in its creation by God. Even Paul in the Epistle to the Romans had recognized that the Gentiles had a moral law written in their own hearts — but he also thought that it was not doing them much good (Rom. 2.14-16; 3.9). When Brunner suggested, following Martin Luther, that from the fact of creation certain institutions were necessary to maintain corporate life, his list was necessarily culture-bound. Brunner's ideas on marriage were not in fact those of the ancient Romans, or of modern Islam, and in one important respect, the permissibility of divorce, they differed from the views of his contemporary, Karl

Barth. There could be no general human ground for saying that a modern Protestant view of marriage was something that necessarily arose out of creation. On the other hand, if the orders were part of revelation rather than part of general human experience, then revelation became a series of commandments, rather than the one divine command.

The notion of the orders of creation thus set up a conflict between the demands of the ordinary daily duties and the sacrificial love suggested by the action of God in Jesus Christ in the Gospel. It could not be part of the normal duties of the state official or the bourgeois family to behave like the Good Samaritan or to take literally all the injunctions of the Sermon on the Mount. Brunner indeed suggested that such total love was not possible in any group situation. 'Real community, love, is never given to a collective body, even if this body were to consist of two people only; real community only exists between the "I" and a single "Thou"' (1937:328).

However the model is structured, it seems that there is an inevitable tension in the Christian notion of social justice, between what is possible at the present time and what a full model of Christian community would be like, if such a thing could really be brought about in the world. Only in occasional periods of prosperity and optimism does this tension seem to disappear from Christian thought.

(iv) Theologies of Liberation

In the post-war period, once the immediate task of reconstruction was over, theology turned to the question of how the action of God could be seen in the events that had just passed, and how that action could be envisaged in the years to come. In Europe the beginning of liberation theology among Protestant theologians may be dated from the publication in Germany by Jürgen Moltmann of *The Theology of Hope* in 1967. Moltmann was much influenced by the Marxist philosopher and historian Ernst Bloch, who published *Das Prinzip Hoffnung* in 1959. From Bloch Moltmann learned to reject the notion of Christian eschatology as a theory of events which at the end of time would break into

13

history from the outside. Rather eschatology was a matter of present hope, even hope against all present reason. 'Hope alone is to be called "realistic", because it alone takes seriously the possibilities with which all reality is fraught' (1967:25). The promise could be expressed only in terms of the present, as affirmation and negation of the present, not as a mystic future. The content of the promise was that the world had a history which was open to God's future.

This dynamic understanding of revelation, not as repeating a story that had been told in the past, nor as a story of a distant future, but as a story of what was possible in the near future stemming from present action, was about real historical possibilities. 'Hope, where it holds to the promises, hopes that the coming of God will bring it also "this and that" — namely, his redeeming and restoring lordship in all things. It does not merely hope personally "in him", but has also substantial hopes of his lordship, his peace and his righteousness on earth' (1967:119). This argument was pursued with a detailed examination of the ground of this hope in the experience of the promises of God in the history of Israel and in the New Testament.

Of Jesus he argued that 'The Christian hope for the future comes of observing a specific, unique event — that of the resurrection and appearing of Jesus Christ' (1967:194). The contradiction between the future of God implied in the resurrection and the state of things in the present time created a tension which gave direction to mission in the present. To understand eschatology was not to have a knowledge of a great plan of God running through history, but to experience in the present the dialectic of the present and the future. The reality of the crucifixion committed the Christian deeply to action in the suffering world, the reality of the resurrection committed the Christian deeply to faith that the 'not yet' constituted a positive promise. A hope which was restricted to the church, or to the inner person without concern for the whole human environment, would be a denial of both the cross and the resurrection.

The calling was to participate in the divine righteousness, which was a power to undertake labour. 'That is why the man who is

14

justified begins to suffer under the contradiction of this world, in which he has a bodily solidarity, for he must in obedience seek the divine righteousness in his body on earth, and in all creatures' (1967:206). But the life of righteousness was the future life, in tension with the historical life which led to death. 'In the darkness of the pain of love, the man of hope discovers the dissension between the self and the body' (1967:213). The new life was the negation of the negative, the progressive widening of the grace inherent in the Christ-event to encompass all things.

The new life was fully understood as the 'kingdom of God'. The leadership of Yahweh in the Old Testament extended from the nomadic tribes of the Hebrews to all creation, but 'the universal expectation has its ground in remembering the particular historic reality of his sovereign action in Israel' (1967:217). Because the lordship of Yahweh became a universal promise in Jesus, the believer was compelled to accept the world in its present reality. 'He becomes homeless with the homeless, for the sake of the home of reconciliation. He becomes restless with the restless, for the sake of the peace of God. He becomes rightless with the rightless, for the sake of the divine right that is coming' (1967:224). In mission, Moltmann distinguished between 'the call' to the New Testament hope, and 'the callings', to service in history. 'The call always appears only in the singular. The callings, roles, functions and relationships which make a social claim on man, always appear in open multiplicity' (1967:333). The reference point must be the one call, but discipleship was a process of change within callings. It was the certainty about the one which made bearable the uncertainty about the others.

What Moltmann's argument lacked was an explicit rooting in the analysis of a particular society, although in a general way he was clearly responding to the needs of theological reconstruction in a Germany that was well-advanced on the task of physical reconstruction.

The theology of liberation really began with the publication by Gustavo Gutierrez of *A Theology of Liberation* in Lima in 1971. Gutierrez took as one of his starting points the failure in practice of policies of economic development to produce the results expected of them. In Latin America the push for self-sustained economic growth had not closed the gap with the more advanced industrial countries; on the contrary the gap had widened. International loans had led to the opening of countries to international investment, but because international economic structures did not change, the whole system had remained exploitative in relation to the poorer countries and 'development' merely increased their dependence on the richer countries. 'The underdevelopment of the poor countries, as an overall social fact, appears in its true light — as the historical by-product of the development of other countries' (1974:84).

But it would be misleading to analyse development simply in terms of economic growth, for growth was only one element in a total social process of the distribution of goods and services, the creation of income and the gaining of access to political power. The imbalance to which the term 'development' referred was also a general cultural gap. 'The poor, dominated nations keep falling behind; the gap continues to grow. The under-developed countries, in relative terms, are always further away from the cultural level of the centre countries; for some it is difficult ever to recover the lost ground' (1974:86). There was a real risk of dividing humanity into two different kinds of beings.

A purely economic analysis of the enforced dependence of the poor countries on the rich countries could be used to ignore the question of political power. The situation required also a class analysis, which would be a political analysis. 'Development theory must now take into account the situation of dependence and the possibility of becoming free from it' (1974:87-88). Because the practical effects of dependence were already felt, Latin America had entered into a revolutionary situation, in which the Cuban revolution had been a catalyst. But the 'spiral of violence', as Dom Helder Câmara, the Archbishop of Recife in Brazil, had called it (1974:40), was not an answer to the total situation. The use of violence in protest against the hidden violence already exercised through the existing institutions might at one time or another be unavoidable, but, as Câmara himself saw, 'liberation' needed to be analysed more deeply.

Gutierrez then addressed himself to the task of defining a theological understanding of liberation which could both be true to the Bible and to the teaching of the Catholic Church, and also respond to the real human situation in Latin America. In this he showed the two marks which have distinguished liberation theology. The first was a concern for a theology which was truly biblical, taking the Bible seriously as a book rooted in and speaking to human history, through creation, through salvation and through eschatology. 'The Word is the foundation and meaning of all human existence; this foundation is attested to and this meaning is concretized through human actions.' (1974:238).

The second mark, arising out of practical experience, was concern for the poor. 'But it will remain for the Church on a continent of misery and injustice to give the theme of poverty its proper importance; *the authenticity of the preaching of the Gospel message depends on this witness*' (1974:288). Again the treatment was strictly biblical; the book ended with an analysis of the biblical meaning of poverty. It ended also with an acknowledgement that finally liberation theology must come from the oppressed themselves.

Some of the thinking which lay behind Gutierrez' work had originated in the official teaching of the Roman Catholic Church. From the Encyclical Letter *Rerum Novarum*, ' On the Condition of the Working Classes', of 1881 onwards, the church was involved in an increasingly committed discussion of social problems. After 1945, however, Catholic theology experienced renewal in all areas of its life, in liturgy, in Bible study, in appreciation of the arts, and in dealing with the immense problems of reconstructing the physical and moral order in Europe. All these practical activities raised theological questions as critical scholarship began to recover some of the nerve lost in the 'modernist' crisis of 1907. These forces came together in 1959 when Pope John XXIII proposed to call an 'ecumenical council', a meeting of all bishops of the Roman Catholic Church. The intention was to complete the work of the First Vatican Council, which had met briefly in 1869-1870 and had managed only to define the powers of the Pope before being dispersed as a result of the

17

Italian occupation of Rome. The Pope intended that what became known as the Second Vatican Council should be an *aggiornamento*, a bringing up to date of the church in all its ways.

The Council met in Rome in a series of sessions between 1962 and 1965 under the presidency of John XXIII and after his death of Paul VI. Three areas of its work were of particular interest for the study of Christian ethics. The first was the 'Dogmatic Constitution on the Church', *Lumen Gentium*, in 1964, in which the church was defined primarily as 'the people of God' (Articles 9-17), rather than as a juridical and hierarchical structure, thus in effect reversing the priorities of Vatican I. The second was the 'Declaration on Religious Liberty', *Dignitatis Humanae*, in 1965, which declared that 'the human person has a right to religious freedom', defined as freedom from coercion in religious matters, both public and private, based on 'the very dignity of the human person as known through the revealed word of God and by reason itself' (Article 2). The third was the 'Pastoral Constitution on the Church in the Modern World', *Gaudium et Spes*, in 1965, which was the only teaching of the Council for which no documentation was provided in advance by the Vatican bureaucracy.

The bishops of the Council demanded in their first session that their work should include discussion of the world-wide social and political problems of which they had first-hand knowledge through the pastoral work of the church in every diocese. Dom Helder Câmara is on record as asking, outside the Council sessions, 'Are we to spend our whole time discussing internal church problems while two-thirds of mankind is dying of hunger?' (Vorgrimler, 1969:11)

Two committees were set up to work on the draft of the Constitution, one on basic theology and one on the urgent practical problems of the family, the world economy and world peace. This method of working, unavoidable in the circumstances, meant that the response to the practical problems was not developed directly from the basic theology. But there was enough common ground for the connections to work in a general sort of way. There was also a problem about claiming the authority of a

Council for the discussion of social issues; for this reason the document was characterized as a 'Pastoral' rather than a 'Dogmatic' Constitution. But, as Joseph Gremillion comments, it remains true that *'Gaudium et Spes* is the first expressly social and cultural-political document to be proclaimed by an Ecumenical Council of the Catholic and Apostolic Church' (1976:139), and its contents are now part of the teaching of the Roman Catholic Church at the highest level of authority.

The Constitution began with a declaration of the interest of Christians in 'The joy and hope, the sorrow and anxiety of the men of our time' (Article 1) and described the task of the people of God as being to discover in the world 'what are the genuine signs of the presence and purpose of God' (11). The emphasis in the opening stages of the document was on what is common to all humanity, leading to a definition of the status of humanity as being made in the image of God (12), though 'wounded by sin' (14). Human beings nevertheless participated 'in the light of the divine mind' and were called on through conscience to embrace what was good freely, though needing the help of grace to come to free action wholly centered on God (16, 17).

This theological anthropology, deriving both from the Old Testament in Genesis 1.27 and from the Catholic tradition of natural theology, laid the necessary basis for an understanding of the work of Jesus as the founder of a new humanity. 'The mystery of man becomes clear only in the mystery of the incarnate Word. Adam, the first man, was a type of the future, that is of Christ our Lord. Christ the new Adam, in revealing the mystery of the Father and his love, makes man fully clear to himself, makes clear his high vocation' (22). Although this and later Articles included reference to other Christologies, it was clear that the choice of a phenomenological starting point for the document as a whole had its root in this theology of Christ as the foundation and the fullest explanation of human community.

Much in the discussion of the practical problems expressed the same viewpoint; the teaching on mutual love in the discussion of marriage (49), the teaching on the proper autonomy and liberty of human culture (59), the teaching on the dignity of the human person and the integrity of human vocation in social and economic life (63) and on the common origin of all wealth as God's gift (69), and the teaching on peace as not 'the mere absence of war' (78), but the fruit of a passion for justice in human order. All these were marks of an acceptance of human affairs in their proper autonomy as part of the fullest understanding of the work of Christ. The point was summed up at the end of the exposition of the basic theology, where Christ was described as 'the end of human history, the point on which the aspirations of history and civilization converge' (45). There was here a conscious parallel with the World Council of Churches' concurrent study on 'Jesus Christ the Lord of History' (Vorgrimler, 1969:19-21).

In the World Council of Churches itself the concern about world poverty in the context of colonialism and neo-colonialism was put on the agenda by a World Conference on Church and Society held in Geneva in 1966. 'We have become increasingly aware of the plight of the developing nations which comprise more than two thirds of the world's population, and yet have access to only one fourth of the world's resources' (1967:209). Because the Bible existed in history and was about history, the believer was necessarily 'a part of the struggle in our time to achieve a responsible society of justice and peace among men, and to discern and realize relative meanings in history' (1967:200).

This conference in fact marked a decisive break from the immediate post-war period when the World Council of Churches had been dominated by delegates from North America and Western Europe; now the concerns were those of Africa, Asia and Latin America, namely the removal of western domination and the search for economic development and social justice. At the Fourth Assembly of the World Council of Churches at Uppsala in Sweden in 1968 world economic development became a major issue, with the bold assertion that 'No structures — ecclesiastical, industrial, governmental or international — lie outside the scope of the churches' task as they seek to carry out their prophetic role in understanding the will of God for all men' (1968:52).

In 1970 the World Council of Churches held a consultation on ecumenical assistance to development projects, which discussed in detail the link between development and social justice. At this meeting Professor Samuel Parmar of Allahabad University spoke of the problems of 'domestic imperialism' and the need to change institutions within developing countries as well as the relationships between more and less developed nations. He pointed to the problems created by the 'green revolution' in agriculture in India, where the social structure had not changed along with changes in techniques; the fact that the bigger farmers had benefitted at the expense of the smaller farmers and landless labourers meant that increased prosperity had increased rather than lowered social tensions. He commented that 'To attain the goal of social justice, it becomes necessary to change the social framework' (1970:54). A high rate of growth by itself would not bring about social change. But high growth without social change could lead to political instability, which itself inhibited further growth. Economic development could produce peace and avoid revolution only if it was itself a process of revolution. 'Development cannot take place without radical changes in economic and social relationships, and diffusion of political power' (1970:55).

He noted also the need to extend the concept of social justice to international economic relationships. 'The burden of debt repayments has increased to the point where nearly half of the current external assistance is used up by developing nations for debt repayments. At this rate by 1980 some developing countries will have to earmark all their aid for repayments, so that the net inflow of external resources will be zero' (1970:52). This problem did indeed emerge in the late 1980's. The effort to increase production by importing technology caused a dual problem; firstly that such technology was capital-using and labour-saving, so reducing the demand for labour and the generation of income; secondly that at the same time the continuing application of technological advances in the more industrialized countries reduced the demand for the raw materials and commodities on the export of which the developing countries depended. Professor Parmar commented that 'International economic justice is the only way to ensure development with international interdependence' (1970:53).

At the same conference Dom Helder Câmara listed some recent reports of conferences on development issues and said, 'If we add the Encyclical Populorum Progessio of Pope Paul VI we can say that for the next few years we Christians do not require any more documents concerning the social sphere. The problem that we now have to tackle is that of putting our fine theories into practice' (1970:63). Much effort has gone into this project, particularly in Latin America, where the second and third General Conferences of the bishops of the Catholic Church (CELAM), at Medellín in 1968 and at Puebla in 1979, paid attention to the analysis of the relation between poverty and the social and political structures in their region. Although Pope John Paul II has condemned what he sees as the Marxist element in some versions of liberation theology, or contextual theology, he also has continued to lay stress on the problem of poverty worldwide.

(v) Liberation and the Integrity of Creation

By the time of the Fifth Assembly of the World Council of Churches at Nairobi in Kenya in 1975, the concern for development and justice had begun to connect with a new and growing concern about resources and the environment. The Geneva 1966 Conference on Church and Society had discussed the possibility of technological advances giving increased economic and political power to an elite, and had called for the widest possible participation in decision-making, remarking that 'we do not know the limits of what man can do for man through scientific technology' (1967:193). At Nairobi Professor Charles Birch of the University of Sydney referred to the need for positive 'de-development' of the rich countries and to the aim of 'a just and sustainable society' for all humanity. 'If . . . we are to break the poverty barrier for almost two-thirds of the earth's people, if we are to continue to inhabit the earth, there has to be a revolution in the relationship of human beings to one another. The churches of the world have now to choose whether or not they become part of that revolution' (1976:23).

The Assembly continued to press on the theme of poverty and social justice. 'Poverty, we are learning, is caused primarily by unjust structures that leave resources and the power to make decisions about the utilization of resources in the hands of a few within nations and among nations, and that therefore one of the main tasks of the Church when it expresses its solidarity with the poor is to oppose these structures at all levels' (1976:123). But it also recognized the existence of alienation and the spiritual dangers of an uncontrolled push for ever greater production. 'We have been alienated from our neighbour, nature, cosmos and God. For many, a glory has passed from the earth' (1976:134).

By 1979, when the World Council of Churches held a conference on 'Faith, Science and the Future' in Boston, the problems of pollution and the exhaustion of resources, the dangers of nuclear technology and waste-disposal, and the need to define 'humanness' in the face of rapid changes in biological techniques had been added to the demand for development and social justice. Speaking on the theme of 'The Transition to a Just, Participatory and Sustainable Society', John M. Francis, himself a nuclear scientist, set the keynote of the new situation. 'The illusion of mastery vested in the conception of more powerful forms of technology has dissolved for the foreseeable future' (1980, Vol. I:178). This is a lesson that has not yet sunk in and it may require substantial changes in what we mean by 'justice'.

The model of social justice sometimes gives the impression of having gone hand-in-hand with the Marxist analysis of society. But contextual theology has always come first of all from the Old Testament focus on the desire for justice for Israel and the New Testament focus on the breaking-down of barriers within the eucharistic community. The first carries with it a sense of the forceful action of God for social change — even changes undesired by Israel; while the second carries with it the sense of a deep commitment through the eucharistic action to the wholeness of each sharer in the eucharist, so that any form of oppression becomes an obscenity within the eucharistic community. Marxist thought can sometimes be used to clarify the analysis of particular conditions, but there is nothing in the general concepts of social justice that cannot be referred directly to the biblical and post-biblical experience of the Christian communities. The development of contextual theology in Asia has paid much more attention to the diversity of cultural and religious traditions as the source of a concern for the poor; Asian liberation theology is even less open than Latin American liberation theology to the charge of being Marxist-oriented (Mackie, 1989; Song, 1988).

The question is, nevertheless, whether the disappearance of the hope of economic growth as the engine of justice, which has been an important part of both Christian and Marxist thought, will leave us with anything to say to people who find their lives left without meaning? Here the latest developments in the model of social justice, which are black theology and feminist theology, raise important questions about the relationship of the growth of the individual person to the definition of social justice. In particular, black theology raises questions about the endless Christian problem of the proper use of force, while feminist theology raises questions about the use of force as a specifically male problem — and notes that black theology has so far been a largely male preserve.

Nowhere has the ambiguity of Christian stances on social justice been experienced more sharply than in the working out by black Christians of black theology. Black theology has unarguably been the voice of the oppressed themselves. Steve Biko, in an article on 'Black Consciousness and the Quest for a True Humanity', first published in South Africa in 1972, identified the need for black people to reject the consciousness imposed on them by whites of being 'inferior' and 'bad'. This lie originated in the need of whites to defend their economic advantages, but in time it became an ideology, a false consciousness which was accepted by both sides for different reasons. Black people had to reject the escapism of running away from themselves and emulating the whites. 'Freedom is the ability to define oneself with one's possibilities held back not by the power of other people over one but only by one's relationship to God and to natural surroundings' (1973:41).

Biko's own death symbolized dramatically the nature of the violence which he faced. Against this violence Biko asserted, not counter-violence, but the importance of 'black consciousness', the recognition by black people of their own potential as human beings. 'At the heart of this kind of thinking is the realisation by blacks that the most potent weapon in the hands of the oppressor is the mind of the oppressed' (1973:41). The demand for freedom of thought, for self-knowledge, and the demand for unity of action of black people were for Biko the expression of the gospel in the actual social location of black people.

It is a demand which many white people would have difficulty in recognising as an expression of the gospel. But black people have had to put the question of racism as a critical question to the Christian faith. 'Blacks ask: What does it mean to believe in Jesus Christ when one is black and living in a world controlled by white racists? And what if these racists call themselves Christians also?' So Allan Boesak began his discussion in *Black Theology, Black Power* (1978:1-2). In a wide-ranging analysis of the problem, mainly in terms of South Africa, but also drawing on North American theologians and civil rights leaders such as James Cone and Martin Luther King, Boesak made clear a distinction also noted by the Latin American theologians, that theologies of liberation see the call of Jesus as a call to change society rather than a call to personal salvation.

It could not be ruled out that such a change might require the use of force, and only the oppressed had the right to raise that question. But what the Christian needed in the construction of the new society was faith and courage rather than force. For the aim was the transformation of society in terms of the most fundamental needs of human beings. 'Black Theology sincerely believes that it is possible to recapture what was sacred in the African community long before white people came — solidarity, respect for life, humanity and community' (1978:152). Neither human experience nor the revealed faith could promise reconciliation without passing through some sort of conflict. But Boesak ended with an African proverb, 'One is only human because of others, with others, for others' (1978:152).

The theology of poverty and the theology of black consciousness have both made a demand for the recognition of oppression on the basis of well-established biblical teachings about compassion and about freedom. Feminist theology, from its particular experience of the suppression of the self, was driven to ask more critical questions about the nature of all human experience, including experience of God. Rosemary Ruether in *Sexism and God-Talk* in 1983 pointed out that the objective sources of theology, namely the scriptures and the various forms of tradition, were all a record of collective human experience of the divine, of the self, of the community and of the world. The experience of women had been an experience of oppression by males, for some in a personal form but for all in the form of the institutions and collective ideas of patriarchally organized societies. This collective experience of women provided a negative criterion by which even the collective representations of God could be assessed. 'The critical principle of feminist theology is the promotion of the full humanity of women. Whatever denies, diminishes, or distorts the full humanity of women is, therefore, appraised as not redemptive' (1983:18-19).

But the fullness of the potential of woman was not yet realised, having never yet existed in history. Women needed a conversion in which they discovered themselves as persons. The first liberation was to disclose the self, to become the centre of one's own identity. Male theologians had always discussed this in terms of 'man' being created 'in the image of God'. Feminist theology made the disclosure by women for women that woman was made 'in the image of God'.

Ruether recognised that anger might be a proper response once consciousness of the actual condition of woman was established. 'Anger is liberating grace precisely as the power to break the chains of sexist socialization, to disaffiliate with sexist ideologies' (1983:186). But along with the negative statement there was also the possibility of beginning a definition of a positive

26

criterion of being. One starting point could be the human relation to nature. Patriarchal thinking on nature had been linear,
dichotomized and exploitative, thinking in terms of use and mastery. Ecological thinking would require a different kind of
thought. 'Converting our minds to the earth means understanding the more diffuse and relational logic of natural harmony'
(1983:91). What was needed was not a move from a masculine
way of thinking to a feminine way of thinking, but a move from
all present ways of doing and thinking to a new psychic integration that would also affect the social world. 'Women want to
integrate the public and the private, the political and the domestic spheres in a new relationship that allows the thinking-rela-
tional self to operate throughout human life as one integrated
self, rather than fragmenting the psyche across a series of different social roles' (1983:113).

So the idea of social justice curves back to a model of salvation
through the notion of a new creation. All the experiences of
tension come back to the call for a new beginning, a making-
new, here in the earth, of all the potentials of all living creatures.
Models of social justice are clearly models of change. Equally
clearly some of the change required will be disturbing and even
frightening. Most frightening of all, however, is the question
whether there is now enough time left to bring about this change.

At the Boston conference of the World Council of Churches
in 1979, Paulos Gregorios, the Syrian Orthodox Metropolitan of
New Delhi, spoke in a sermon on Revelation 12.1-6 of the basis
of our hope. 'The new humanity, about to be born, is in God's
hands, and its destiny is to be before the throne of God. But let
us not make any mistakes with our science and technology and
play into the hands of the fire-dragon' (WCC, 1980; Vol. 1:379).
The time of the fire-dragon is now upon us. Whether by nuclear
war, or by the exhaustion of resources, or by the 'greenhouse
effect' and other forms of pollution, we have reached the point
where the human hope of continuing to inhabit this fragile earth
requires a serious reversal of values, from those which promote
conflict and excess to those which promote co-operation and the
thoughtful use of resources. A profound change in the way we

envisage ourselves as persons in community is now required. What are the resources within the Christian tradition for a new way of thinking about the nature of human beings within their natural environment? To answer this question requires a return to the beginning.

2
The Bible as the Source of Authority in Ethics

The Bible is a journey through time. Both Jews and Christians see themselves as a pilgrim people, whose journey is recorded in the Book and still continues into a future which is not yet fully defined. The Christian tradition is the process by which the knowledge of the living God has been expressed in successive contexts. The Bible is therefore the beginning of a process of self-understanding carried on by the Jewish and Christian communities, basically by the telling of stories. 'Most, perhaps all, of the writings that now make up the New Testament, and a great many of the other earliest Christian writings as well, had as their primary aim the shaping of the life of the Christian communities' (Wayne Meeks, 1987:12). The thread that runs through the Bible stories is the experience of the word of God as a summons to action. 'Yahweh said to Abram, "Leave your country, your family and your father's house, for the land I will show you"' (Gen. 12.1). The summons to have the courage to go out into a new situation is the beginning of the biblical faith.

(i) The Covenant
The Jewish and Christian tradition has its roots in primitive culture, even before the distinctions of the 'religious' and the 'secular' emerged. Those of the tribes who moved into Palestine more than 3,000 years ago were concerned with the land, with the people already in possession of it, and with the relationship of that possession to the god or gods who ruled the land. The full processes by which the Hebrews emerged as 'Israel' and came to terms with the problem of the meaning of their possession of the land are not now recoverable (Martin, 1989). But by the end of the Hebrew Bible whatever god or gods the various groups originally followed had become the God of the Hebrews, Yahweh, the Lord who led and protected, who acted in love and mercy, and who asked for pure worship and social obedience in response to these gifts.

This transition was a remarkable achievement. It is embedded in an equally remarkable liturgical act. The feast of 'Passover', a presumed fertility rite of nomadic herding tribes, in which a lamb or goat would be sacrificed to ensure the fertility of the flock in the new season, became the foundational rite of the Hebrew people's new sense of themselves as the people called by God to settle in the land of Canaan. In Exodus 12, when the last of the plagues was about to come upon the Egyptians, which was the death of the first-born of humans and of domestic animals, instructions were given for the people to keep on this last night in Egypt. First an animal was to be selected, as for ritual slaughter. 'It must be an animal without blemish, a male one year old; you may take it from either sheep or goats' (12.5). The blood of the animal was to be put on the doorposts and lintel of each house of the Hebrews, so that death would pass them by. Then the animal was to be eaten roasted, with unleavened bread and bitter herbs. The meal was to be eaten with everyone ready for departure. 'You shall eat it like this: with a girdle round your waist, sandals on your feet, a staff in your hand' (12.11). And once the people were out of Egypt, the Lord's 'passover' was to be remembered. 'For all generations you are to declare it a day of festival, for ever' (12.14).

The rite as it now stands in Exodus 12 is clearly already more than a historical remembrance. The attention to detail ('Do not eat any of it raw or boiled, but roasted over the fire, head, feet and entrails ' (12.9)) suggests a liturgical performance. But the existence — and the persistence — of the liturgical remembrance is itself a tribute to the historical reminiscence of the original events.

In these original events was laid the beginning of the movement which created Judaism as one of the world's great religions.

The later Book of Deuteronomy describes the heart of the Passover meal in the home. 'In times to come, when your son asks you, "What is the meaning of the decrees and laws and customs that Yahweh our God has laid down for you?" you shall tell your son, "Once we were Pharaoh's slaves in Egypt, and

Yahweh brought us out of Egypt by his mighty hand'" (6.20, 21). The consequence of this historical remembrance was that 'For us right living will mean this, to keep and observe all these commandments before Yahweh our God as he has directed us' (6.25). This response to God who was active in leading the people was the centre of the ethical monotheism of the Hebrew religion. The actual shaping of Judaism, however, was a long process.

From the beginnings of 'Israel' in Palestine, around 1400 BC, to the Hellenistic period which began with Alexander the Great conquering Syria in 333 BC, the Hebrew Bible covers a period of more than 1,000 years. The last books to be admitted, Ecclesiastes and Esther, were written perhaps around 250 BC. The Hebrew understanding of God was a mixture of the theology and ritual that the migrants brought with them into Palestine, the religion and culture of the people already in and around that land, and above all the historical experience of living as a people in this land in response to this God.

First of all, God was seen as active in all of history. The final form of the Biblical faith began with the Exodus migration of the people from Egypt and saw that movement as deliberately arranged by God. While other religions were concerned to maintain the stability of the necessary cycles of birth and death, seed time and harvest, the Hebrews also saw their God as initiating change for positive purposes. This God asked the people to take risks and to trust that the results would be good. The great agreement, the Covenant on Mount Sinai in the desert before the entry into Palestine, expressed the mature form of that faith:

> Moses then went up to God, and Yahweh called to him from the mountain, saying, 'Say this to the House of Jacob, declare this to the sons of Israel, "You yourselves have seen what I did with the Egyptians, how I carried you on eagle's wings and brought you to myself. From this you know that now, if you obey my voice and hold fast to my covenant, you of all the nations shall be my very own for all the earth is mine. I will count you a kingdom of priests, a consecrated nation". These are the words you are to speak to the sons of Israel'. (Exod. 19.3-6)

31

This promise was offered as an act of grace, in unmerited loving-kindness towards the Hebrew peoples. In return God required faithful witness both in worship and in social justice in the community.

The duties of the agreement were summarized in the Ten Commandments, the 'Decalogue' of the covenant on Sinai (Exod.20.1-17):

> You shall have no gods except me.
> You shall not make yourself a carved image or any likeness of anything . . .
> You shall not utter the name of Yahweh your God to misuse it ...
> Remember the sabbath day and keep it holy . . .
> (Exod. 20.3-11)

These first four teachings established the nature of God as one, as holy and as relating to the people in worship. The prohibition of images was the prohibition of images of false gods for use in worship. The keeping of the sabbath, from Friday evening to Saturday evening, was a weekly re-enacting of Israel's relationship to God: a pause given to God which made a claim on God's action in creating the world (Exod.20.11) and on God's action in bringing the people out of Egypt into Palestine (Deut. 5.15). What remained was the moral demand.

The following six commands to honour parents, not to kill unlawfully, not to commit adultery, not to steal, not to bear false witness and not to covet anything that belonged to another (Exod. 20.12-17) came from a society that still made no distinction between the religious, moral and legal requirements in human life. Yet between them these commandments touched all the bases of human existence: the family, organized society and the integrity of the person. The law of the covenant, though clearly the product of a patriarchal society, showed a remarkable breadth of moral potential.

The history of the Israelites up to the fall of Jerusalem in the face of the Babylonian attack in 587 BC follows the working-out of this covenant through particular social, political and religious institutions. The story is recorded only in part, but it is clear that there were different expectations about the relationship between God and the people among various groups in different periods and that there were changes in these expectations as history moved on.

The tribes which lived in Palestine separately or as a loose federation became a kingdom under Saul, reached a high point under his successor David, then split into two kingdoms on the death of David's son Solomon. In 721 BC the northern kingdom, Israel, was swallowed up by Assyria, and in 587 BC Jerusalem, the capital of the southern kingdom of Judah, was taken over by the Babylonian empire, its leaders exiled and its Temple destroyed. Each step in this history raised questions about the nature of the covenant promises.

If the Hebrews were aware of the absolute sovereignty of God, they also had plenty of examples of the stubbornness of the social order in the face of God's commandments. The great preachers who are known as the 'Later Prophets' arose in protest against breaches of the covenant promise, against impure worship and against neglect of the poor, the widow, the orphan and against unjust dealing in business and in the courts of law.

Amos, working in the northern kingdom around 750 BC, attacked a society that was prosperous and self-confident in its own economic and military strength. His prophecy was an attempt to bring the people back to the God who led them in the wilderness. The people of the northern kingdom stood condemned 'because they have sold the virtuous man for silver and the poor man for a pair of sandals' (Amos 2.6). A worship which does not lead to social justice is false.

> I reject your oblations,
> and refuse to look at your sacrifices of fattened cattle.
> Let me have no more of the din of your chanting,
> no more of your strumming on harps.
> But let justice flow like water,
> and integrity like an unfailing stream. (Amos 5.22-24)

Hosea, a prophet in the northern kingdom working a little later than Amos, when the north was already under visible threat from

Assyria, also offered no immediate comfort.

> Wherever they turn, I will spread my net over them,
> I mean to bring them down like the birds of heaven,
> I will punish them for their perversity. (Hos. 7.12)

But for Hosea the notion of punishment led on to a hope of restoration. This was not be be earned by any good deed on the part of the people. The hope lay in God's nature as love.

> I myself taught Ephraim to walk,
>
> I took them in my arms;
> yet they have not understood that I was the one looking after
>   them.
> I led them with reins of kindness,
> with leading-strings of love. (Hos. 11.3,4)

God threatens punishment, but the image of mothering prevails. Yahweh decides not to give way to anger, not to destroy the kingdom, 'for I am God, not man' (Hos.11.9). This restraint arises from God's holiness, not from any lingering remnant of goodness in the people. Grace arises from God's nature as creator and redeemer, before which even justified destruction in some sense gives way.

Nevertheless, the possibility of God's withdrawal, the concealment of the Presence, was always implicit in the covenant as the necessary negative aspect, the negative which affirms the reality of the agreement. The absolute sovereignty of God demanded that Israel's failure to keep the promises of the covenant be punished. Israel had accepted its election but had failed to live out its election in practice. It was necessary for God to be God and so to appear negatively to the northern kingdom as a judge. The withdrawal of protection made sense within a positive purpose, the recalling of Israel to the promises which would enable them to live more fully a life of response to this active God. The image of mothering shows God's dealings with Israel through the analogy of personal relationship, but shows also that such a relational theology may still include the necessity to recognize the cost of what is done.

In the southern kingdom of Judah Isaiah of Jerusalem received his call to preach in 740 BC. Drawing on a tradition of assurance of the permanence of God's promises to the house of David, he mixed his announcement of judgment with a promise of renewal.

> Though your sins are like scarlet,
> they shall be as white as snow;
> though they are red as crimson,
> they shall be like wool. (Isa.1.18)

The punishment would be a cleansing and a refining of the people to whom God was bound in promise and in love. Isaiah seems to have remained convinced that Jerusalem itself would never be taken. It would have been small comfort to him to know that eventually the city would fall not to Assyria but to Babylonia. Even so the threat of judgment was clear enough.

> Very well, I will tell you
> what I am going to do to my vineyard:
> I will take away its hedge for it to be grazed on,
> and knock down its wall for it to be trampled on. (Isa.5.5)

It fell to the next major prophet to deal with the final disaster for the southern kingdom. Jeremiah was called to preach in 627 BC when, in spite of its restiveness under subordination to Assyria, Jerusalem had still not been conquered by a foreign invader. The fact that the monarchy and the Temple remained intact was taken to be a sign of the continuing presence of God with the people. To Jeremiah fell the task of giving the word of God that even these institutions could and would fall. 'Steal, would you, murder, commit adultery, perjure yourselves, burn incense to Baal, follow alien gods that you do not know? — and then come presenting yourselves in this Temple that bears my name, saying: Now we are safe — safe to go on committing all these abominations!' (Jer.7.9, 10). Such confidence was misplaced. It did not

35

save those who trusted in an earlier place of worship. 'Now go to my place in Shiloh where at first I gave my name a home; see what I have done to it because of the wickedness of my people Israel!' (Jer.7.12)

The old cultic site of Shiloh was no guarantee against failure to keep the covenant promises. Neither could the existence of the Temple in Jerusalem create such a guarantee. The covenant promises brought judgment as well as hope and the judgment would not necessarily be favourable.

Seeking salvation in the covenant promise could be a high-risk occupation. Some leaders understood this well enough. King Josiah (640-609 BC) led a movement of reform based on renewed attention to the covenant (II Kings 22). The danger in which the kingdom stood through its present disobedience was seen at that time. But the death of Josiah in battle with the Babylonians weakened the movement for renewed purity and let the more material trust in earthly institutions predominate.

So the elements came together for the greatest challenge experienced by the people who had first settled as Hebrew tribes in Palestine and had established a great kingdom. Now they had to live through the breaking-down of everything they had created — and yet to see this also as the work of God. The God who led them into the land was also the destroyer. Jeremiah, for whom the work of preaching was agonising in this crisis (Jer. 15.10; 20.14-18), had to announce submission to the coming destruction of the city. 'Those who stay in this city will die by sword, by famine, or by plague; but anyone who leaves it and surrenders to the Chaldeans now besieging it will live; he shall escape with his life' (Jer.21.9). An empire which was not a part of the covenant promise became an instrument of the covenant to punish the covenanted people.

(ii) The Law

It was in the experience of exile and the destruction of the institutions of Judah that the faith of the Israelite peoples took on the wider religious form called Judaism. The link of the faith with the land and with the institutions of monarchy and Temple was not broken. But when the purity of the faith rested with the 'remnant', as they came to be called, in exile in Babylon, rather than with the people who remained in the land, the emphasis shifted to what could be preserved in exile.

In the latter part of the Book of Jeremiah and in Ezekiel there appears the theme of a promised new covenant. 'I shall give you a new heart, and put a new spirit in you; I shall remove the heart of stone from your bodies and give you a heart of flesh instead. I shall put my spirit in you, and make you keep my laws and sincerely respect my observances' (Ezek. 36.26, 27). In time the new covenant became the basis for a wide range of expectations. 'The need for renewal of the near-severed relationship gives rise to the concept of a "new covenant" and consequently to the Qumran sect and ultimately to Christianity' (Segal, 1980:68). Most immediately, however, it seems to have moved the responsibility for responding to God away from the institutions of monarchy and Temple and towards the individual. The promise was that the the Law would be written in the heart of each person. 'There will be no further need for neighbour to try to teach neighbour, or brother to say to brother, "Learn to know Yahweh!". No, they will all know me, the least no less than the greatest — it is Yahweh who speaks — since I will forgive their iniquity and never call their sin to mind' (Jer.31.34).

This was obviously a picture of a future ideal situation rather than a description of present reality in whatever period. But it corresponded in intention to the main institutional change of the exile, the shift from Temple sacrifice to worship and teaching in a more domestic situation which eventually became the basis of the synagogue. It is difficult to be sure about elements of continuity and change in this period, because the evidence from pre-exilic times and from the period from the exile to the end of the Hebrew Bible does not give much detail about observances at particular times and places. Certainly the pre-exilic prophets demanded individual as well as institutional obedience to the covenant. But in the exile the life of response presumably became centred on the synagogue and the family. In this a great positive decision was affirmed, that God could be served outside the land. The exile was thus affirmed as a positive experience within the covenant promise.

This new understanding of the covenant centred in the synagogue on the reading of Torah, which was primarily the first five books of the Hebrew Bible, Genesis to Deuteronomy, attributed to Moses. Although Torah translates as 'law' it is important to keep open the wider sense of the word. 'The rabbis never speak of Torah as the means to salvation, and when they speak of salvation at all, the way of Torah "which is your life" (Deut.32.47), is that salvation' (Gaston, 1979:51). Torah is a living experience. The interpretation of the Books of Moses and of the later writings of the Hebrew Bible, through the tradition of discussion by scholars, always aimed to produce an understanding of the word of God for the present time. Torah is thus the name not only of an established writing but also of a process of dynamic interpretation in a community.

To keep Torah is to be a member of a community which lives within God's promise of salvation. When Torah is breached, repentance brings restoration. The laws are the sign of God's graciousness, God's loving intention that human beings should live in a way that shares in that grace. The teaching of Torah is based on the dignity of human beings, from their creation in the image of God (Gen.1.27) to their becoming sharers in God's purpose through the covenant.

When the people accepted the responsibility for their own freely chosen disobedience, by seeing the events of the exile as the operation of the covenant, they came to a wider understanding of the covenant promise, but they also set up a new problem. The concern for human dignity on a universal scale sharpened the question of the prevalence of evil. If God was not simply the God of the land, but worked through the great empires of Assyria and Babylonia, then God's activity must be seen in the whole of creation. It became difficult to interpret all human events simply in terms of the Israelites' own obedience or disobedience. Evil was a universal phenomenon. In the words of a modern Jewish scholar, 'One great cry resounds through the Bible: The wickedness of man is great on the earth' (Heschel, 1956:375). Life on earth was infinitely precious because it was the opportunity to choose good and reject evil. Abraham Heschel writes of human life, 'It is the eve of the Sabbath, on which the report is prepared for the Lord's day; it is the season of duty and submission, as the morrow shall be that of freedom from every law' (1956:398). So Judaism came to concentrate on the individual act. What was redemptive was a good deed, an action in accordance with Torah which was carried out with full attention. 'It is the act, life itself, that educates the will. The good motive comes into being while doing the good' (Heschel, 1956:405).

Human beings were corruptible, God was gracious, and between these two was the commandment, the knowledge of God's will as a deed which can be done. Judaism concentrated on actual failures rather than a theory of original sin and on the good that can be done rather than the failure to become perfect. 'At the end of days, evil will be conquered all at once; in historic times evils must be conquered one by one' (Heschel, 1956:409). In this sense Judaism was deeply affirmative of human life and the observance of Torah is a source of joy.

> The precepts of Yahweh are upright,
> joy for the heart;
> the commandment of Yahweh is clear,
> light for the eyes. (Psalm 19.8)

Torah was in no way hidden; anyone willing to take an interest in Judaism could know it and keep it. The final destruction of the Temple in 70 AD only put the seal on a tendency that was launched with the exile, that the Israelite religion had the capacity to become a profoundly democratic faith, without priest or hierarchy, but rather 'a kingdom of priests, a consecrated nation' (Exod.19.6).

After the end of the Hebrew Bible, the rabbis taught mainly by the authority of their own wisdom and learning, though always within a tradition. On the whole Judaism survived without councils or creeds. In its widest sense Torah became the name for a process of teaching which mediated between the Hebrew Bible, the later tradition and the contemporary problems. It was opinion always in the process of formation, revering the past but revering also the presence of God in the questions of daily living.

Torah was also open in the sense that it could be stated very simply. 'Listen, Israel: Yahweh our God is the one Yahweh. You shall love Yahweh your God with all your heart, with all your soul, with all your strength' (Deut.6.4, 5). Deuteronomy 6, verses 4 to 9, constituted the 'Shema', the morning and evening confession of faith of Judaism. Love of God implied love of neighbour. Indeed, in the rabbinic interpretations of Torah, sins against God were more easily forgiven than sins against fellow human beings, for the latter required restitution as well as repentance. No one earned their salvation by good deeds, but good deeds and repentance for bad deeds were required in order to stay within the covenant community. E. P. Sanders comments that 'Human perfection was not considered realistically achievable by the Rabbis, nor was it required' (1977:137).

In keeping Torah, Judaism met constantly with the problem of suffering. On the whole, justice was expected in this world, even if such justice could never be complete. Suffering, even 'undeserved' suffering, was seen as cleansing those whom God loved. Nevertheless, the nature of the covenant promise always tended to imply that the suffering which came upon the people as a whole was a punishment for disobedience. So the prophets had viewed the fall of the northern and southern kingdoms. But it could not be denied that this mass suffering fell upon good and bad alike, on those who kept Torah as much as on those who did not. To this problem there were three possible answers. The first was a round denial.

> Now I am old, but ever since my youth
> I never saw a virtuous man deserted,
> or his descendants forced to beg their bread;
> he is always compassionate, always lending:
> his children will be blessed. (Psalm 37.25)

This answer may have been true for almost all of the people in times of peace and prosperity, and it could always be true for some individuals. But not everyone who suffered could be accused of particular unrighteousness in proportion to their degree of suffering, and no satisfactory moral account of general human suffering could be given on this basis.

The second answer was that suffering was to be accepted, as being a test or a discipline. Within certain limits this was plausible on the analogy of parent and child. 'Learn from this that Yahweh your God was training you as a man trains his child, and keep the commandments of Yahweh your God, and so follow his ways and reverence him' (Deut.8.5, 6). God's leading the people forty years in the wilderness, keeping them fed and clothed, was both a punishment and a caring; it provided a model for other circumstances. But insofar as the human experience of suffering went way beyond anything that could be understood morally as necessary training, the Hebrew Bible had a teaching of the simple acceptance of suffering, based on the otherness and unknowability of God, in which it must be trusted that the way chosen by God was right. This was the answer in the two speeches of God in Job 38-42. Job finally submitted to this view.

> I know that you are all-powerful:
>   what you conceive, you can perform.
> I am the man who obscured your designs
>   with my empty-headed words. (Job 42.2, 3).

More often, however, Israel cried for vindication, for judgment to be declared in God's court against her oppressors, recognizing that much suffering was caused by deliberate human action about which human beings have choice.

> Rise, Yahweh, God raise your hand,
> do not forget the poor!
> Why does the wicked man spurn God,
> Assuring himself, 'He will not make me pay'?
> (Psalm 10.12, 13)

Most characteristic of Hebrew faith at this point was the will to hold on to faith in God's goodness towards the people, whatever their trouble in the world might be.

The third answer was that the suffering of human beings could in some way be redemptive for others. In the four passages known as the 'Servant Songs' (Isa. 42.1-4; 49.1-6; 50.4-9; 52.13-53.12) the writer of the second part of Isaiah showed a mysterious figure who by suffering redeemed Israel.

> We had all gone astray like sheep,
> each taking his own way,
> and Yahweh burdened him
> with the sins of all of us. (Isa. 53.6)

There is no certainty about the interpretation of this figure, whether the servant was a historical person, possibly a prophet, or a future leader, or a personification of Israel. Christians later applied the verses to Jesus, but it is possible also within Jewish thought to read them as a statement of vicarious atonement, suffering by one person which is effective for the healing of another. Phillip Segal comments that the 'figure here is unique in that he dies *in behalf* of the people, carrying *their* guilt' and regards the verses as being 'of the utmost significance to both Judaism and Christianity' (1980:104).

There was also implied in the servant songs a salvation which extended beyond Israel itself.

> It is not enough for you to be my servant,
> to restore the tribes of Jacob and bring back the survivors of
> Israel;
> I will make you the light of the nations
> so that my salvation may reach to the ends of the earth.
> (Isa. 49.6)

The theme of God's salvation coming to many peoples through Israel appeared in the third part of the Book of Isaiah (chapters 56 to 66). In the 'Wisdom literature' (Proverbs, Job, Ecclesiastes and some Psalms) there was an emphasis on God as creator of the universe and so of the whole human race. Segal attributes this partly to the influence of the Greek world on Judaism after

400 BC. 'Fused with the biblical idea that all humans are created in the image of God, hellenistic ecumenism eventually expresses itself in its fullest form in the Judaic-Christian idea of human brotherhood' (1980:152). Other tendencies in Judaism worked in the opposite direction, towards the separation of those who kept Torah from those who did not (Ezra; Nehemiah). As Segal points out, Christianity later experienced the same tension. In any case, Torah was given, not to an ethnic group, but to those who had faith in the creative and redemptive activity of God and who accepted obedience to the teaching as the best way of response.

(iii) Ethics in the Old Testament

Because of this long history, it would be difficult to claim that there is an Old Testament 'ethic'. Judaism is in a sense an ongoing debate about ethics. Nevertheless there may be some value in attempting a sketch of the teaching in the Old Testament relating to the three major ethical areas of sexuality, property and political power, as showing both the foundations which were already given for a Christian ethic and as a basis for understanding the changes that came about with Jesus' preaching of the kingdom of God.

Sexuality

The fundamental fact of Old Testament society in its treatment of sexuality is that of patriarchy. In all practical arrangements the odds were weighted against women. The aim of the arrangements was to secure reproductive success in terms of the male line. For this purpose the woman joined the man's family group, though Genesis 2.24 hints at a history of other customs. For this purpose also she could be divorced, if she proved barren, and later also for other reasons: legislation in Deuteronomy refers to a husband finding 'some impropriety of which to accuse her' for the purpose of divorce (24.1).

Sexual activity by the male was limited only by the barriers which defined kinship and categories of created being. Leviticus 18 laid down the relationships and Leviticus 20.8-21 added the penalties for transgression, either the death penalty or outlawry, for a range of activities, from adultery with a married woman, through incest and male homosexual acts to intercourse with animals. Where the death penalty applied, the partner also must die, including even the animal partner. To transgress against these divisions of kinship and of species was to transgress against holiness, against the creative but terrible power of God (Douglas, 1966).

These categories did not in practice allow the male a great deal of room for manoeuvre. For a Hebrew woman to become a prostitute was also a form of incest in terms of the people as a whole (Lev. 19.29). What remained was the maintaining of more than one wife, or the use of foreign women as prostitutes, or the use of a woman on a regular basis as a concubine. The story of Abraham, Sarah and Hagar (Gen. 16) showed the use of a servant to achieve reproduction when a wife was barren: Leviticus 18:18 forbade taking 'into your harem a woman and her sister at the same time'; I Kings 11.1-13 saw Solomon's many wives and concubines as giving rise to the problem, not of polygamy, but of the influence of foreign wives in turning the male to false worship.

What was not clear was how far the average Hebrew male was able to practice either polygamy or divorce. Both had economic implications, since divorce involved returning to the divorced wife's father the betrothal gift. To have many wives or concubines would be a sign of wealth and power, but there is little evidence about the lives of those who were neither wealthy nor powerful. Elkanah, the father of the prophet Samuel, is one of the few who is recorded as having two wives (I Sam. 1.2). Roland de Vaux concludes from the available information that 'It is clear, however, that the most common form of marriage in Israel was monogamy' (1961:25).

For the woman there was only the choice of marriage or of virginity in her father's house. The virginity of an unbetrothed woman was protected by a law that a seducer must marry the woman or pay the sum fixed in compensation to her father, if her father refused the marriage (Exod. 22.15-17). Deuteronomy

22.28-29 later converted this into compulsory marriage and the payment of compensation and added that the seducer was not allowed to divorce the woman at any time in the future.

Marriage was almost certainly the better choice. The woman was listed among her husband's possessions in the Decalogue (Exod. 20.17). But in the much later epilogue to the Book of Proverbs the 'good wife' appeared as a person of dignity and responsibility, exercising control over her household and receiving praise from her sons and her husband (31.10-31). In a community where almost everyone lived by continuous physical labour it was not an ignoble ideal.

There is nevertheless a difficulty in knowing what these legal provisions and generalised ideals meant in terms of practical human relationships. Hints of human problems broke through in the legislation itself. Deuteronomy 21.15-17 dealt with the fact that a man with two wives was likely to love one more than the other: this law required him to give the first-born son the first-born's double share, even though he be the son of the less-loved wife. Deuteronomy 24.5 laid down that 'If a man is newly married, he shall not join the army nor is he to be pestered at home; he shall be left at home free of all obligation for one year to bring joy to the wife he has taken'. The Song of Songs, though it takes its place in the Old Testament now as an allegory of the love of Israel and Yahweh, was equally clearly in its origins a song of human love and jealousy:

> For love is strong as Death,
> jealousy as relentless as Sheol. (Song of Songs 8.6)

What unified and gave form to these human passions was not the detail of the law but the overwhelming sense of the nature of God as loving-kindness. By the use of terms such as 'faithfulness', 'righteousness' and loving-kindness' the Old Testament taught that the nature of God was fidelity. It was the fidelity of God that set up the Covenant and from the Covenant there followed the moral requirement for human beings also to show fidelity, both to God and to one another. The stories of Ruth and Naomi (Ruth 1) and of David and Jonathan (I Sam. 18.1-5; II Sam. 1.17-27) were human examples of the fidelity which was proper to those who loved God. Increasingly as the Old Testament history progressed the marriage relationship was seen as a symbol of the relationship between God and Israel, whether in the breach of relationship in Hosea 1-3 or in the restoration of relationship in Isaiah 49.14-23. In the post-exilic Book of Malachi, the image of the broken marriage led to the pronouncement 'For I hate divorce, says Yahweh the God of Israel' (2.16). It seems likely that this increased stress on the marriage of Yahweh and Israel may have had some connection with an increasing respect for the state of marriage as a relationship between human beings. If this were so, the dominance of Yahweh in the theological relationship posed no challenge to continuing patriarchy in the human relationship.

With Malachi the process of reflection in the Old Testament on sexual relationships came back to its origins in the story of creation. 'Did he not create a single being that has flesh and the breath of life? And what is this single being destined for? God-given offspring' (Mal. 2.15). The Biblical sense of the unity of female and male, however varied its social expressions, sprang from the primeval story of God's free act in creating Adam and Eve for companionship (Gen. 2.18-25). Near the end of the Old Testament period, in the Genesis 1 account of the creation, male and female were shown as created in the same moment to represent equally the image of God in the world (Gen. 1.26-28).

The relationship of female and male was uniquely important because of the function of sexuality in reproduction. But the covenantal love which had the potential to transform the marriage relationship from the function of reproduction to the experience of love also had implications for all other relationships within the covenantal community. The fellow-Israelite was always a brother, 'You must not bear hatred for your brother in your heart. You must openly tell him, your neighbour, of his offence; this way you will not take a sin upon yourself' (Lev. 19.17). Even one who was still in a state of enmity was to be treated with equity (Exod. 23.4-5; Prov. 25.21-22). A foreigner who was resident in the covenantal community was to be treated with the same care (Exod. 22.20; Lev. 19.33-34). The fundamental moral criterion of the Old Testament was the recognition of the covenant community, the demands of which arose not simply from the fact of life together, but more crucially from the fact that the covenant life together was made possible only by the free gift of God.

Property

Israel's earliest dealings with property were as a tribal community, but the effect of life in Palestine was in time to create a society with economic and political divisions into rich and poor, powerful and powerless. In the period of the monarchy the social structure of Israel shifted considerably. 'A world which consisted merely of family groups, where servants lived with the master of the house, passed away and in its place there arose a society divided into king and subjects, employers and workmen, rich and poor. The transformation was complete, both in Israel and Judah, by the eighth century B.C.' (de Vaux, 1961:22). The weakening of the sense of the tribal community gave scope for the rise of an individual moral consciousness, but it also left the individual and the small family more at risk from changes of fortune or from economic pressure.

The fundamental theological principle of property was that all the good that came from the earth came as God's gift. The human commitment to 'fill the earth and conquer it' (Gen. 1.28), or to 'cultivate and take care of it' (Gen. 2.15), arose from what distinguished human beings from other animals, the capacity to work. The exercise of labour, of intelligent control, was the reason for creating a rational animal, but the animal was also created as spiritual, able to know and be known by God. Consequently the human creature was able to know itself as responsible, as being under authority, sharing in a creative purpose greater than itself. The task of stewardship of the whole earth was the task of the whole human race, male and female. The fall from this responsibility in Genesis chapter 3 made the task harder than it need have been, but the world did not become foreign to

47

the human being. It remained what it always was, God's sole creation, under no other power, open to human potential.

In this world labour was proper to human beings and might be expected to produce the necessities of food and clothing and shelter. Since not all could labour equally, customs or laws were required to assure the results of labour to those who needed protection. An early piece of legislation concerned the harvest.

> When you gather the harvest of your land, you are not to harvest to the very end of the field. You are not to gather the gleanings of the harvest. You are neither to strip your vine bare nor to collect the fruit that has fallen in your vineyard. You must leave them for the poor and the stranger. I am Yahweh your God.
> (Lev.19.9-10)

Where an Israelite fell into debt, no interest was to be charged on the loan (Exod. 22.24b-25). Where a garment was taken as a token pledge from a poor person, it was to be returned before sunset each day, because of the person's need (Exod. 22.25b-27). The ground for this was Yahweh's compassion. 'If he cries to me, I will listen, for I am full of pity'. The stranger must not be oppressed, because the Israelites themselves were once strangers in Egypt; the widow and orphan must not be treated harshly (Exod. 22.20-24a).

The effect of this early legislation was to preserve as far as possible that equality of social relationships which arose from the theory that all had come equally into the land as tribal settlers under the leadership of God and indeed had escaped from slavery in Egypt only by God's mighty hand. The protests of the prophets and the cry of the oppressed in the Psalms nevertheless testified to the troubles that the poor and the weak actually experienced.

> Happy the man who cares for the poor and the weak:
> If disaster strikes, Yahweh will come to his help. (Psalm 41.1)

> For I know that your crimes are many,
> and your sins enormous;

persecutors of the virtuous, blackmailers,
turning away the needy at the city gate.
No wonder the prudent man keeps silent,
the times are so evil. (Amos 5.12-13)

One strand of the future hope included a decision in favour
of the poor by the recognition of their human need and dignity.
In First Isaiah the work of the messiah was promised to bring a
judicial decision in favour of the poor.

He does not judge by appearances,
he gives no verdict on hearsay,
but judges the wretched with integrity,
and with equity gives a verdict for the poor of the land.
(Isa. 11.3-4)

In Second Isaiah the messianic time was seen as a time of plenty
for the hungry.

Oh, come to the water, all you who are thirsty;
though you have no money, come!
Buy corn without money, and eat,
and at no cost, wine and milk. (Isa. 55.1)

This messianic promise was dependent on a return to Yahweh,
on putting first the covenant promise of God.

Why spend money on what is not bread,
your wages on what fails to satisfy? (Isa. 55.2)

The actual imbalance of forces in the community was recognized by the principle of the 'sabbatical year' in which Israelites
who had been made bondservants for debt were to be set free
(Exod. 21.1), fields were to be left fallow and the produce which
came naturally was to be left for the poor and the wild animal
(Exod. 23.20-11). Deuteronomy added the remission of debts
every seventh year and pleaded that this should not lead to a
reluctance to lend as the seventh year approached (15.7-11).
The 'jubilee year' at the end of seven weeks of years (Lev. 25.8-

19) seems to have been a late addition to the text, expressing messianic hopes rather than reflecting actual past practice (de Vaux, 1961:175).

It is not clear how far the sabbatical year was actually put into effect, but the existence of the legislation at least demonstrated an intention to put into working form the basic principle of human stewardship of the earth and the fact that the promised land itself was a gift (Jer. 34.13-14). The principle did not deny the right to own property, but this right was always to be kept subordinate to the needs of all the human beings within the community of Israel. It did deny the right to accumulate at all costs in the face of the needs of the widow, the orphan, the stranger and those who had fallen into debt.

The notion of the poor as being of special concern to God arose from the certainty of God's prior activity in creation and in the covenant actions by which Israel was saved from Egypt and brought to its special position in Palestine — a position of trust which depended on continuous responsive activity. Care for the poor was not first of all a matter of human compassion, but a matter of the human response to God's creative act. Within the covenant community the fulfilment of all depended on equity towards even the least. Poverty was not made holy in itself. The fundamental vision was still that of human labour making the earth fruitful. The Book of Proverbs taught against idleness (10.4), but also against the corrupting effect of riches (11.28) and warned,

> To mock the poor is to insult his creator,
> he who laughs at distress shall not go unpunished.
> (Prov. 17.5)

It was clear to the post-exilic community, as to the earlier prophets, that many who were poor were so not by their own fault, and that many were poor through the deliberate action of others, particularly those who accumulated wealth. Indeed, accumulation was the primary sin against the poor.

> Woe to those who add house to house
> and join field to field

until everything belongs to them
and they are the sole inhabitants of the land. (Isa. 5.8)

Such accumulation overturned the fundamental order of the
covenant, in which the human beings together accepted responsibility for the creation at the hand of God, making the earth
fruitful by their labour and returning praise to the Creator. In
overturning the order of creation, those who oppressed the poor,
those who built up riches for themselves without concern for
others, not only risked their own lives, but risked bringing disaster upon the whole created order.

Political Power
Israel's primary political experience was that of liberation, claims
H. W. Wolff. 'Israel derives its history, not from any mythically
celebrated and politically tested monarchy, but from a group of
slaves who had been liberated from Egypt' (1974:193). The community began as a loose federation of tribes, bound together by
allegiance to the liberator God rather than to political institutions. It was led by the elders who were heads of families and by
appointed judges and their scribes (Joshua 24.1). These tribes
followed a common customary law and sometimes acted in groups
under a common leadership (Judges 4 and 5), but this was not
the normal form of leadership. 'The only authority manifest in
Israel at that time was charismatic' (de Vaux, 1961:93).

Even when the monarchy was established under Saul, the role
of the kings was to hold power under Yahweh. Deuteronomy
17.14-20 showed the king to be appointed by Yahweh, 'one from
among your brothers' (17.15), to be kept under restraint in respect of number of cavalry, number of wives and the demands of
the royal treasury. The king's principal function according to
Deuteronomy was to learn and to follow the law of Yahweh. 'It
must never leave him and he must read it every day of his life
and learn to fear Yahweh his God by keeping all the words of
this Law and observing these laws' (17.19).

As with the laws on property and the poor, so Deuteronomy's
ideal of the king as a representative figure, a first among equals,

51

may not have corresponded closely with the practice. The king, after all, had control of the army, the taxes and the royal estates, and he appointed the full-time judges in the various areas. The ideal nevertheless was believed to be rooted in the foundational experience of the people of being rescued from Egypt by a God-appointed leader, Moses, and it gave at least some basis for the prophets' criticism of royal injustices (Jer. 22.13-19).

The function of the king was indeed to be a 'saviour': to represent the welfare of the people in his own person and to ensure justice. Psalm 72, possibly used in the enthronement ceremony, began,

> God, give your own justice to the king,
> your own righteousness to the royal son,
> so that he may rule your people rightly
> and your poor with justice. (Ps. 72.1-2)

Such virtue would overcome enemies (72.7-11) and even ensure agricultural prosperity (72.16).

The final phase of Old Testament political experience was that of a community without political power, bound together by religious faith and religious institutions. The restoration of Jerusalem after the exile was undertaken by commissioners appointed by foreign rulers, first Cyrus and then Darius, yet even this work was ascribed to Yahweh. 'But now, suddenly, Yahweh our God by his favour has left us a remnant and granted us a refuge in his holy place; this is how our God has cheered our eyes and given us a little respite in our slavery' (Ezra 9.8). So alien rule became bearable and arguably even irrelevant to Israel's calling as a religious community.

In all this history there was no suggestion of pacifism as a political objective. The promise of peace was for the future as a gift from Yahweh (Psalm 72.7); eventually it became a sign of the time of the Messiah. The task was rather to know when action was in accordance with God's will and when it was not. All human power was suspect in itself.

> A large army will not keep a king safe,
> nor does the hero escape by his great strength;

it is delusion to rely on the horse for safety,
for all its power, it cannot save. (Psalm 33.16-17)

The satire on the king of Babylon (Isa. 14.3-21) was a satire on
all pretensions to a power that was not God-given. The real opportunity for peace would come only in the time of complete acknowledgement of God.

They do no hurt, no harm,
on all my holy mountain,
for the country is filled with the knowledge of Yahweh
as the waters swell the sea. (Isa. 11.9)

This long and varied political history of Israel gradually built
up a strand in the Old Testament which saw the whole of humanity as having a common need of release from oppression.
Even the rules dealing with slaves showed some sense of a common humanity in God: in the Decalogue the slave was to share
in the sabbath rest (Exod. 20.10) and in the Deuteronomic legislation on the sabbatical year the bondsman released after six
years was not to go empty-handed, 'as Yahweh your God has
blessed you, so you must give to him' (Deut. 15.12-14). The rule
of Yahweh operated as a source of restraint upon the oppressor
and of hope for a different future.

H. W. Wolff concludes, 'Thus the Old Testament sees men in
the midst of social tensions as being on the road to freedom,
between the declaration of Yahweh's early acts in salvation history and those future acts which prophecy has proclaimed'
(1974:205). Even the masters of slaves belonged to a people who
had been slaves and but for God might be slaves again. As Old
Testament thought turned increasingly to the apocalyptic future, so that future set a standard for the present to attain.

After this
I will pour out my spirit on all mankind.
Your sons and daughters shall prophesy,
your old men shall dream dreams,
and your young men shall see visions.

Even on the slaves, men and women,
will I pour out my spirit in those days.
I will display portents in heaven and on earth,
blood and fire and columns of smoke.
(Joel 2.28-31)

(iv) The New Covenant

By the beginning of the first century AD the Rabbis were teaching, on the basis of the Hebrew Bible, that God had chosen Israel as a special people. The choice was made out of God's own perfect freedom of action, not for any merit of Israel. In response to this loving act of God the Jewish people were expected to respond with pure worship and with the maintenance of a balanced social order. It was expected, humans being what they are, that individuals and sometimes the whole people would fall short of this standard. For this there was provided a means of maintaining the covenant, through repentance, through restitution to persons who had been harmed, and through the corresponding acts of worship, principally sacrifices.

Rabbinic Judaism was a religion of grace rather than of legal obligation. N. H. Søe, writing as a Christian student of ethics, says, 'The central teaching of the Pentateuch is not God's strict or even merciless punishments, but His trustworthiness, His faithfulness to His covenant, notwithstanding all the grumbling and transgressions of His people' (1968:307). At the same time Judaism was very much a religion of this world. The working-out of God's grace through the covenant was expected in terms of earthly happiness or unhappiness, though this was conditioned by a recognition that suffering might have a cleansing effect on the believer, and that some retribution for sin might have to await a further judgment beyond this world.

The transition from the old covenant to the new covenant of Jesus was therefore not a transition from 'Law' to 'Gospel'. Rather it was a transition from grace through Torah to grace through the name of Jesus. As Søe continues, 'And it is just the same in the New Testament. Everything is here directly centered around the name of Jesus Christ'.

But what does this mean? So far as Jesus himself is concerned it is very difficult to answer the question, because all the material that now exists under the heading of 'the New Testament' is part of the record made by the early church after the experience of Jesus' death, the apparent failure of his life, the experience of new life in the community after the resurrection of Jesus, and the beginnings of the success of Christian mission in the wider world beyond Jerusalem and Galilee.

Critical scholarship allows at least two things to be said out of this material about Jesus himself.

The first is that he did not intend to found a church. There is no hint that Jesus envisaged a body of 'Christians' splitting off from Judaism to form a separate assembly. Rather he seems to have predicted the end of Judaism itself in its present form and its replacement by the open rule or 'kingdom' of God. In this kingdom the righteous would receive justice and the unrighteous would be condemned.

The second point is that Jesus seems to have envisaged himself as having the central role in preparing for this kingdom. It was this that was the cause of offence between Jesus and the Jewish leaders in Jerusalem. In effect Jesus announced that in this final moment of judgment the act of following him replaced the system of atonement through the Temple and the observance of the Law. He himself was the point of entry for the new relationship with God. It was sufficient reason for the Jewish authorities to regard him as a blasphemer and a rebel. The Roman authorities needed no more than an indication of a movement and a leader to cause them to cut off the leader as a potential source of trouble.

In practical terms the whole mission became a failure when Jesus was executed. Only slowly did those who had been his followers realize that there was another way of reading the whole situation. There is a record of this debate in Luke 24.13-35, where the mysterious stranger met on the road to Emmaus explains to two of the followers how it had been predicted in the Hebrew Bible that the Messiah must suffer. The stranger, who promptly disappears, is recognized as the risen Jesus in the eucharistic act of breaking and blessing bread.

What in fact the followers became convinced of was that Jesus lived. Paul was clear that the resurrection body was not the same as the earthly body. 'Whatever you sow in the ground has to die before it is given new life and the thing that you sow is not what is going to come . . .' (I Cor. 15.36, 37). What mattered was the double conviction that in the resurrection appearances the followers were encountering the same person, and that because Jesus lived, they lived also. As Paul put it in the Letter to the Romans, 'You have been taught that when we were baptised in Christ Jesus we were baptised in his death; in other words, when we were baptised we went into the tomb with him and joined him in death, so that as Christ was raised from the dead by the Father's glory, we too might live a new life' (Rom. 6.3, 4).

This new relationship was brilliantly symbolized for the church by the move from the Jewish liturgy of the Passover to the Christian liturgy of the resurrection. Whenever the eucharist was celebrated — and the evidence is that it was celebrated continuously from the time the disciples became convinced of the resurrection — the action proclaimed the living presence of Jesus. When bread was taken, blessed, broken and distributed, when wine was taken, blessed and passed round, when the words were spoken, 'This is my body' and 'This is my blood', the church both remembered the events of the last supper with Jesus and his suffering and death, and asserted the living presence of its risen Lord.

Swept away in this movement was all the detail of Jewish sacrificial worship. The Passover, the annual remembrance of the escape from Egypt which was the foundation of the Jewish sense of being a nation under God, was transformed into a weekly and even daily remembrance of the self-offering of Jesus. Even the day of the weekly observance was changed from the Sabbath, the seventh day of creation, to Sunday, the first day of the new creation, the eighth day of the week.

Whether the Christians wished it so or not, by keeping the eucharist they separated themselves from Judaism. For the bread and wine symbolized the one self-offering by which Jesus went to his death. As the Letter to the Hebrews said, 'By virtue of that one single offering, he has achieved the eternal perfection of all whom he is sanctifying' (Heb. 10.14). The offer of one act of repentance, forgiveness and communion with God was now open to all human beings simply in the name of Jesus.

It was this separation of Christians and Jews that was the difficult question for Paul. After all, he himself was a Jew, trained in the rabbinic teachings. As he wrote, in the Letter to the Romans, 'What I want to say is this: my sorrow is so great, my mental anguish so endless, I would willingly be condemned and cut off from Christ if it could help my brothers of Israel, my own flesh and blood' (Rom. 9.2). But why should God's promises, given first to the Jews, now be fulfilled in those who were rapidly becoming a non-Jewish group?

The only possible explanation that occurred to him was that by this move God was preparing something better for both Christians and Jews. The new thing was a new and simpler way of entry to salvation. As he now saw it, from the standpoint of a follower of Jesus, the problem about salvation was two-fold: that the Law should not be abolished and that the promises to Israel should not be broken.

On the one hand, the Law was not abolished by Jesus' death and resurrection, but fulfilled. It was precisely the condemnation of the Law on human sin that Jesus accepted in accepting his death. Yet on its own the Law could be no more than a form of condemnation. No one in practice, thought Paul, could claim to live a life that was perfect by the standard of Torah. The mere knowledge of good and evil could not in itself bring salvation. In the Letter to the Romans he described from his perspective as a Christian the state of someone who knows what good is but finds her or himself unable to do it. 'What a wretched man I am! Who will rescue me from this body doomed to death? Thanks be to God through Jesus Christ our Lord!' (Rom. 7.24, 25). Only the appeal to Jesus would really work.

The ability to know good and the tendency to do evil were both part of the same human nature. For Paul freedom came not from knowledge but from empowerment. The power of the

57

Spirit which raised Jesus from the dead would also allow God to effect in the human being what the human being could not do alone. But this meant first that the human being must know what the previous failure was, and second that she or he must accept the power of God's love to forgive and overcome that failure. The way into new life was first to know the self as forgiven, and then to know the extent of the sin. This double dynamic was already recognised within the Law, but for Paul it had become clear that only by participation in the risen life of Jesus could the dynamic actually work for everyone.

So Paul came to the other half of his argument, which was that the promises made to the Israelite people were not broken. Those who kept the faith of Abraham were not those who were in physical descent from Abraham, but those who still had the courage to set out from home to find the promised land. The rejection of those who held to the Law without Jesus would not last for ever. 'God has imprisoned all men in their own disobedience only to show mercy to all mankind' (Rom. 11.32).

It was easy for later Christian writers, without Paul's rabbinic background, to come to regard the Jews as representing a wilful persistence in rejection of the one chance of rescue. The opposition of Jews and Christians in the early Roman empire was a complex matter, since in much of their belief and practice the churches stayed close to Judaism. At times it was a question of a struggle for political influence as much as it was a theological dispute. But the ground was now being laid for a theological bias of Christianity against the Jews. Matthew's indictment of the 'scribes and Pharisees' (Matt. 23.13-39) and John's delineation of 'the Jews' (John 6), helped to create a stereotype which had grievous results whenever in western Christendom political pressures made it convenient to find scapegoats through anti-Semitism.

The irony of this situation lies in the fact that the central ethical message of the New Testament can be summed up in the single word 'love'. Paul makes this clear in the hymn on love in I Cor. 13, Matthew makes it clear in the parable of the Last Judgment in Matt. 25.31-46, Luke makes it clear in Jesus' first sermon in Luke 4.16-22, and John makes it clear in the last discourse in John 15-17, ending with the words:

> I have made your name known to them
> and will continue to make it known,
> so that the love with which you loved me may be in them,
> and so that I may be in them. (John 17.26)

Since the letters of Paul, and much of the material in the gospels, originate in a period when there were still plenty of people around in Jerusalem and in Galilee who had known Jesus himself, it might well be argued that the young communities would not have accepted as central to their message an ethic about loving the neighbour which was not consonant with what they knew of Jesus. The fact that all knowledge of Jesus had to be reread in the light of his death and resurrection helps to account for the variety in the New Testament writings, but there is no reason to suppose that the communities were not looking also for a continuity with the historical Jesus. Nor is there any reason to doubt that they found that continuity in a reformulation of the Jewish ethic of neighbour love.

The love of the neighbour and the love of God were not to be separated. They began together in the love within the community. As Paul reminded the believers in Corinth, the Christian thanksgiving meal was a participation in Christ. 'The blessing-cup that we bless is a communion with the blood of Christ, and the bread that we break is a communion with the body of Christ' (I Cor. 10.16). This was also a belonging to one another. 'The fact that there is only one loaf means that, though there are many of us, we form a single body, because we all have a share in this one loaf' (I Cor. 17). Similarly, in the image of the church as the body of Christ he stressed the unity in diversity of the Christian community. 'In the one Spirit we were all baptised, Jews as well as Greeks, slaves as well as citizens, and one Spirit was given us all to drink' (I Cor. 12.13).

In the great hymn to love in the next chapter, Paul explored the possibilities of the Spirit-filled community. 'If I have all the eloquence of men or of angels, but speak without love, I am simply a gong booming or a cymbal clashing' (I Cor. 13.1). He wrote of the patience of love and its kindness, its absence of jealousy, its hope, its endurance. He wrote too that in human experience the fullness of love in the universe had to be taken on trust. 'For our knowledge is imperfect and our prophesying is imperfect; but once perfection comes, all imperfect things will disappear' (I Cor. 13.9, 10). But a time would come when all would be made clear. Until then, the qualities of faith, hope and love were required for the Christian life — and the greatest of them was love.

It might seem that this hymn to the very personal qualities of faith, hope and love must be in contradiction to the emphasis in the Gospel according to Matthew on the fulfilling of the Law. Jesus as a teacher of the Law said at the beginning of the Sermon on the Mount, 'Do not imagine that I have come to abolish the Law or the Prophets. I have not come to abolish but to complete them' (Matt. 5.17). This is possibly because Matthew was addressing a community which stayed close to Judaism and consequently was concerned to stress a continuity between the Torah and Jesus.

Yet the treatment of the Law in the Sermon on the Mount (Matt. 5-7) raises problems for this interpretation of Matthew's purpose.

In the first place it should be noted that the Sermon opens with the Beatitudes which, like I Corinthians 13, are concerned with personal qualities rather than particular actions. 'How happy are the poor in Spirit . . . the gentle . . . those who mourn . . . those who hunger and thirst for what is right . . . the merciful . . . the pure in heart . . . the peacemakers . . . those who are persecuted in the cause of right' (Matt. 5.2-10). If this is the Law, it is a very particular reading of the Law, though one not entirely absent from the Rabbinic tradition.

In the second place, it should be noted that when treated as law, the particular requirements of the Sermon pose severe problems. As direct moral demands, the teachings of the Sermon seem immoderate. From a prohibition of murder it moves to a prohibition of calling another 'a fool'; from a prohibition of adultery to a prohibition of lust in the heart; from a provision for the divorce of a wife by a husband to a prohibition of divorce and remarriage for either; from the limiting of revenge to an equal exchange of 'an eye for an eye' to a prohibition of offering resistance to evil; from a command to love the neighbour to a command to love the enemy. All these moves constitute a radical reading of the Jewish ethic.

The whole movement can be summed up in the final words of this section of the Sermon, 'You must therefore be perfect just as your heavenly Father is perfect' (Matt. 5.48).

Not all the ethical material in the New Testament has this radical character. The First Letter of John clearly intends the love of the brother which is the hallmark of the new community to be a love of those who are within the community.

> In this way we distinguish the children of God
> from the children of the devil:
> anybody not living a holy life
> and not loving his brother
> is no child of God's. (I John 3.10)

The detailed instructions of the First Letter to Timothy on women's dress (I Tim. 2.9), on the behaviour of church officials (I Tim. 3), and on the rank of 'widow' and 'elder', are simply good practical advice. Even the lists of good and bad activities in the major letters of Paul (such as I Cor. 6.9, 10 and Gal. 2.21) are not fundamentally different from similar lists given by other writers on morals of the period. There is a broad agreement among serious writers on morals in the ancient world, whether Jewish, Christian or pagan, that family relationships should be sustained, that truth should be told, fair dealing should be maintained, and that drunkenness and debauchery are not worthy of rational beings.

On the other hand the New Testament writers retained a sense that in Jesus the kingdom of God had already come, though it was not yet open and visible to all. The power was already present and they experienced it. The resurrection alone was sufficient assurance of that. The ethical problem lay in the fact that the radical demands of the New Testament seemed to be based on the expectation of the kingdom coming quickly in full. Only so were they sustainable. Once that expectation disappeared the ethical demands might be impossible and even irresponsible. Yet the young communities stubbornly held on to the promise of the New Covenant, with its understanding that the kingdom had already arrived in the life, death and resurrection of Jesus, even in advance of a final consummation. Those who lived between the resurrection and the eschaton were convinced that the kingdom was already present. The song of Mary in the birth narrative of Luke used quotations from the Old Testament to establish that the expected future action of God must be considered a present reality.

> *He has pulled down princes* from their thrones *and exalted the lowly.*
> *The hungry he has filled with good things,* the rich sent empty away. (Luke 1:52,53)

The kingdom had come already because great things were being done in the Spirit. The Acts of the Apostles recorded of the first converts, 'These remained faithful to the teaching of the Apostles, to the brotherhood, to the breaking of bread and to the prayers. The many miracles and signs worked through the apostles made a deep impression on everyone' (Luke 2:42, 43). In this early charismatic community the fulfilment of the radical ethic did not seem to be a problem.

What the young Christians were clear about was that in Jesus they had a measure of what humanity was to become. In the Spirit of Jesus they encountered a power which would enable them to fill up that measure. The radical ethic was not intrinsically impossible, but it had to be seen in the double timescale of the present activity and the future fulfilment of the kingdom. This inevitably meant a tension between the present and the future.

(v) Ethics in the New Testament

Christian ethics had to be created by balancing the two principles of order and of change. Order, because God had created the world and the creation was still good, in part and in potential, in all the institutions of human community. Change, because what already existed was not yet fully conformed to the future order of God. So there was the paradox that the kingdom created an imperative that was too radical to be obeyed as a rule. To love the enemy, to refuse to resist evil by violent action, to be faithful in human relationships and to put no trust in possessions was to challenge the every-day reality of the social order and to call for its transformation into something new. Yet even within the period covered by the New Testament some sort of indication of what the new order required had to be sketched out.

Sexuality

In the new covenant the image of God was transferred from Eve and Adam, humanity in its natural state, to Jesus Christ, the image of humanity in its future state.

> He is the image of the unseen God
> and the first-born of all creation . . . (Col. 1.15)

Reflection by the first Christians on the significance of Jesus led to the conclusion that the whole creative process had to be seen in a new light. In the risen Christ, humanity could now be seen in the light of its future as well as of its past. The past was not swept away, but transformed by the new significance of human life as being capable of the resurrection life.

Essentially sexuality was not a major concern in the New Testament. Christians inherited the Jewish conviction that sexuality was good in itself. Jesus was radical in his openness to the potential of the image of God in women as well as men and in enemies as well as friends, as is suggested by the two stories concerning Samaritans (the 'good Samaritan', Luke 10.29-37, and the woman at the well, John 4.5-30). All the evidence about Jesus is already a part of Christian tradition in the Gospels and the letters; nevertheless what comes across from all the sources is a radical reassertion of God's demand for fidelity in relationships as the centre of Christian life. If there is any ethical teaching which can safely be attributed to Jesus himself, it is the radical demand, in terms of current practice, that promises be kept.

> But from the beginning of creation *God made them male and female. This is why a man must leave father and mother, and the two become one body.* They are no longer two, therefore, but one body. So then, what God has united, man must not divide. (Mark 10.6-9)

One effect of this was greatly to improve the situation of women, who were now entitled to put much greater trust in the promise of mutual fidelity. 'Jesus did not proclaim a new sexual ethic as such; rather, he centered attention on the best thinking of his day by placing men and women on the same level not merely in theory but also in real life' (Kosnik, 1977:20).

By returning to the theology of creation, Jesus affirmed that sexuality was part of God's founding intention and an opportunity to make progress in the life of covenantal fidelity. What was required was not any kind of law, but a simple willingness to persist, for the same reason that God persisted with Israel, because the nature of love was to overcome by faith in the beloved — whatever the beloved might be.

Equally, marriage was not to be seen as more than a part of earthly experience: 'For at the resurrection men and women do not marry; no, they are like the angels in heaven' (Matt. 22.30); celibacy was a possibility (Matt. 19.10-12): and the disciples were praised for giving up their families for the sake of Jesus' mission (Matt. 19.27-30).

Yet this affirmation that the social institution of marriage was a pathway for covenantal fidelity did not in itself provide the details of an ethic. The ensuing debate about the nature of Christian life was perhaps reflected in Matthew's exception to the rule forbidding divorce.

> It has also been said: *Anyone who divorces his wife must give her a writ of dismissal.* But I say this to you: everyone who divorces his wife, except for the case of fornication, makes her an

adulteress; and anyone who marries a divorced woman commits adultery.
(Matt. 5.31-32, quoting Deut.24.1)

Though it is not clear what *porneia*, the word translated here as
'fornication' means (more broadly it can be translated 'uncleanness' and might mean 'incest'), there is at least a possibility that
the phrase here and at Matthew 19.9 is an addition by a Christian community that was already finding the absolute prohibition of divorce too heavy a burden. If so, we have here an early
example of a process that certainly existed — and was necessary
— quite soon afterward in the life of the church, the process of
Christian law-making.

In replying to questions from the Christian community in
Corinth Paul was quite clear that he was involved in the business
of Christian law-making. Having dealt with the teaching against
divorce and noted that what is forbidden has two stages — separation and remarriage — all this as a teaching 'from the Lord' (I
Cor. 7.10-11), Paul went on to give teaching in his own name on
a new issue, whether Christian converts should remain in union
with spouses who were unbelievers, and concluded in favour of
maintaining the union where possible, because of the influence
that the Christian partner could have on the spouse and the
children (I Cor. 7.12-16). This need to tackle new situations was
a major factor in the development of Christian ethics.

For Paul, however, the need was not for a new set of rules but
for a new way of thinking about the whole framework of life.
The return of the Lord was to be expected soon. Consequently
all human activities were to be subordinated to the demands of
the eschaton.

> Brothers, this is what I mean: our time is growing short. Those
> who have wives should live as though they had none, and
> those who mourn should live as though they had nothing to
> mourn for; those who are enjoying life should live as though
> there were nothing to laugh about; those whose life is buying
> things should live as though they had nothing of their own;
> and those who have to deal with the world should not

become engrossed in it. I say this because the world as we
know it is passing away.
(I Cor. 7.29-31)

Consequently the specific advice Paul had to give in this chapter needs to be treated with some reserve. Paul himself was clearly
in favour of celibacy (I Cor. 7.7), but he was not prepared to call
marriage sinful (I Cor. 7.25-28). Because sexuality was such a
powerful force, wives and husbands should not refuse one another, except by mutual consent for an agreed period of prayer.

Paul's teaching on sexuality was an amalgam of the radical
thinking which began with Jesus and the older inhibitions of
patriarchy. In the Letter to the Galatians he asserted the ontological equality of every baptised person with every other. 'All
baptised in Christ, you have all clothed yourselves in Christ, and
there are no more distinctions between Jew and Greek, slave and
free, male and female, but all of you are one in Christ Jesus'
(Gal. 3.27-28). Just as this ontological status did not immediately
initiate a social revolution to free slaves, so the situation of women
remained ambiguous, even within the church. Women were
admitted to the eucharist equally with men, but were they admitted to the ministry?

Paul reasserted the tradition of patriarchy in I Corinthians
11.2-16, where he argued that woman was not made directly in
the image of God (11.7), and that if a woman prophesied she
should keep her head covered because of the angels (11.10). If
this is a reference to the mythology of Genesis 6.1-4, as seems
probable, it is far removed from the argument on Christian freedom in the Letter to the Galatians. Even more difficult is the
clash between this passage and I Corinthians 14.34-40, which
forbids women to speak in church at all, on the basis of the
Jewish Law. For this reason some commentators regard the latter
passage as an addition to the Pauline text. Whatever the status
and explanation of these two passages, they are at least a reminder that at no point does the New Testament contain a systematic and coherent exposition of 'Christian ethics'.

Between Paul's urgent expectation of the arrival of the eschaton
and the later, more settled life of the churches came the most

substantial passage on Christian marriage in the New Testament, the Letter to the Ephesians, 5.21-33. Whether or not this letter was by Paul himself, it showed clear marks of Pauline theology, not least in the treatment of marriage. Beginning with mutual obedience, 'Give way to one another in obedience to Christ', the letter developed the theme of the church as the bride of Christ, completing the Old Testament image of Israel as the bride of Yahweh and showing Christian marriage as a human analogy of the relationship of Christ and the church. In terms of mutual covenantal fidelity, the passage enlarged the message already given in the teaching attributed to Jesus on divorce and in Paul's comments in I Corinthians 7. The emphasis put on the love of the husband for his wife may indeed be a new note in the culture of the ancient world. Wolfgang Schrage comments that 'The admonition calling on husbands to love their wives, in the sense demanded by the context of the whole of Ephesians, is something new and unique in the ancient world' (1988:253).

It would have made more sense theologically if the author of Ephesians had been able to say that the husband should love his wife as Christ loved the church and that the wife should love her husband as Christ loved the church. But embedded patriarchy did not permit this. Instead the astonishing and quite illegitimate claim was made that one human being could stand to another as Christ stands to humanity, without a mutuality of this in-Christ love. The conflict with the radical sanity of Paul in I Corinthians 7.3-5 is instructive about the way that thinking in the church was going. The image of God in Jesus Christ was now to be applied to one half of the human race but not to the other.

After this the churches settled down to less urgent expectations of the eschaton and more detailed regulation of their own life. In I Timothy 3.1-13 instructions were given on the qualifications for elders-in-charge and for deacons; in I Tim. 5.3-25 on the behaviour of widows and elders; and in I Tim. 6.1-2 on the behaviour of slaves to masters, but not of masters to slaves, unlike Ephesians 6.5-9. The proper management of family life and respect for established orders of society were becoming the new criteria of a Christian ethic.

In general, where the New Testament did give moral instruction, it was not noticeably different from that which was supplied by serious-minded pagan philosophers. 'You know perfectly well that people who do wrong will not inherit the kingdom of God: people of immoral lives, idolaters, adulterers, catamites, sodomites, thieves, usurers, drunkards, slanderers and swindlers will never inherit the kingdom of God' (I Cor. 6.9). The difference was not so much in the sort of things which might be done, but in the power which was given by the Holy Spirit for change. 'These are the sort of people some of you were once, but now you have been washed clean, and sanctified, and justified through the name of the Lord Jesus Christ and through the Spirit of our God' (I Cor. 6.10-11). There were, however, more serious matters than sexual sins which might stand between the new convert and the fullness of the power of Jesus Christ.

Property

The first stance towards possessions in the New Testament was a radical subordination of the material world to the coming of the kingdom of God. The open reign of God constituted a reversal of all values, among them the belief that the possession of material objects constituted a route to happiness. Possessions were now to be put to the work of their true owner, God.

This meant that possessions were to be seen fundamentally in the form of gifts. As a gift of God the material world would be available to the children of God to meet their essential needs.

> That is why I am telling you not to worry about your life and what you are to eat, nor about your body and how you are to clothe it. Surely life means more than food and the body more than clothing! . . . Your heavenly Father knows you need them all. Set your hearts on his kingdom first, and on his righteousness, and all these other things will be given you as well. (Matt. 6.25; 32b-33)

In the same way the children of the kingdom were to pray, 'Give us today our daily bread' (Matt. 6.11), referring not only to the needs of the day, but also to the history of salvation, when

Yahweh fed Israel with manna in the desert (Exod. 16), and through the bread of the eucharist to the messianic banquet, the meal of the great Tomorrow when God's reign would be fully known. The belief in sufficient provision for the present day was also an act of faith in the past history and the future promise.

The faith in future provision, however, would only work if the material world was seen as a gift also in the sense of something to be given. 'Give to everyone who asks, and do not ask for your property back from the man who robs you' (Luke 6.30). Charity was the foundation of the new ethic, but what was at issue was more than the helping of those in need, as the second half of Luke's sentence made clear, though Matthew reads, 'if anyone wants to borrow, do not turn away' (Matt. 5:42). What was at stake was the sovereign freedom of God over all material things, a freedom the followers of Jesus had to share with regard to that which passed through their own hands. The second half of the sentence also served as a warning that the followers of Jesus might not receive entirely what they prayed for. Reliance on God was not a route to material prosperity.

The question may be asked, whether the synoptic Gospels do not contain a more serious rejection of material things? 'No servant can be the slave of two masters: he will either hate the first and love the second, or treat the first with respect and the second with scorn. You cannot be the slave both of God and of money' (Luke 16.13). 'Mammon' is the term used here and at verses 9 and 11 where the Jerusalem Bible translates 'money'. Wolfgang Schrage comments, 'Here, as in rabbinic usage, it means not just money in the narrow sense but all one's possessions, everything of monetary value, one's total resources. It is not limited to especially great wealth, but refers to possessions of all kinds without regard for quantity and value' (1988:102).

Other sayings and stories made the same point: the rich farmer who died suddenly without using his stored-up wealth (Luke 12.16-21); the rich man and the beggar Lazarus (Luke 16.19-31); the rich young man who wanted to become a disciple but who turned away when told to sell everything he had (Mark 10.17-22); and the subsequent saying attributed to Jesus that 'It is easier for a camel to pass through the eye of a needle than for a rich man to enter the kingdom of God' (Mark 10.23-27). The disciples, expressing amazement that anybody could be saved under these circumstances, were told that for human beings it was impossible, but that for God all things were possible.

It is clear from these passages that, firstly, active discipleship in the sense of sharing in the immediate mission of Jesus before the crucifixion meant giving up all possessions and family responsibilities. The first who were called abandoned even the tools of their trade — boat and nets — to follow Jesus (Mark 1.16-20). On the sending-out of the Twelve they were told, for this particular journey, to 'take nothing for the journey except a staff — no bread, no haversack, no coppers for their purses' (Mark 6.7-8). The version in Matthew added, 'for the workman deserves his keep' (Matt. 10.9-10).

This gives a clue to the second point, that not everyone associated with Jesus was called to the same absolute renunciation. Some had to go on working, raise families, have a surplus from which others could be helped. Such were the women, including Mary Magdalene, Joanna and Susanna, who provided for Jesus and the Twelve 'out of their own resources' (Luke 8.1-3). The missionaries were to be present only as bearers of the message, not as craftsmen or traders. Those who heard were to put their goods at the disposal of the mission, but also to continue to sustain daily life for themselves.

The third point is that any concern for material possessions which was not about daily sustenance and the forwarding of the work of God was highly dangerous. Sexuality might be a passing problem, but the concern to accumulate material things cut the soul off from God absolutely,. It negated precisely that which was central, the conscious awareness of the supremacy of the present rule of God. The use of 'mammon' in Luke 16.13 carried with it a sense of money as an idol, a power over against God. Wolfgang Schrage comments on the mission of the Twelve, 'Here as elsewhere the law of love is the absolute norm, to which all other considerations are secondary. This love knows nothing of inviolable property rights and distribution of wealth, but controls and restricts the use of possessions lest they become a source of idolatrous dependence' (1988:106-107).

The radical subordination of the material world to the coming of the kingdom of God in the synoptic Gospels also accounted for the special place given to the poor.

> How happy are you who are poor; yours is the kingdom of God.
> Happy you who are hungry now: you shall be satisfied.
> Happy you who weep now: you shall laugh. (Luke 6.20-21)

Those who had nothing were nearest to the kingdom. Having no material distractions they were the most ready to listen to the Christian mission. Having experience of suffering, they were the most anxious for release. The blessings to the poor and woes to the rich were given to those, respectively, who accepted their life at the hand of God, however harsh, and those who set their sights on their own ability to accumulate. It was not that the state of being poor was in itself blessed, nor that the state of being rich was in itself evil, but that the sets of values associated with the two conditions were more and less amenable to the possibility of an action of God in the world. As Martin Hengel comments, 'God is near to the poor, the despised, the sick, as they stand before him with empty hands, like the prodigal son standing before his generous father' (1974:30).

The preferential option for the poor in the synoptic Gospels was not about social change to give the poor an equal share of economic resources and political power. The reversal which Luke proclaimed in the Magnificat, of the downfall of the mighty and exaltation of the lowly, of the feeding of the hungry and the sending away empty of the rich (Luke 1.52-53), was effected by the birth of Jesus. It was the proclamation that all humanity, poor and rich, was capable, within the limits of its createdness, of bearing the being of God and was henceforth to be known by that possibility and not by its particular material conditions.

This recognition of the human potentiality of God-bearing, symbolized liturgically by baptism into Christ's death and rising to life, also had an economic and political implication, that to deal with the poor man or woman was to deal with Jesus Christ. As David Mealand remarks at the conclusion of his study of the treatment of the poor in the Gospels, 'the New Testament gives no comfort to those who think that religion or morality can turn a blind eye to oppression, injustice or flagrant inequalities' (1980:98).

How did the young Christian communities carry out this essentially radical policy of subordinating possessions to the demands of the kingdom of God? The earliest practical record of those communities in the letters of St Paul pays very little attention to the matter. The earliest letters, I and II Thessalonians, laid stress on the need to uphold the credit of Christians in the community in general by 'living quietly, attending to your own business and earning your living' (I Thess. 4.11). The dangers of idleness and sponging on others were mentioned twice more (I Thess. 5.14; II Thess. 3.7-12). Paul himself worked with his hands as a tentmaker (Acts 18.3) and reminded both the community at Corinth and the community in Thessalonica that he was not a financial burden as a missionary (II Cor. 12.13-15; I Thess. 2.9).

Though the first Christians covered a wide social spectrum, from slaves to persons of substantial property, their base was among the urban artisans and the professional class. Here the Jewish respect for work as a part of God's order in creation would strike a sympathetic note. Nevertheless, where support was freely offered, it might also be freely accepted (Phil. 4.10-20). In particular, Paul pressed the needs of the community in Jerusalem, suffering in conditions of famine (Romans 15.25-28). As he explained to the Corinthians, this service was a matter of giving concrete expression to the ontological reality of union in Christ. 'Remember how generous the Lord Jesus was: he was rich, but he became poor for your sake, to make you rich out of his poverty' (II Cor. 8.9).

All of this was written under the same expectation of the imminence of the eschaton that marked the teaching of Jesus himself. Along with his exposition of the ethics of sexuality, Paul also relativized the transaction of business: 'those whose life is buying and selling things should live as though they had nothing of their own' (I Cor. 7.30). Slaves were a form of property, but even the status of slave was not to be a matter of great concern. 'Let everyone stay as he was at the time of his call. If, when you were called, you were a slave, do not let this bother you; but if you should have the chance of being free, accept it' (I Cor. 7.20-21). The Letter to Philemon, however, showed a strong pastoral concern about the fate of a runaway slave who had now become a Christian and whose master was also a disciple of Paul. Here Paul made it clear that the relationship in Christ should prevail over the law and custom of master and slave. The kingdom of God was always to be the final test of behaviour.

That the young communities experienced tensions between rich and poor is clear. In the First Letter to the Corinthians Paul had to deal with such tensions in the context of the eucharist (11.17-34). The Letter of James attacked head-on those who despised the poor within the church. 'Listen, my dear brothers: it was those who are poor according to the world that God chose, to be rich in faith and to be the heirs to the kingdom which he promised to those who love him' (James 2.5). The rich came in for sharp condemnation (James 5.1-6).

These signs of tension contrast with the most tantalizing of all the New Testament passages about possessions. In Acts 2.42-47, immediately following the mass conversions of the day of Pentecost, there is a brief account of the life of the very first Christian community, which includes the words, 'The faithful all lived together and owned everything in common; they sold their goods and possessions and shared out the proceeds among themselves according to what each one needed' (2.44-45). This picture was repeated in Acts 4.32-35 and reinforced with two stories, of Barnabas who sold a field and contributed the proceeds, and of Ananias and Sapphira who claimed to have contributed everything but kept back a part, and were punished with death (Acts 4.36-5.11).

Acts 2.42-47 certainly presented a picture of what the first Christian community *ought* to have been like: the difficulty is to know how far it represented reality. On the one hand the circumstantial detail about Barnabas, Ananias and Sapphira may suggest an element of historical reality. On the other hand, the problems of Paul at Corinth in the eucharist and the need for a collection for the Christians in Jerusalem, the problem of the distribution to the widows in Jerusalem (Acts 6.1-7), together with the complaints against the rich later in James, all indicate that such an experiment, if it ever took place, must have ended very quickly. For one thing, the sheer size of the church in its rapid expansion among the gentiles must have made such intimacy of feeling increasingly difficult. For another, the first intensity of eschatological expectation must have eased quite soon and given way to more practical questions, as in the letters to Timothy.

The experience of Acts 2 was not so much an experiment in communism that failed, as an experiment in brotherly and sisterly love that was premature. If it truly took place, it foundered on the rock of perfectionism, the assumption that every Christian was already perfected in the kingdom of God, rather than trying to learn from the beginning the ways of the kingdom. It may have foundered also on another rock that Paul had warned about, that the life of the kingdom was about the hard work and good citizenship that first of all produces something to be shared.

Yet that experiment remained the light at the end of the tunnel, the sign of the future in which all effort would be for the sake of mutuality, not individual possession. For this reason the Christian tradition left it in place, as an essential part of the first 'day' of the church, which was the new day that was yet to come in the kingdom of God.

Political Power

The question of political power in the New Testament is first of all the question of a conflict between the kingdom of God and all political powers. For the worldly organs of power were not to be improved by Jesus' teaching, but to be replaced by the open rule of God. There was to be no further place for the exercise of power as formerly known on earth. From now on, every earthly exercise of power was to be in antagonism to the kingdom or in direct obedience to it. But the nature of power in the kingdom made it an impossible form for the earthly powers to follow. According to John, Jesus washed the disciples' feet, saying, 'If I, then, the Lord and Master, have washed your feet, you should wash each other's feet' (John 13.14); he chose the company of outcasts and sinners, leading to complaints from respectable folk (Mark 2.15-17), and told the sons of Zebedee that in their request to sit at his side in glory in heaven they misunderstood his mission, 'No, anyone who wants to become great among you must be your servant, and anyone who wants to be first among you must be slave to all' (Mark 10.43b-44).

The mark of the operation of the new kingdom was to be justice. Those who were deserving in God's sight would receive their reward, those whose value was in their own estimation or in the accumulation of material possessions or earthly power would have a rude awakening. The earthly order existed only to be overthrown. It had one remaining function: to crucify Jesus and so to reveal its own nature fully.

After Pentecost the Christian communities continued on the whole to regard the existing world order as one which was to be swept away. For the present the justice of the kingdom of God was to function within the communities themselves. So Christians were not to take one another to court, for earthly law was superseded by the law of *agape*, the perception of one another within the measure of God's justice. Those who were to judge the world in future by the law of *agape* were certainly competent to settle their own disputes (I Cor. 6.1-8).

This left the Christians with two problems. The first was about the nature of God's justice within the Christian bodies. Clearly in terms of the Sermon on the Mount the justice of the kingdom was creative rather than a matter of strict reward or punishment. The labourer who worked for the last hour of the day was to receive the same pay as those who worked for the whole day (Matt. 20.1-16); the son who wasted his inheritance had his return celebrated (Luke 15:11-32). *Agape* did not demand a strict account of what a person deserved, but rather responded with the utmost generosity to their conversion to love. As the communities developed into rule-making and rule-enforcing bodies this charismatic generosity had to give way to more measured forms of justice. So questions of the nature of power within the church began to arise. The concern of I Timothy 3.1-13 with the qualities of ruling elders and deacons is the beginning of this process.

The other problem was more momentous. The young Christian communities, even at the beginning, could not confine the question of power to their own internal order. Each community had to define its own relations with the state, both the Roman empire and the local powers. The situation of a minor sect of the Jews within the empire was not good. The Jews themselves were only just tolerated, in view of their past tendency to religiously-based rebellion. A group which the Jews themselves did not exactly welcome could not expect better treatment from the officials of the empire.

For this reason the first Christians walked a tightrope. For the sake of their own mission they desired the maximum tolerance from the government. So I Peter, written perhaps in a time of persecution under Domitian or Trajan, urged 'For the sake of the Lord, accept the authority of every social institution: the emperor, as the supreme authority, and the governors as commissioned by him to punish criminals and praise good citizenship' (I Pet. 2.13-14). At the same time, Christians were 'slaves of no one except God' (I Pet. 2.16). The earthly institutions had practical advantages for Christians but no holiness of their own.

The benefits of Roman rule were in fact considerable; it brought open communications, substantial trade and a uniform legal system, at least for Roman citizens, though its demands for taxes were also heavy. Roman rule permitted a variety of religions, but asked for one thing from everyone, the worship of the emperor as the personification of the empire itself. The state was the ultimate authority for all activities within the culture. To refuse the very minimal signs of worship was to refuse to accept the authority of the state as such.

Christian monotheism, on the other hand, like Jewish monotheism, asserted the ultimate authority of one God, even over the state itself. The Christians did not have a problem about the Roman occupation of Palestine, but they did have a problem about the Roman claim to exercise ideological control in the area of religion, insofar as religion touched on the political interests of civil and military service. Two further New Testament passages deal with this issue, the story of the coin to pay tax (Mark 12.13-17) and Paul's remarks on government in the Letter to the Romans (13.1-7). Both look at first sight as though they are urging obedience to the government; both turn out on closer examination to be rather more subtle.

> Next they sent to him some Pharisees and some Herodians to catch him out in what he said. These came and said to him, 'Master we know you are an honest man, that you are not afraid of anyone, because a man's rank means nothing to you, and that you teach the way of God in all honesty. Is it permissible to pay taxes to Caesar or not? Should we pay, yes or no?' Seeing through their hypocrisy he said to them, 'Why do you set this trap for me? Hand me a denarius and let me see it'. They handed him one and he said, 'Whose head is this? Whose name?' 'Caesar's' they told him. Jesus said to them, 'Give back to Caesar what belongs to Caesar — and to God what belongs to God'. This reply took them completely by surprise.
> (Mark 12.13-17)

The story in Mark was meant as a trap by the Pharisees and the Herodians. If Jesus supported the refusal to pay tax to the emperor's agents, an unpopular tax to an occupying power, he would put himself at odds with that power and so be in danger of arrest. If he supported the payment of the tax, he would become a collaborator and so lose influence with most of the people of the land. Jesus' mission was neither to support nor to reject the occupying power, but to announce the end of all such power. By asking for a coin from his questioners (Mark 12.15b), Jesus immediately implicated them in their own trap, for to possess a coin bearing Caesar's image was already to be on terms of acceptance with the occupying power. To return to Caesar that which bore his image and title was to allow the present situation to continue in all its ambiguity, while to give back to God what

77

belonged to God was to reassert the priority of the announcement of the kingdom over all other concerns. For the kingdom was to be the end of all collaboration and of all nationalism as well.

The situation was a little more difficult for Paul, since after Jesus' passion and resurrection God's open rule had not yet come. As a Roman citizen Paul was quite ready to claim some of the benefits of Roman government (Acts 22.25-29) and at the end of his ministry he appealed to Caesar for judgment (Acts 25.10-12). In the Letter to the Romans, between two expositions of Christian love (12.1-21; 13.8-10), he set out the nature of Christian obedience to the secular authorities as a part of Christian service to God.

> You must all obey the governing authorities. Since all government comes from God, the civil authorities were appointed by God, and so anyone who resists authority is rebelling against God's decision, and such an act is bound to be punished. Good behaviour is not afraid of magistrates; only criminals have anything to fear. If you want to live without being afraid of authority, you must live honestly and authority may even honour you. The state is there to serve God for your benefit. If you break the law, however, you may well have fear: the bearing of the sword has its significance. The authorities are there to serve God: they carry out God's revenge by punishing wrongdoers. You must obey, therefore, not only because you are afraid of being punished, but also for conscience' sake. This is also the reason why you must pay taxes, since all government officials are God's officers. They serve God by collecting taxes. Pay every government official what he has a right to ask — whether it be direct tax or indirect, fear or honour. (Rom. 13.1-7)

It was not the purpose of the Christian mission, as Paul understood it, to offer any new political or economic powers in place of those that already existed, or to question the legitimacy of the existing powers on the basis of their commitment to justice. It would, in any case, have been a rash endeavour for such a tiny sect, but that was not the point. The point was that God's kingdom was still awaited, and was coming quickly (Rom. 13.11-14).

In this situation the practice of obedience was a temporary device. The power of the state could not be avoided in the present time. The structure of order created by the state, including the collection of taxes, was created by God (Rom. 13.1, 2, 6). From the service of God, 'by offering your living bodies as a holy sacrifice, truly pleasing to God' (Rom. 12.1) to the service of the state, since 'all government comes from God' (Rom. 13.1), the line of obedience was not based on the state's own claims but on the necessities of God's mission. Not even a Christian government could claim, on the basis of Paul's argument, to be anything but a temporary expedient. Yet government as such was also intended by God as part of the human attempt at fulfilling the image of God. As Wolfgang Schrage puts it, 'The state, too, is provisional, belonging to the world that is passing away, not final and absolute but temporary and transitory'. But he adds, this does not mean that the state is negligible, it has its place precisely because it is part of the interim period that leads to the eschaton. 'Christians can and must respect the provisional order of God's created world and not be too hasty in ignoring or sabotaging their implicit obligations to the state' (1988:236).

Under the pressure of persecution a later generation of Christians experienced the Roman state much more directly as an oppressor and an enemy. In the Revelation of St John the present world order did not lead into the kingdom of God but was a malign beast (Rev. 13), destined to be replaced by an entirely new order. 'Then I saw *a new heaven and a new earth*; the first heaven and the first earth had disappeared now, and there was no longer any sea. I saw the holy city, and the new Jerusalem, coming down from God out of heaven, as beautiful as a bride all dressed for her husband' (Rev. 21.1-2).

In the New Testament there was not a single view of the state, but a series of responses according to local conditions. All the sources were agreed, however, that in times of peace the state might be an ally to Christian work, as I Timothy suggested prayers for those in authority, 'so that we may be able to live religious and reverent lives in peace and quiet' (I Tim. 2.1-2). No Christian source suggested that the state itself was holy or to be obeyed at all costs; all saw it as relative to the power of God; some saw it as a direct enemy.

Did the possibility of resistance to political power stretch as far as violent resistance? In New Testament terms this question cannot be answered, because it mistakes the purpose of the mission of Jesus. The preaching of the kingdom of God was not about what Jesus and his followers proposed to do, but about what God had already decided to do. Resistance to the arrest of Jesus (Luke 22.49-51) would not only have been futile in practice, but also an evasion of the calling to announce the kingdom to the end. There is no doubt that the central action of the Christian faith was an act of non-violent resistance, in the sense that Jesus refused to buy peace by giving up his claim to preach the kingdom. The kingdom of God could not be brought in by force. The ethic for individuals of forgiving enemies (Matt. 5.38-48) was based on the same principle that the love of God could not be proclaimed by the use of force.

Whether there remained, in the interim, a 'proper use of force' by Christians was a question that the New Testament simply did not address. The necessity of a defensive form of force to protect the innocent could plausibly be argued, but there was no question that the kingdom itself could not be promoted by forceful means.

3
Ethics in the Church

The history of the treatment of particular ethical issues in the church reveals elements both of continuity and of change. The continuity has been that of the fundamental principles of biblical ethics in relation to sexuality, possessions and political power. The change has come from the attempt to define these principles in practice in different historical contexts. Sometimes the constraints imposed by the historical context have done grave damage to the biblical principles; sometimes the principles have broken through as something radically new in a fresh context; sometimes questions have arisen that have had no parallel in biblical experience. At all times Christians have gone about their business with as much faithfulness to the Bible as their circumstances have allowed.

(i) The Early Church

In moving from the people and the law of Judaism to the wider pagan world the young Christian communities set themselves a problem. What was the status of a Christian in the wider society? The Hebrew Bible aimed always in principle at an integration achieved by separating the Jews from surrounding peoples. Within the separated people all the institutions of government, law, economics, Temple cultus, synagogue, family and personal ethics were meant to form a unity. Even with centuries of foreign domination the ideal of a separated people was not lost.

In the Diaspora, the communities of Jews settled outside Palestine, a certain amount of distinctiveness was maintained by obedience to Torah. Indeed this distinctive life style of high moral standards was what attracted many pagans to become hearers of the Law, even though they were not willing to join fully in the Jewish way of life. In addition, the Roman empire's way of dealing with the Jews as a separate religious and ethnic group reinforced the sense of separate identity, sometimes more than the Jews themselves would have wished, as in the refusal of full citizenship to the Jews of Alexandria.

The new Christians did not have this obligation of separateness. Once the crucial decision was taken that the followers of Jesus did not have to become Jews in all respects, the Christians found themselves in an ambiguous position in civilized society, in it but not sure that they wanted to be of it. It is not certain what the social stratification of the first converts was, but it is probable that they were in some sense marginal people, high achievers but of low or uncertain social status, such as freedmen who were successful in business or women who found themselves running their own estates. They were certainly urban rather than rural and by no means confined to slaves or small artisans.

Christianity spread rapidly in the Roman world. In the three hundred or so years from the end of the New Testament to the death of St Augustine of Hippo in 430 AD the Christian communities changed from being a small and illegal sect of the Jews to being members of the sole official religion of the Roman empire. Their numbers were perhaps not very large absolutely until Christianity was finally tolerated by and subjected to the official direction of the emperor Constantine from 313 onwards. In Rome in 251, one of the points in history where a rough calculation can be made, it has been suggested that there may have been around 15,000 to 20,000 Christians in a population of some 700,000 (Grant, 1978:7). This would be a large number, but still far from a mass movement.

What gave it importance was that it affected what today might be called the professional classes. R. M. Grant remarks that 'We regard it not as a proletarian mass movement but as a relatively small cluster of more or less intense groups, largely middle class in origin' (1978:11). He comments that in a hierarchically organized society the conversion of the emperor was necessary if Christians were to take control of society as a whole. Up to that time, in spite of their own splits and dissensions, the Christians were a movement that was small but vigorous, economically prosperous but not powerful politically, though the policy of toleration adopted by the Emperor Gallienus in 260-261 showed that they were sufficiently numerous in the eastern provinces of the empire to be of significance when the government were considering allies for defence against external enemies.

While Constantine is often given the credit or the blame for integrating Christianity into the governmental system of the empire, it is probable that the Christians' own social progress would have made that decision sooner or later inevitable. Indeed the failure of Julian the Apostate in 361-363 to reinstate paganism may suggest that the older forms of paganism were in any case in decline and ripe for replacement, whether by Christianity or by some other new and vigorous religion, such as Manichaeism which was now spreading from the east, just as Christianity itself was later to be replaced in North Africa by Islam.

This social process by which Christianity replaced paganism settled one of the questions of early Christianity: whether the communities were to be a 'church' or a 'sect', whether they were to separate themselves from society or take responsibility for it. The answer was that they were to become one of the major institutions supporting the social order.

Undoubtedly the first move was for some degree of separation. In the early years, as the gentile mission gathered pace and the converts were less and less trained in the moral law of Judaism, ethical teaching required more and more insistence on the difference between a moral and an immoral life. Only rarely did the note of free acceptance in Christ appear. The degree of rigour required varied from writer to writer. Except for those who later physically separated themselves by going off into the desert, the line of demarcation between Christians and others was not clear-cut. What resulted was not so much a complete separation as a process of mutual criticism and affirmation. Tertullian, who died in 220, was a representative of that fierce North African temperament which did much to shape early Christianity. In a work called *The Apology* he emphasized the distinctive nature of the Christian communities. 'We are a body knit together as such by a common religious profession, by unity of discipline, and by the bond of a common hope' (Forell, 1971:12). These Christians met together to wrestle violently with God in prayer and lived a close-knit common life. 'All things are common among us except our wives' — this Tertullian wrote in contrast to the pagans, who were in his eyes willing enough to be sexually promiscuous but all too unwilling to share their material possessions with those in need. Indeed Tertullian remarked that one of the charges laid against Christians was 'See, they say, how they love one another', meant as a word of contempt for their charitable actions.

This close-knit community had its darker side. Those who fell from its high standards were to be cast out, anticipating the judgment to come. The question of the relationship of forgiveness to community discipline was always difficult. But the weapon of exclusion did not sit easily with a faith whose basis was reconciliation. Tertullian in time gave up on the standards of mainstream Christianity and joined the more rigorous sect of the Montanists, though he quarrelled with them also before his death.

As Christianity began to conquer the economic and political structures of the Roman empire a reverse movement took place within Christianity itself. The penetration of civilized society was matched by a withdrawal into the deserts of Judea and Egypt of the hermits who became the founders, unwittingly, of the monastic system. In its early stages the withdrawal was no doubt influenced by the experience of persecution, but it is also clear that the ascetic calling to life as a hermit was a genuine new movement with its special calling.

Athanasius records of St Antony of Egypt, who died in 356, that at around the age of twenty he received a call in the words of the Lord, 'If you would be perfect, go, sell what you possess and give to the poor, and you will have treasure in heaven', and again, 'Do not be anxious about tomorrow', and that he then gave away his possessions and took up the discipline of solitude and prayer, growing a little food, wrestling with demons and giving advice to all who came for it.

The discipline was primarily training for battle, for the wrestling with the demons which was the front line of the battle against the forces of evil. The form in which this battle was reported was different from the form which might be used today. But the battle was recognisably one which any human being might face in any generation, the struggle with a force which is against the good, whether it be interpreted in terms of interior or of exterior warfare. The movement of withdrawal to undertake this warfare was established as a Christian experience by two features. The first was an absolute dependence on God in Christ. In a long address in the middle of the *Life*, Athanasius presents Antony as saying of the demons, 'We need, therefore, to fear God alone, holding them in contempt and fearing them not at all' (1980:54).

The second feature was that the life of the hermit was founded on reconciling love. Athanasius recorded of Antony that 'he was tolerant in disposition and humble of soul' (1980:80-81) — though it should be noted that his tolerance did not extend to the Meletian schismatics or the Arian heretics. Antony indeed was one of the most doughty supporters of what eventually survived as the 'catholic' faith. But within that faith the first rule was love. A story from the collected sayings of the desert hermits illustrates the fundamental sanity of the life:

> There were two elders living together in a cell, and they had never had só much as one quarrel with one another. One therefore said to the other: Come on, let us have at least one quarrel, like other men. The other said: I don't know how to start a quarrel. The first said: I will take this brick and place it here between us. Then I will say: It is mine. After that you will say: It is mine. This is what leads to a dispute and a fight. So then they placed the brick between them; one said: It is mine, and the other replied to the first: I do believe that it is mine. The first one said again: It is not yours, it is mine. So the other answered: Well then, if it is yours, take it! Thus they did not manage after all to get into a quarrel. (Merton, 1974:67)

The movement to the desert, at least in its later stages, was probably a reaction against the Christian empire of the successors of Constantine. The desert ascetics were not anti-social. 'The society they sought was one where all men were truly equal, where the only authority under God was the charismatic authority of wisdom, experience and love' (Merton, 1974:5). They were indeed obedient to the bishops — but the bishops were rarely to be found in the desert.

In time there grew up alongside the hermits another system of 'cenobitic' monks, those who lived together in an ordered life under a rule and a superior. In the eastern church St Basil the Great (c.330-379) set out a rule which deeply influenced all later monasticism. For Basil solitude meant withdrawal from the world in the heart rather than physical removal to the desert. It meant freedom from possessions, from family, from learning; it meant a balanced life of prayer and manual work; the study of the scriptures; moderation in food and drink; simplicity in clothing; quietness in manners. The inner withdrawal was accompanied by a life of studied moderation rather than a striving for great ascetic achievement.

In the western church the rule of St Basil was built on by St John Cassian (c.360-435) and St Benedict of Nursia (c.480-c.550). While many influences went to make up later western monasticism, with its devotion to learning and to the celebration of the liturgy, at its heart there was always the fundamental perception of the *Rule* of St Benedict that the monastic life was not a way for heroes, but a way for ordinary human beings whose particular calling was to train the will to obedience to God through the obedience and reverence of each to each in the community and to those for whom the community must have a special care, the sick and the poor who were the guests of Christ in the monastic community. Rowan Williams comments,

> Benedict's monks are not heroes of the will nor, in that deeply ambiguous phrase so beloved of spiritual writers, 'athletes of the spirit'. They persevere by grace, in hope and desire. And, more importantly still, the whole monastic emphasis on *attention* to the brethren serves to reduce the emphasis on the self and its solitary battles and direct us to the importance of learning how to *respond*.
> (1979:104)

(ii) Ethics in the Early Church

The developing theory of the monastic life set up a problem which distorted Christian ethics in the west for the next thousand years. This was the theory of the double standard or two counsels, or ways of life. One was the monastic way, based on poverty, chastity and obedience, which aimed at contemplation as the highest good. The other was the secular way, the way of daily life in the world, involved in marriage and child-bearing, trade and other labour, liable to taxes and military service. The tendency was to claim the monastic way as the higher way, the way of perfection, not available to the ordinary Christian, so putting the duties of ordinary life on a lower level. The Orthodox Church never made this mistake, because it saw all knowledge of God as rooted in the one community of the eucharist, equally open to all. This meant that the secular experience of marriage had as much potential for the ontological experience of Christ as had the monastic commitment. John Zizioulas comments on monastic sanctification, 'What I wish to underline, however, is that no "spirituality" is healthy and truly Christian unless it is constantly dependent on the event of ecclesial communion. The eschatological community *par excellence* is to be found in the eucharist, which is thus the heart of all ecclesiology' (1985:131, note 19). He also notes of marriage that 'Linked with the eucharist it becomes a reminder that although the newly married couple have been blessed in order to create their own family, nevertheless the ultimate and essential network of relationships which constitutes their hypostasis is not the family but the Church as expressed in the eucharistic assembly' (1985: 61, note 61).

The eastern church was influenced by the faith that all human life had an infinite possibility of self-transcendence within the eucharistic community. St Gregory of Nyssa (c.330-c.395) in his *Life of Moses* developed the idea that human beings have a capacity for self-transcendence, which has no limits, because God has no limits, 'the continual development of life to what is better is the soul's way of perfection' (1978:133). Although monastic life directed attention especially to contemplation, yet for Orthodox theologians mystical theology was the height of theology for everyone. Though St Gregory was writing for monastics there was no reason in Orthodox theology to suppose that perfection was not in principle attainable by those in the active life. The area of mystical knowledge was the church as a whole rather than the monastery as such.

Sexuality

Considerable effort in recent years has gone into the attempt to define how the people of antiquity understood the body and its sexual activities. Central to the discussion has been the fact that in the third and fourth centuries after Christ there was an increasing stress upon abstinence from sexual activity. A significant moment came when the Council of Elvira decreed, around 306 AD, that 'Bishops, presbyters , deacons, and others with a position in the ministry are to abstain completely from sexual intercourse with their wives and from the procreation of children'. It added, 'If anyone disobeys, he shall be removed from the clerical office' (Article 33; Womer, 1987:78). James Brundage comments, 'Although some patristic writers argued that virginity was a highly meritorious Christian virtue, no mainstream authority prior to the canons of Elvira demanded celibacy, even from the clergy' (1987:75).

There was, of course, a tradition of sexual asceticism already available to Christian thought within Judaism in the Essene community of Qumran in Judea and other groups elsewhere; some aspects of the prophetic tradition also had ascetic implications, but as Christopher Rowland remarks, 'Rigorist and separatist tendencies in the quest for divine holiness gave to these groups an elitist quality which inevitably separated them from the mainstream of Jewish practice' (1988:50). Something of this rigorist tradition may have entered into parts of the New Testament itself.

There was also support for abstinence in the classical tradition of philosophy. Many philosophers, including the Stoics and the Platonists, saw sexual desire as an impediment for those called to the highest level of human life, which was *theoria* or the pure contemplation of universal truths. Even the Greek view of homosexuality can be shown, in the philosophical discussion of those relationships thought to be honourable in themselves, to require that the physical pleasure be seen as a step in the transition to the highest philosophical aim of a relationship based on abstinence and a renunciation of physical desire (Michel Foucault, 1984: 264-269).

This, however, was for the few. For the many of the population as a whole, sexuality of all kinds was part of the basic facts of life. For the state, sexuality was something to be regulated in the interests of the preservation of property and the maintenance of domestic and public power; otherwise it was to be indulged according to what was fitting to the sex and social status of the individuals involved. John Boswell notes that 'Romans were concerned to see that their rights over their spouses and children (of either sex) were not violated, that their offspring married into situations which enhanced their prestige (or wealth), and that they themselves avoided any overt violations of the rights of others which might be unjust (or incur retribution)' (1980:62, note 4).

By the first century the Roman state was beginning to provide by statute for the control of marriage, which was previously regarded as a private arrangement between families (Brundage, 1987:32-38). It remained, however, a contract which could be dissolved through the formal repudiation of one spouse by the other. Apart from the general legal implications of contracts, the law also sought to protect minors and to define what was fitting for the free, mainly male, citizen. In this period Roman law did not take notice of homosexuality as such, but provided barriers against the seduction of minors, rape and the prostitution of citizens equally with respect to heterosexual and homosexual behaviour. Only in the sixth century were homosexual relations specifically prohibited (Boswell,1980:71).

Alongside the legal provisions there were also questions of custom and of expectation. This is a much less well-defined area. It is extremely difficult to know what was the quality of personal relationships at various social levels in the ancient world. Written records necessarily refer mainly to those who could read and write or who had the wealth to go to law. There is, however, evidence to suggest that in the first to the third century, well

89

before Christianity became a major social influence, there was already a tendency to lay greater emphasis on marriage as a personal relationship. The marital affection required by Roman law as a part of the marriage contract received greater emphasis, with a higher expectation of durability in the marriage. Indeed Michel Foucault has argued that with the changes in the view of sexuality taking place from the third century BC to the fourth century AD, it would be difficult to posit a specifically Christian or Judaeo-Christian sexual ethic. 'Certain important events stand out such as the guidelines for conscience laid down by the Stoics and the Cynics, the organization of monasticism, and many others. On the other hand the coming of Christianity, considered as a massive rupture with earlier moralities and the dominant introduction of a quite different one, is barely noticeable' (1985:25).

What is clear is that the Christian faith itself began with a firm commitment to the goodness of marriage, albeit in a patriarchal context, as part of its Jewish heritage, directly affirmed by Jesus himself in the texts on divorce, and by the Pauline corpus, with some reservations, in I Corinthians 7.1-11 and Ephesians 5.21-33. Within the New Testament there was also an ascetical strain, again in I Corinthians 7.6-9; in Mark 10.28-31, the call to give up family to follow Jesus; and in Matthew 19.10-12, the saying on celibacy. By the fourth century this had turned somehow into an ideal of celibacy and even virginity, which at least in the west was treated as a higher state than marriage. So Jerome, arguing the point with Jovinian at the end of the third century, claimed that 'He puts marriage on a level with virginity, while I make it inferior; he declares that there is little or no difference between the two states; I claim that there is a great deal' (Letter 48 to Pammachius, 2; quoted in Pagels, 1988:95).

The combined authority of St Jerome, St Ambrose of Milan and St Augustine of Hippo enforced Jerome's point of view on centuries of subsequent Christian teaching. Augustine is generally cast as the villain of this piece and certainly it was he who produced the final formulation of a theology that connected sexuality fundamentally with sin, but he wrote under the influence of a tradition that had already established a powerful mechanism to deal with sin, particularly sexual sin. In the first four centuries the problem whether sin after baptism could be followed by repentance and reconciliation to the Christian community found two answers. The minority party held that sin meriting excommunication could not be followed by a return to the church at all. The majority opinion allowed reconciliation, but only after a considerable period of penance, and then only once in a lifetime. So the Council of Elvira ruled that 'If a woman conceives in adultery and then has an abortion, she may not commune again, even as death approaches, because she has sinned twice' (Article 63: Womer, 1987:81). As John Mahoney comments, 'The final result seems to have been that great numbers of ordinary Christians must have lived in what could only be called a permanent state of ecclesiastical delinquency' (1987:4). Many indeed postponed the act of reconciliation or of baptism until they were near death.

In the *Confessions*, St Augustine contributed to this situation a very sensitive account of the development of a personality. In his investigation of his own experiences and his capacity for self-revelation he was closer to the mind of the seventeenth century than to the ancient world. Walter Allen has noted the *Confessions* as one of the few works of antiquity comparable to the universal human content of Daniel Defoe's *Robinson Crusoe*. A comparison more apt than it may seem at first sight, since the *Confessions* also contain a good deal of literary artifice (Allen, 1958). Certainly Augustine had a good story to tell, of his relations with his mother and father, his development as a philosopher, his conversion to Christianity, his speculations on the nature of memory and of time, and his experience of the power and care of God. What comes over most strongly is his sense of sin, from the anguish over the childhood episode of the stolen pears to his concern over enjoying church singing rather than letting his mind be led on to thoughts of God. 'Have pity on me and heal me, for you see that I have become a problem to myself, and this is the ailment from which I suffer' (*Confessions*, X 33: 1961:239).

The problem which troubled Augustine most was that of carnal desire. Partly this arose from his own experience of keeping a mistress for fifteen years — by whom he had a son, Adeodatus — and putting her aside when the time came to make a proper marriage. Partly also it arose from his wrestling with the question of the origin and the transmission of sin. For many years he was under the sway of his own desires. His friend Alypius, who finally persuaded Augustine not to marry, and other friends were examples of chastity. 'But I was far from being the equal of these noble spirits. I was bound down by this disease of the flesh' (*Confessions* VI, 12; 1961:128). Part of the problem with the disease of the flesh was that Augustine enjoyed it. 'As a youth I had been woefully at fault, particularly in early adolescence. I had prayed to you for chastity and said, "Give me chastity and continence, but not yet." For I was afraid that you would answer my prayer at once and cure me too soon of the disease of lust, which I wanted satisfied, not quelled' (*Confessions* VIII, 7; 1961:169).

Now in his maturity Augustine struggled and suffered more deeply from his inability to will the refusal of sexual desire. 'Yet I did not do that one thing which I should have been far, far better pleased to do than all the rest and could have done at once, as soon as I had the will to do it, because as soon as I had the will to do so, I should have willed it wholeheartedly.' (*Confessions* VIII, 8; 1961:171). Quoting the Letter to the Romans, 7.17, he decided that *'My action did not come from me, but from the sinful principle that dwells in me.* It was part of a sin freely committed by Adam, my first father' (*Confessions* VIII, 10; 1961:173). After this came his experience of conversion, where in a garden, hearing what seemed to be the voice of a child saying 'Take it and read, take it and read', he opened the Bible at the Letter to the Romans 13.13-14 and reading the injunction to put aside revelling and drunkenness and to put on Jesus Christ he felt his heart filled with the power to do so (*Confessions* VIII, 12; 1961:177-179).

This left Augustine with the problem of free will. Where was it summoned from so suddenly? In meditating on this question in later years, Augustine gradually drove back the scope of free will in the human being. Others had been concerned about this, but it was Augustine who took the fatal step for western theology of linking the defect of the will, originating in Adam, with the transmission of human nature through the sexual act. He reasoned that since human beings were created by God, they were created with a capacity to respond to God as fully as their condition required. But actual human experience showed that all human beings committed sin. The possibility of sin arose from the reality of the freedom given to the first human beings to make their own choices, but once the choice against God had been made, the solidarity of human beings was such that human beings no longer had the possibility of not sinning. Human personality suffered a transformation and this transformation was passed on from generation to generation through the sexual act. Augustine did not disapprove of marriage; biological reproduction was itself good, including the upbringing of children; the fidelity sworn and maintained between the couple was good; and the sacrament, the effect of marriage as a sign of the union of Christ and the church, was also good.

What was not good was sexual desire in itself, for such a power over human nature and especially over human reason could not have been a part of human personality as originally created. Sexual desire itself was one form of a wider problem of desire. Eugene TeSelle comments, 'It is to be noted, however, that concupiscence, though it consists chiefly of sexual desire, is not that alone, for there are many other ways in which the animal aspects of the soul can escape rational control and tempt man' (1970:317).

What thus entered Christian theology was a fundamental reason for mistrusting sexuality, a mistrust fed by the fact that Christian teachers were now almost exclusively celibate males. Augustine's increasingly pessimistic view of human freedom also had political implications, and perhaps even political origins, as Elaine Pagels argues. 'Throughout western history this extreme version of the doctrine of original sin, when taken as the basis for political structures, has tended to appeal to those who, for whatever reason, suspect human motives and the human capacity for self-government' (1984:149).

Neither St Augustine nor any other writer of the patristic period was concerned to spell out a systematic account of Christian ethics. Their work was always directed to particular problems in particular contexts. Nevertheless an overall impression built up that sexuality was sinful in general, though permitted for the purpose of procreation, but even then not to be enjoyed in itself. As Derrick Sherwin Bailey remarks, 'The significance of sex in the personal life of the individual was never appreciated, nor was sexual intercourse seen to possess any meaning or even importance in the experience of husband and wife as "one flesh", save for the purpose of procreation' (1952:55).

With this view of heterosexual activity it is no surprise that Christian thought could find no place for the possibility of seriously-felt same-sex relationships. On the other hand, as John Boswell points out, 'It is indeed too often overlooked that just as there was a pagan ascetic and antierotic tradition, so was there a Christian tradition of tolerant and positive attitudes towards love and eroticism, represented by such figures as Ausonius, Sidonius Apollinaris, Saint John Damascene, Marbod of Rennes, Saint Aelred of Rievaulx, et al.' (1980:163). Many Christians in the early centuries must have shared in such an acceptance of the positive nature of human sexuality, both heterosexual and homosexual.

Property

The ascetic movement with respect to sexuality in the early church had its parallel in attitudes to possessions. Those who went into the desert to become the first Christian hermits were not only seeking silence and freedom from distraction for prayer but also making a gesture of unconcern for material things and for worldly power. Some who did not follow into the desert taught the same lesson. As Minucius Felix put it, 'we would rather despise riches than possess them', sounding, as Martin Hengel comments, 'almost like a Cynic philosopher' (Hengel, 1974:51; the quotation is from Octavius 36, 5). As with abstinence from sexuality, so abstinence from possessions was specially pressed upon the clergy; by the fourth century St Ambrose of Milan was instructing them that 'We do not use the logic of the world, which says one should accumulate wealth, but we follow God's

wisdom, which counts as valueless the possessions of this world'
(*The Duties of the Clergy*, Book III, chapter 2; Womer, 1987:105).

The aim for those who were not clergy or lay monastics, however, was not the abandonment of possessions, but a form of self-
sufficiency which, coupled with giving to the poor, did not necessarily rule out the control of substantial property. As the Christians became a larger element in society it became more difficult
to maintain an argument for rigorous separation. In time Christians acquired wealth, not only as individuals but also as churches,
although this was technically illegal until the time of Constantine.
What became the major Christian view of wealth, that the important point was not possession of riches but the spiritual attitude
to them, was propounded by Clement of Alexandria, who lived
from around 150 to 215. In his time Alexandria was one of the
richest cities of the Roman empire and one of the great centres
of learning, both pagan and Christian. It is not surprising that it
was in this city that Clement wrote on *The Rich Man's Salvation.*
He approached the problem through the story in the Gospel of
Matthew of the young man who came to Jesus and asked what he
must do to be saved, beyond keeping the Ten Commandments
(Matt. 19.16-22). Jesus' reply was 'If you wish to be perfect, go
and sell what you own and give the money to the poor, and you
will have treasure in heaven; then come, follow me'. But the
young man gave up at these words, 'for he was a man of great
wealth'.

The point of the story in Matthew seems to be that this was
required for someone who wished to participate directly in Jesus' mission: not everyone whom Jesus helped was given an instruction about perfection. But the following saying of Jesus to
the disciples, 'it will be hard for a rich man to enter the kingdom of heaven' and the disciples' surprise (vv. 23-26), shows
where the saying was particularly aimed. This was not good news
for Alexandria. Clement took the line that what was in question
was the way a rich person used possessions and the degree of
attachment by which he or she was bound to them. 'He is to
banish those attitudes towards wealth that permeate his whole
life, his desires, interests and anxiety' (11; Womer, 1987:44). He

continues with a remark which combines a hard realism with a genuine spiritual perception: 'There is nothing marvellous or enviable about having no money, unless true life be the reason for it'. The condition of poverty was not in itself more godly than the condition of wealth: it could lead to bitterness as much as humility, to depression as much as to holy joy. Poverty voluntarily undertaken brought joy; involuntary poverty required rather relief. In so far as attachment to the elements of material life was the greatest barrier to joyful reliance on God alone, the poor might be under less temptation, but envy and desire might be equally strong at any level of income.

There is in *The Rich Man's Salvation* the air of one who protests too much. The wealthy must not fling away their possessions but keep them in stewardship for those with genuine needs. 'How could there be any sharing if no one possessed anything?' (13; Womer, 1987:45). Nevertheless the argument had a solid base. No one before the nineteenth century could force a way out of the problem that Clement saw: that the relief of the poor depended on the ability of productive capacity to provide relief, and that efficient productive capacity depended in the main on the good business methods of wealthy individuals.

As Charles Avila remarks, the early Christian thinkers were not social theorists, nor strictly speaking philosophers, but theologians, preachers and pastors. Nevertheless they left a corpus of sermons, essays and incidental references which 'leaves no room for doubt as to the importance they attached to their treatment of the ownership idea-practice-and-institution for the lives of the people of their time' (1983:11). Avila refers to the difficulties created throughout the early Christian period for the peasants through taxes, forced labour and destructive methods of agriculture, and claims that by the sixth century, 'at least one-fifth of agricultural lands had been abandoned by cultivators, exhausted by exorbitant taxes and rents' (1983:31). The system of farming by slavery or by the serfdom of tenants bound to a particular estate gave no incentive for technical innovation or capital investment; tenants who could not even keep food enough for themselves for the winter fled to the towns to beg or starve or become criminalised.

It may be this social background which accounts for the fact in the fourth century particularly three leading thinkers sought to lay down the ground rules for the treatment of property, namely, St Basil the Great, St Ambrose of Milan and St John Chrysostom. Their common argument was that nature had provided freely for all and that the accumulation of riches could only be the result of force or deceit. As St Ambrose puts it,

> The philosophers also believe that justice requires that public property be treated as public and private property as private. But this is not what nature illustrates, for nature has provided all things for common use. God has decreed that all things are produced so that food is available to all and the earth is possessed by everyone equally. Natures provides for everyone, but greed has restricted the supply to only a few.
> (*The Duties of the Clergy*, Book I, chapter 28; Womer, 1987:98)

St Basil referred to the rich as robbers and St John Chrysostom preached total sharing at Antioch and Constantinople at the end of the fourth century. Yet their efforts were without any marked success. There are two ways of looking at this history. One is to say, with Charles Avila, that there was an early Christian socialist doctrine, which became a kind of secret in the church. 'Thus the message of the primitive church and the patristic philosophy of ownership, both of which contradicted the practices of the institutional church, were progressively buried and forgotten' (1983:153). The other is to suggest that the Christians had no practical alternative to the institutions of private property, slavery and serfdom.

In the absence of the very notions of 'capitalism' and 'socialism' their concentration on the demand for benevolence on the part of the individual owner of wealth may have looked less like avoiding the problem and more inevitable than it does today. As an established movement the Christians were necessarily conservatives, drawing their economic ideals from the society of which they were now the masters. Even the ideal of natural justice was a reflection of the surrounding society. 'To put it simply, the Christian attitude towards property tended to be an aristocratic one, and the criticism of avarice was an important aspect of it' (R. M. Grant, 1978:123).

Political Power

By the end of the fourth century the Christians had a problem in political theory as well as economic theory. The political stance of Judaism, that the ruler was appointed by God to unite the people in a single liturgical, political, economic and ethical obedience, had been tenable only for the people in the land of Palestine, and for them in their later history only in theory. Political obedience in the diverse religious and political cultures of the Roman empire could not call on the same commitment. While the New Testament generally recognized the necessity of obedience to earthly rulers (Rom. 13.1-7; I Pet. 2.13-17), it is also clear that from the teaching of Jesus onwards Christians made a sharp distinction between the kind of obedience owed to God and the kind of obedience owed to an earthly ruler (Mark 12.13-17). The Christians were not looking for trouble with the state, and were mostly anxious to avoid persecution. In times of persecution the deliberate seeking of martyrdom was forbidden. The arguments of Tertullian and Origen about the nature of Christian citizenship showed a desire even among the more rigorous for a form of co-existence with the state.

While he was still an orthodox Christian, in *The Apology*, Tertullian considered the problem of the relationship between Christians and the state. Christians attracted some suspicion and resentment from other citizens because they did not contribute to the upkeep of the temples, which functioned on the religious side to protect the interests of the Roman empire as a whole, and they also refused to take on public office when eligible for it. This was a serious matter, for the Roman empire lacked a bureaucracy in the modern sense of a permanent administrative class and so had difficulty in providing good administration. Leading citizens were required to performs terms of public service, not unlike the modern draft for military service. It was impossible for the Christians to undertake this service because any dealing with the state involved a minimal but unacceptable recognition of the state religion.

Christian apologists consequently argued that though Christians refused this service, and refused military service for the same reason, nevertheless they contributed substantially to the well-being of society. Tertullian as a rigorist was particularly well-placed to argue from the high moral standards of the Christians. 'Well, in your long lists of those accused of many and various atrocities, has any assassin, any cutpurse, any man guilty of sacrilege, or seduction, or stealing bathers' clothes, his name entered as being a Christian too?' (Forell, 1971:46). He argued that Christians worked hard and that while they did not pay temple taxes, they were highly conscientious in paying other taxes, so that the state gained more than it lost from them.

Tertullian deeply disapproved of public amusements such as acting, chariot racing and the games and said so in *On Pagan Shows*, because of the kind of company that was kept there and because such frivolous activity distracted people's attention from the proper business of human beings, which was giving glory to God. His driving principle was always the prospect of final judgment. 'Let us mourn, then, while the heathen are merry, that in the day of their sorrow we may rejoice; lest, sharing now in their gladness, we share then also in their grief' (Forell, 1971:50). But this did not mean that Christians did not share other human activities. 'We sail with you, and fight with you, and till the ground with you; and in like manner we unite with you in your traffickings — even in the various arts we make public property of our works for your benefit' (Forell, 1971:45). Rigorous though he was, Tertullian was no desert father, fleeing large-scale human community altogether.

The reference to fighting presumably meant in such circumstances as attacks by robbers or pirates since Tertullian was one of those most opposed to official military service. Christians put up a variety of arguments to justify their refusal to fight. A hundred years later Origen defended it on the ground that Christian prayer was freely given for the success of the state in arms and that the state recognized that the priests at certain pagan shrines should keep their hands free from human blood and perform no military service. 'And none fight better for the king than we do. We do not indeed fight under him, although he require it; but we fight on his behalf, forming a special army — an army of piety — by offering our prayers to God.' (*Against Celsus*, Book VIII; Forell, 1971:58).

With the victory of Constantine, the problem became not simply one of states which were overtly hostile to the Christian faith, but of states which caused difficulty to Christian faith by their friendship. Now either the Christian communities became so integrated that what possibility existed for a prophetic voice was allowed to pass by, or the Christians were so charmed by their success in society that they gave in to the temptation to assume a Christian form of power and to run the state for the benefit of Christian organizations alone.

It was this last possibility that began to open to the Christians in the ancient world at the point of their highest success. In the year 381 the Western emperor Gratian ordered pagan sacrifices to stop and had the Statue of Victory, the symbol of the integration of the old Roman religion and the state power, removed from the Roman Senate House. After Gratian's death in 384 an appeal was made by Symmachus for the restoration of the statue, on the ground that there were many ways to the truth of the one creator. The plea for religious toleration, so often made in modern times by Christians of minority views against Christians of majority views, and by Christians of all views in Communist and other totalitarian states, fell on this occasion on hostile ears. St Ambrose, the bishop of Milan, persuaded the emperor Valentinian under threat of excommunication to refuse. It was, as W. H. C. Frend comments, 'an ignoble but decisive' victory over the old religion (1982:186). Six years later Ambrose used the same power, at risk to his own life, to rebuke the emperor Theodosius for his massacre of the citizens of Thessalonica, writing '. . . if you purpose being present, I dare not offer the Sacrifice. That which may not be done where the blood of one innocent person has been shed, may it be done where many have been slain?' (1982:184).

While accepting the responsibility of rebuking emperors, the western church lost forever the innocence of not calling on the civil and military power for its own ends. What Ambrose began in refusing the plea of Symmachus, Augustine of Hippo reinforced in using the power of the state in his struggle against the Donatists. The African church had long been divided about the nature of the purity of the church, in a dispute running back to the problem of how to deal with those who had conformed to paganism in the persecution under the emperor Decius in 250-251. By the time of Augustine, who was bishop of Hippo from 395 to his death in 430, the rigorists were organized in a separate church, called after its founder Donatus. The schism was not merely a matter of words. Property was annexed or destroyed and even blood was shed on both sides. In these circumstances it was not unnatural for Augustine to look for help to the civil power.

In justifying the arrest of a presbyter of the Donatist church, Augustine appealed among other things to the parable of Luke 14.15-24 in which the invited guests refused to turn up for a wedding and the lord of the feast sent out for others to be compelled to come from the highways and byways. The story in its setting in the gospel narrative of the journey to Jerusalem probably referred to the calling of the Christians when Israel had refused to hear the good news, but Augustine applied it to the catholic church as a justification for compelling the schismatics and heretics to come in. 'They should not be complaining that they are being compelled but taking note of the goal towards which they are being compelled' (Letter 185, Wiles and Santer, 1975:239). Since salvation operated only within the church and only within the 'catholic' as opposed to 'Donatist' church, the compulsion which ensured salvation was a loving act. But this argument depended upon an absolute assurance of being right. Under the pressure of controversies and with the advantages and disadvantages of the new interest of the state in the Christian communities as part of the official structure of law and order, a new Christian identity had been formed.

Near the end of Augustine's life the Christians found that the commanding heights of political power they had so recently scaled were crumbling under them. The entry of Alaric the Goth into Rome in AD 410 was a shock comparable to the fall of Jerusalem in 587 BC. Though Rome was no longer the political capital, since the court was at Ravenna, and though, as it turned out, Alaric and his army wanted the fruits of power rather than the destruction of the system, nevertheless the fall of Rome marked a profound change in the history of the ancient world. As Peter Brown comments, 'On a deeper level, Rome symbolized the security of a whole civilised way of life'. Its fall was 'an ominous reminder of the fact that even the most valuable societies might die' (1967:289).

While Christians could take this and the following calamities in North Africa as a just judgment of God upon their sins and divisions, to pagans it seemed more likely that the calamity had come because the Christians had abandoned the old Roman religion.

Between 413 and 425 St Augustine wrote his response to the dissolution of the old Roman power. In *The City of God* he argued that there was no necessary link between religious faith and political success. Human beings had the opportunity of two sorts of service. The first was the service of God, which was directed to the heavenly city, the new Jerusalem promised in Revelation 21.1-8. The second was the service of human ends in the earthly city, the ends of politics and economics, of self-aggrandizement and the desire for possessions, of lust and vice. 'Two loves therefore have given origin to these two cities, self-love in contempt of God unto the earthly, love of God in contempt of one's self to the heavenly. The first seeks the glory of men, and the latter desires God only as the testimony of the conscience, the greatest glory. That glories in itself, and this in God' (*The City of God* XIV, xxviii; 1945:58-59). These two cities were not the state and the church, but those who lived within both the state and the church having their eyes fixed on their own ends, and those who lived within both the state and the church having their eyes fixed on the final end in God.

Augustine used a wealth of historical examples to show that it was not a disaster for the Christians that Roman rule had begun to fail. On the contrary the disaster for Christians would be to put any trust in earthly things, whether the building of a city or the building of a political constitution. Eugene TeSelle comments, 'To him earthly tasks could not have ultimate significance, for it was not easy to see how the building of the earthly city could make much difference to the final outcome' (1970: 271). So at the close of the Roman era Augustine set the Christians' minds on the cosmic task of obedience to God, not only through but also against the run of human history.

The City of God is not a book on politics in the modern sense. Only a few pages deal with obedience and political institutions (*The City of God* XIX, xiv-xvii). What Augustine achieved was to demolish once and for all the argument that Christians could form a political community on the Jewish model, even with a universal basis. Never again would theology be able with a clear conscience to align itself totally with a single political programme or single set of political institutions. In Augustine's argument past history showed that possibility to be illusory in practice and fundamental theology showed it to be too limited in principle, because the aim of human history rested in a future far beyond human history.

The very grandeur of the conception, however, carried with it two dangers. The first was that the judgment upon human history was so radical that it could overlook the need to make an ethical evaluation of the affairs of the earthly city. Realism about the limits of politics could easily be used to justify submissiveness to the earthly power in all its affairs. The other danger was that the priority of the heavenly city, in other hands than Augustine's, could be made to yield a theory of the domination of the earthly church over the earthly state. Augustine wrote at a moment when the power of both earthly institutions was being shaken, to show that neither institution was the ultimate design of God. As Sir Ernest Barker comments, for the first time the earthly state is not seen as the final aim of human society. 'Rome has fallen: Christ has risen. The process of history is a process making for His Kingdom' (Introduction to *The City of God*, 1945, Vol. One;

xxi-xxii). The later history of the western church was to show what a very complex resource this political theory could be.

From the point of view of the western tradition the first great phase of Christian history came to an end in Augustine. His achievement was immense in terms of the range of questions to which he attempted an answer. It was immense also in achieving a synthesis of theology and philosophy for his time. Eric Osborn concludes that 'His account of Christian morals builds together earlier ideas into a final synthesis of early Christian ethics. As Clement and Origen had fused the Platonic account of good with the Pauline account of grace, so Augustine develops this theme in an all-embracing system' (1976:145-146). But as Osborn also comments, the synthesis did not last. Whatever shape Christian identity was to take in the future, it could not rest in the shape hammered out by the last catholic bishop of Hippo.

(iii) A Universal Theology

After the barbarian invasions at the end of the period of antiquity, the church in North Africa survived only in small pockets in Egypt, Palestine, the Lebanon and Ethiopia, while Northern Europe had a long slow climb to make to the point where it could claim to be a Christian culture. But in the eighth century an old concept came to new life. In Rome the popes still ruled in theory as agents of the Byzantine emperor in Constantinople. In 753 Pope Stephen II visited the king of the Franks, Pepin III, to make an alliance which divided power in northern Italy between pope and king. R. W. Southern comments:

> The long drawn-out consequences of this realignment for both the unity and the disunity of Christendom were enormous. For the first time in history the pope had acted as a supreme political authority in authorizing the transfer of power in the Frankish kingdom, and he had emphasised his own political role as successor to the emperors by disposing of imperial lands in Italy. These were steps of the highest importance for the future. They were moreover highly treasonable. (1970:60)

When Pepin's son Charlemagne was crowned Holy Roman Emperor on Christmas Day in the year 800, the event witnessed to the power of the idea of a universal society, transferred from the old Roman empire, now located only in the east, to the new northern political power. 'Christendom', the idea of the unity of religion and politics in a single, all-encompassing, unavoidable order, was beginning to come to birth.

It was, however, a slow birth. In the tenth and eleventh centuries the Carolingian empire weakened and the powers of the Emperor and the subordinate kings passed effectively to the local nobility, the great landowners and the knights who owed service to them. The kings had welded the roving tribes into territorial communities, but in so doing they undid themselves, for in an age of poor communications, thinly-spread populations and many enemies, power became concentrated at the most local level, where defence could be organised rapidly and exactions could not be checked by a remote even if theoretically higher authority. The organisation of life around the self-sufficient manor, whether of a lord or of a monastery, limited the need for trade and reinforced the emphasis on the purely local institutions. Feudalism was a war-lord society, modified only slightly by the efforts of the church, since the church was run by members of the same families as the military aristocracy.

The system of mutual obligations which constituted feudalism, based on territory and service, varied from place to place and from time to time, but in the main related to land tenure, the 'fief' or 'feud'. At the bottom were those who had no rights, beyond the right to mere existence, the serfs. In the early Middle Ages the majority of the people were serfs working on the land. Above the serfs were a layer of freemen, whose freedom had no great value unless by tenure of land they could make a living and keep a defined place in the system; any economic misfortune could force freemen into serfdom. Above the freemen were the small class of the nobility, whose right to extract profit from serf and freemen included also an obligation to defend the system as a whole against outside attack and exaction. Though towns existed they were small and acted mainly as service areas for the countryside, providing no alternative source of cultural values or political power. At its best feudalism could be seen as a system

105

based on respect for law.

> The higher one rose towards liberty, the more the area of
> action was covered by law, the less it was subject to will. The
> knight did not obey fewer laws than the ordinary freeman,
> but very many more; the freeman was not less restricted than
> the serf, but he was restricted in a different, more rational
> way. Law was not the enemy of freedom; on the contrary, the
> outline of liberty was traced by the bewildering variety of law
> which was slowly evolved during our period. (Southern,
> 1953:105)

In this sense feudalism, though a local system, drew on universal
values of law and rule.

For the church the change from empire to feudal system was
potentially a disaster, for power over its own institutions began
to pass from the at least theoretically sacred kingship that it had
created to a far from sacred baronage. The officers of the church,
both secular and monastic, were deeply embedded in the feudal
kinship system. But a time came when these officers began to
look for protection against local political powers to the one place
which had some sort of claim to a counter-balancing authority,
the church in Rome whose sacral power anointed emperors.

The development of the papal claim to political authority was
gradual, never fully admitted in principle by the political powers,
and exercised with varying effectiveness. The problem really arose
because ecclesiastical jurisdiction could not be separated effectively from secular jurisdiction. The church provided the person-
nel for such bureaucracy as feudal society required, it undertook
all the work of education and welfare and by its ownership of
land it constituted a major economic power in its own right. No
king could leave such power untouched, and no king could attempt to set boundaries to such power without appearing also to
strike at ecclesiastical privileges. No pope could refuse such a
challenge. At its highest the papal claim was stated by Boniface
VIII in the bull *Unam Sanctam*, directed at King Philip IV of
France in 1302. Referring to the doctrine of the two swords,
spiritual and temporal, the Pope asserted that the temporal sword

was also in the power of Peter. 'Wherefore both are in the power of the Church, namely the spiritual and material swords; the one, indeed to be wielded for the Church, the other by the Church; the former by the priest, the latter by the hands of kings and knights, but at the will and sufferance of the priest' (Forell, 1971:146-147).

The eventual failure of the papal claim arose from the very natural opposition it created in the political authorities to whom it was directed. There was also an opposition generated in ecclesiastical institutions at lower levels by alarm at the Roman will to centralisation. That opposition lost the fight within the institution of the Roman Catholic Church, but one of the great 'might have beens' of history is whether the attempt in the thirteenth century to control the popes by means of a General Council of the Church could in any way have averted or modified the effects of the sixteenth century Reformation. Until the Reformation destroyed the basis of the question, it is doubtful if either side could have claimed a final victory in the battle to exercise the ultimate control over the universal society which western Christendom saw itself to be.

The political concept of the papal empire found its parallel in theologies which provided a universal system of explanation from the eternal and invisible God, through the workings of nature and the workings of human nature, illuminated by revelation, down to the smallest question of ethics or belief. The great Christological controversies were long over. The western Church had a largely settled system of doctrine. The eastern Church could safely be ignored or even treated as an enemy. The systematic Latin mind now set itself to building a final theologico-political system.

St Thomas Aquinas stands in the middle of the intellectual movements of the Middle Ages. On the one hand he was the inheritor of the long tradition of Christian dealings with Platonism, in which the perfection of the Idea or Form was superior to the possibilities of individual existence, though Christian Platonism in no way denied the goodness of substance within creation at its own level. On the other hand Aquinas himself was one of those who responded to the shift of attention to the works of Aristotle, a change which in time led to concentration on the particular and the individual, and so to experimental science. Paradoxically, the theologian of universal order was also one of those who did most to cause that order to be overthrown by another order, less favourable to Christian or any other metaphysics.

Positively, St Thomas took Aristotle's philosophy and rewrote it in a Christian sense. Etienne Gilson remarks:

> First, the philosophical reformation achieved by Thomas Aquinas is a moment in the history of theology before being one in the history of metaphysics. Secondly, even on the level of pure philosophy, his doctrine cannot be understood as a further stage in the progressive discovery of Aristotle by the Latins. Thomism was not the upshot of a better understanding of Aristotle. It did not come out of Aristotelianism by way of evolution, but of revolution. (1955:364-365)

The major contribution was the definition of God as 'the pure act of existing'. Rather than the Being preceding action of Platonism, Aquinas' God was the Act which preceded being. But this God who for Aristotle was only the mover of creation was for Aquinas also the creator. The God of Aquinas was the god of Aristotle transformed into the I AM THAT I AM of the Hebrews (Exod. 3.14). This God of Aquinas confronted the human being with the question of existence: not the 'how' of creation but the 'why' of existence became the question to which God formed the answer.

The pure act of existing which is God could not be known directly by human reason, but could be known to some extent, thought Aquinas, by analogy with that which human reason does encounter and know. For God, as the infinite fullness of being, contained within the act of existence all the possibilities of being, including all the possibilities of the created world. There is no way in which it could be said that it was necessary for the God of Aquinas to create a universe. The creation was a free act of God's will. But since the creation, so far as human reason could determine, did exist, its being must follow from the nature of the Being of its creator. This creation, which was infinitely below its creator, nevertheless had the signs of the creator within it. Below the angels, the highest form of creation was the human being and in the human being the rational soul gave form to everything that constituted a human being. F. C. Coplestone says of the concept of the rational soul, 'It is the principle or component factor of a living thing which first makes it a living thing and which lies behind, as it were, all that thing's vital activities' (1955:159).

Lower beings had their own souls, 'vegetative' for plants, 'sensitive' for animals capable of sensation and other higher activities; only the human being also had a 'rational' soul. The soul was dependent upon the body for its knowledge of the material world. The capacity of the body for sensation came from the existence of the body and was necessary for the soul. The rational soul had, however, its own capacity for the intellectual knowing of universals: it could recognize similarities of being, using the information which came to it through the body. So the mind could make judgments which connected sense-impressions with universal forms. In this way the rational soul could make judgments about the world and the self.

Aquinas' understanding of human nature thus placed human beings firmly at the point of maximum ability to interpret the creation within the creation. By looking at what was created, human beings could arrive at true, though limited, knowledge of their own nature and of the nature of other created existences, and so could arrive at a knowledge, by analogy, of the being of God. The problems, of course, lay in the giving of definition to the particulars of this knowledge.

In ethics this philosophical programme implied that the creature had access to two levels of understanding of God's will, starting with its own basis in created nature, but supplemented by divine revelation. For each existence was created by the Eternal Law in relation to a 'form' or intention of God. This 'form' had no separate existence outside the particular existences, but it was also not exhausted by any particular existence or

109

collection of existences. Moreover the form would be present as a possibility even though any particular existence — say, an individual tiger — might be very far from the fullness of the form. In plants and animals such divergence from the form intended by God would be simply an imperfection. 'A thing is said to be good when it is as it ought to be in order to fulfil its own essence, and the exigencies of its nature...' (Gilson, 1936:326).

Human beings might also suffer from such unwilled imperfections shared with the animal creation. But human beings also had imperfections which might be capable of being changed by decisions of the human will. Human reason, unlike the animals, was able to perceive an 'ought' as a requirement for decision. This 'ought' could arise from looking at what an actual human being, a 'particular' was, and seeing what a human being, the 'form' of a human being, should be. Once seen, it was possible for a person to choose to follow the 'form', which was God's intention for the human being. The refusal to follow the 'form', once seen, would be sin. To perceive the form was to·perceive the law of one's own nature, the 'natural law'.

It may be confusing to call the imperatives which arise out of this perception of the 'form' of a human being, or of any other existence, a natural law. For law implies a more precise and detailed definition than can be deduced from this knowledge. What is perceived is not a rule or an imperative but rather a purpose or goal, a hint of the possibilities created by the touch of the divine within the creature.

However, St Thomas, building on a tradition already established by the pagan philosophers and by earlier Christian writers, in particular St Augustine, did use the term 'law', both of the universal creative act and of the human perception of that act within the creation. The initial creative act itself was beyond comprehension. This total divine intention Aquinas called 'eternal law'. Etienne Gilson comments:

> The eternal law is the dictate of the divine providence, and therefore of the divine reason, governing the perfect community which we call the universe. Inasmuch as man is subject to

this eternal law of divine providence, there is in him an imprint of it which is called natural law. Moreover, inasmuch as
he is a rational creature, man is subject to the eternal law in a
particularly excellent way. He does not simply undergo it, as
all natural beings do. He also knows it and wills it.
(1955:381)

There was, however, a further problem. Even that limited knowledge of the divine nature which would be proper to human
beings in their own nature was distorted by the actual existence
of sin. Since the rebellion of human beings against God in the
beginning, a sufficient knowledge of the 'form' was not available
to them. A further indication of God's intentions for human
beings and for the whole creation had to be provided. This
second provision was the 'divine law', the knowledge of God's
nature and of the obligations of human beings given in the
Bible. The act of God in Jesus paralleled and completed the
original creation in such a way that it brought into being a new
creation. The law of this new creation went so far beyond the
knowledge of the eternal law in nature that it could be known
only by revelation — which itself needed interpretation through
the church, the continuing body of Jesus Christ on earth.

Within the eternal law, known through natural law and through
the divine law of revelation, there was also and finally human
law. Human law was created by the decisions of particular human communities about the proprieties of human behaviour,
but these decisions could always be more or less in line with
God's intention in creation and in revelation. Human law could
vary according to the needs of particular communities in particular epochs, but it was always open to being judged by the
criteria of natural and divine law, and Aquinas argued strongly
in favour of limiting change as much as possible. So, finally, the
nature of God connected with the making of positive law: nothing in the human community could be outside the concern for
the fulfilling of the intentions of the eternal law.

Order thus descended from the creative intention of God who
was 'pure act' into the creation, where it was experienced by
everything that was created, each in its own way, but most fully

by the capacity for reason which was given in the soul of the human being. This universal order constituted the fundamental moral law for human beings. It was not first of all a set of rules, but a recognition of the good which was the ultimate purpose of the nature of each human being. God 'commanded' certain behaviour only in the sense that such behaviour would lead to the greatest good for each being according to its own nature. Equally, other behaviour was 'forbidden' because it lacked the power to fulfil the potential of the human being. Consequently, to sin against God was always to sin against one's own nature, to cut the link between the creative intention and the present reality. To fulfil one's own nature truly was also to be obedient to God.

The attraction of this moral theory was that it provided an assurance of order penetrating into the nature of each being according to its own abilities, and in human beings particularly through the power of reason. The knowledge of this order provided a protection against any arbitrary or unlawful interference with the nature of each being. It implied — or could imply — a deep respect for the inbuilt potential of creation to be itself. The human being was an interpreter of the given nature of beings, not simply the master of them, although it was also part of the nature of human beings to have possession of material things and dominion over other creatures. This dominion, which Aquinas derived both from the human ability to make use of other elements of nature and from the command in Genesis 1.28 to 'fill the earth and conquer it', was clearly shown in the Genesis passage to relate to the human status as the 'image and likeness' of God, that is, a status of ruling in the name of God for God's purposes.

Of the effects of the natural law which were true for everyone, St Thomas specified the inclination to the preservation of one's own life; the inclination to sexual reproduction and the rearing of offspring; and the inclination to know the truth about God and to live in society. The preservation of one's own life and the reproduction of the species were inclinations shared with all other living creatures; only the inclination towards God and towards ordered society were peculiar to human reason. These principles of the natural law were not banal, but they left a great many moral questions unanswered.

St Thomas himself was aware that the working out of the natural knowledge of God's will became more provisional the further it descended into particulars, but the problem with natural law was precisely that in practice it needed an arbiter and so fell under the control of the church authorities. From being an appeal to what all human beings of good will can know of God by the light of reason, it became a sub-division of Christian doctrine. John Mahoney, while regarding the effect of the notion of natural law within the Catholic Church as being to preserve attention to the power of human reason in general and to the possibility of appeal to universal moral principles in particular, nevertheless comments,

> On the whole it has been the fate of Aquinas' natural law teaching in moral theology that the logical appeal and coherence of his system has been stressed, while the provisionality and contingency of conclusions as they come closer to individual situations, features which he himself carefully built into his theory, have been either neglected or ignored. (1987:80)

(iv) Vision and Discipline in Spirituality

During the Middle Ages the tradition of spirituality in the western church to some extent lost contact with systematic theology. Theology took the path of 'nominalism', an extreme individualism which broke up the universe of Aquinas and in doing so laid the foundations of modern science. As systematic theology became more arid, there was a great flowering of spirituality based upon emotion. The Franciscan movement, with its love of nature, including human nature, and its passionate devotion to the person of Jesus, helped to humanize the church. In *The Canticle of Brother Sun* St Francis of Assisi made the glory of creation the context for a proper understanding of humanity.

> Praised be You, my Lord, through our Sister Mother Earth,
> who sustains and governs us,

and who produces varied fruits with coloured flowers and
herbs.

Francis praised God for the sun and moon, for wind and water,
fire and earth, and for life and death, for forgiveness and acceptance.

> Praised be You, my Lord, through those who give pardon for
> your love and bear infirmity and tribulation. (1982:39)

Francis himself was said to have received in his body the 'Stig-
mata', the wounds in hands and feet and side which Jesus suffered on the cross. This claim bore witness to that devotion to
the humanity of Jesus which was a marked feature of the modern form of devotion now beginning to develop; it was to be
seen more fully in the popular work called the *Imitation of Christ*,
attributed to Thomas à Kempis.

The Beguine movement which flourished among Flemish-speak-
ing women in the twelfth and thirteenth centuries showed a
similar emotional force. In the early thirteenth century Hadewijch
wrote of 'Lady Love':

> The madness of love
> is a rich fief;
> Anyone who recognized this
> Would not ask Love for anything else:
> It can unite opposites
> And reverse paradox.
> I am declaring the truth about this:
> The madness of love makes bitter what was sweet,
> It makes the stranger a kinsman,
> And it makes the smallest the proudest. (1980:206)

The social reasons for such movements were no doubt complex. The monasteries which had done so much for the church
and society of the early Middle Ages had largely become the
victims of their own success. 'These puritans of the monastic life
incurred the penalty of puritanism; they became rich because
they renounced the glory of riches, and powerful because they

invested wisely' (Southern, 1970:260). Solid physical labour, good farming methods, careful accounting and the accumulation of capital rather than conspicuous expenditure had made early capitalists of them. The reform movement of the Cistercians, begun at Cîteaux in 1098, in time had the same problems as the Benedictine order from which it came. Similarly the first followers of St Francis of Assisi embraced the Lady Poverty joyfully, but even within the founder's lifetime the full radical nature of the challenge could not be sustained.

Nevertheless the new orders of friars, not living within one settled community but travelling to wherever God's work was to be found, were able to minister to a new society which was developing in the ambitious and less rooted spirit of the towns. The Franciscans were founded in 1209 as mendicant preachers of poverty and the love of Jesus, the Dominicans in 1216 as opponents of heresies; both became involved in the educational enterprises of the new universities. Being relatively free from the control of the local bishops and clergy, the new orders were able to be innovative and intellectually exploratory.

Few teachers were more radical in their thought than Meister Eckhart, a German Dominican who taught for part of his career in Paris. In his sermons and other writings Eckhart used language which suggested that God the Father brought God the Son to birth in each human soul. In a sermon on spiritual virginity he defined a virgin as 'a person who is free of all alien images' (1981:177). This emptiness was to become filled with pure spiritual power from God. 'And I have often said that there is a power in the soul that touches neither time nor flesh. It flows from the spirit and remains in the spirit and is wholly spiritual' (Eckhart, 1981:179).

Eckhart's language was so extravagant that it is difficult to see what his doctrine might be. He did not teach that God was in any sense mixed or confused with human nature, but he did have some sort of doctrine of an issuing-forth of spirit from God and return of spirit to God. 'And as he gives birth to his Only-Begotten Son into me, so I give him birth again into the Father' (1981:194). Here the truth of God was in principle unknowable by human rationality and could be arrived at only by a penetration into darkness to the God beyond God. In the western church, where philosophers were applying themselves to denying reality in metaphysics, it left the individual mind seemingly too much on the loose.

This was no great problem when the teaching was given in guarded language, from ascetic to ascetic, as in the anonymous fourteenth century English work, *The Cloud of Unknowing*. The advice to 'beat with a sharp dart of longing love upon this cloud of unknowing which is between you and your God' (Anon., 1981, p.145; ch.XII) was clearly an expression of personal prayer. When Eckhart said 'But in the breaking-through, when I come to be free of will of myself and of God's will and of all his works and of God himself, then I am above all created things, and I am neither God nor creature, but I am what I was and what I shall remain, now and eternally' (1981:203), he may have been saying the same thing, but it looked more theologically threatening. Rowan Williams comments that 'Eckhart's real problem was the lack of vocabulary. Western Catholicism by 1300 was rapidly losing the means to express theologically the basic principle of its life, the *ekstasis*, emptying, displacement of self in response to the self-emptying love of God, the communion of God and humanity by the presence of each in the other' (1979:136-137).

Yet it was always possible to balance radical experience of God with a sane theology. Dame Julian of Norwich, the greatest of the English mystics, who was born in 1342 and was recorded as still living in her cell attached to the church of St Julian in 1413, had as strong a sense of the love of God as Eckhart, but argued in a more pastoral frame of mind.

On May 13, 1373, after an illness, Julian began to receive a series of visions of Christ's suffering, having previously prayed for an experience of the passion of Christ. The experience was described in vivid detail. 'And at this, suddenly I saw the red blood trickling down from under the crown, all hot, flowing freely and copiously, a living stream, just as it seemed to me that it was at the time when the crown of thorns was thrust down upon his blessed head' (ST III, 1978:129). Along with the visions

Julian also experienced a sense of her own sharp battle with the sources of evil, together with a sense of the ever-powerful love of God in Jesus. 'I saw that he is to us everything which is good and comforting for our help' (ST IV, 1978:130). The capacity for such visions creates a problem for the twentieth century consciousness, but a good case can be made out for Julian's essential sanity even in the visions. Paul Molinari in a study of the visions comments that 'Her descriptions reveal her as capable of profound emotion, but yet without the least hint of emotional instability or indecision' (1958:10).

More important, however, was the quality of Julian's theological reflection on what she had seen and felt. The *Showings*, or *Revelations of Divine Love*, were written by Julian in two versions, a short text (ST) soon after the visions and a longer text (LT) some twenty years later, with a deeper theological exposition.

Julian's theme was the encompassing love of God. 'Know it well, love was his meaning. Who reveals it to you? Love. What did he reveal to you? Love' (LT 86; 1978:342). This love was the same love which God had for human beings before the creation. But it was the experience of the love of Jesus which fully explained the love of the Trinity. 'We know in our faith that God alone took our nature, and no one but he' (LT 80; 1978:335). Jesus carried the burden of sorrow for the human situation of being cut off, through ignorance, from the bliss of the Trinity; he carried not only his own sorrow for other human beings, but also the sorrow which all ought to feel for themselves.

God took the initiative toward humanity in Jesus, but could not and would not force us to be what we were not yet able to be. Love worked first to cause the human being to seek the God who waited. The balance of seeking and waiting was crucial to Julian's theory of the Christian's relationship to God. She dealt with it particularly through the image of Jesus as our mother. The image of the mother was not a property of Jesus to be set over against the other two Persons of the Trinity, rather it was a property of the Godhead which was expressed towards human beings in Jesus. It was the work of Jesus to bring us back 'by the motherhood of mercy and grace into our natural place, in which

117

we were created by the motherhood of love, a mother's love which never leaves us'. Moreover, the love of a human mother received its inmost meaning from the love of God. 'The mother's service is nearest, readiest and surest; nearest because it is most natural, readiest because it is most loving, and surest because it is truest . . . But our true Mother Jesus, he alone bears us for joy and for endless life, blessed may he be' (LT 60; 1978:297-298).

The image of God as mother was also connected to Julian's understanding of the church, in which the Christian was nourished through the sacraments.

> The mother can give her child suck of her milk, but our precious Mother Jesus can feed us with himself, and does, most courteously and most tenderly, with the blessed sacrament, which is the precious food of true life; and with all the sweet sacraments he sustains us most mercifully and graciously, and so he meant in these blessed words, where he said: I am he whom Holy Church preaches and teaches to you.
> (LT 60;1978:298)

The question posed by such a strong image was whether the salvation offered by God could ever fail. For the mothering arose out of the very nature of God. 'It is his office to save us, it is his glory to do it, and it is his will that we know it . . .' (LT 61; 1978:302). The classic problem of the theology of grace was that the human being needed to be given love in order to be able to love in return. Julian recognized that in the drawing of the individual towards God there were often failures on the road. This led to a further affirmation. 'And by the experience of this falling we shall have a great and marvellous knowledge of love in God without end; for enduring and marvellous is that love which cannot and will not be broken because of offences' (LT 61; 1978:300).

Could such love be broken for any human being, or for anything in creation? Formally Julian's theology was entirely orthodox: as she remarked from time to time, 'But in everything I believe as Holy Church preaches and teaches' (LT 9; 1978:192). Yet the experience of prayer uniting the soul with God carried with it both a sense of the love of God being so strong that nothing could stand against it and a sense of God being so holy that even the slightest ill-doing must be a very terrible thing. This created a tension about the future. Julian's basic perception was that it was not the nature of God to destroy. 'And despite all this, I saw truly that our Lord was never angry, and never will be' (LT 46; 1978:259). Indeed, for Julian it was impossible even to conceive of wrath in God. 'For truly, as I see it, if God could be angry for any time, we should neither have life, nor place, nor being' (LT 49; 1978:264). The impossibility of God's anger followed from the littleness of the creation in comparison with God.

And in this he showed me something small, no bigger than a hazelnut, lying in the palm of my hand, as it seemed to me, and it was as round as a ball. I looked at it with the eye of my understanding and thought: What can this be? I was amazed that it could last, for I thought that because of its littleness it would suddenly have fallen into nothing. And I was answered in my understanding: It lasts and always will, because God loves it; and thus everything has being through the love of God. (LT 5; 1978:183)

The immensity of God compared with the littleness of creation combined with the theme of the foreknowing and the foredoing of God to create in Julian a sense of awe before the mystery of creation, sin and redemption. Her final answer was reserve before a mystery (LT 32), but she concluded also that sin could have no permanent existence. For she saw, not the work of creatures, but the work of God in the creature. 'And I was certain that he does no sin; and here I was certain that sin is no deed, for in all this sin was not shown to me' (LT 11; 1978:197-198). Here her mystical theology reached its creative height and came to a tension between creation and salvation that could be resolved in only one way. 'But Jesus, who in this vision informed me about everything needful to me, answered with these words and said: Sin is necessary, but all will be well, and all will be well, and every kind of thing will be well' (LT 27; 1978:224-225).

Julian reflected further on this problem in an extensive passage (chapters 51 to 55 in the Long Text) concerning the vision of a lord and a servant, in which the servant runs off eagerly to do the lord's bidding, but from his very eagerness falls into a steep ravine and lies injured, not knowing of his lord's closeness and loving will to restore him.

> And in this an inward spiritual revelation of the Lord's meaning descended into my soul, in which I saw that this must necessarily be the case, that his great goodness and his own honour require that his beloved servant, whom he loved so much, should be highly and blessedly rewarded forever, above what he would have been if he had not fallen, yes, and so much that his falling and all the woe that he received from it will be turned into high, surpassing honour and endless bliss.
> (LT 51; 1978:269)

The servant is both Adam and Christ. In this double identification Julian conceived salvation, not as an act done by Jesus for humanity, but rather as an act done by Jesus in humanity. Because of her sense of the identification between God and the humanity God had lovingly created, she took the act of love which was the self-giving of Jesus back to the beginning of humanity. 'When Adam fell, God's son fell; because of the true union which was made in heaven, God's Son could not be separated from Adam, for by Adam I understand all mankind' (LT 51; 1978:274). She frequently used the phrase 'all who will be saved', as part of her reserve before the mystery of salvation. Yet clearly she found no ground for any distinction between those to be saved and the whole of humanity. Though she made repeated acts of submission to the teaching of the church, this great mind could not surrender the conviction that the unity of creation and the unity of salvation flowed from a single act of love, the love of the Trinity flowing out to that which had endlessly been seen not only as created but also as saved.

It was not that Julian was weak on a sense of sin — throughout the *Revelations of Divine Love* the great problem with which she wrestled was how sin was possible in the face of God's love. But taking sin with great seriousness, she was forced by her own experience of God in prayer to treat the love of God as higher still. Julian was not lacking in an understanding of the creature as made, or of the gap between creation and creator, but her guiding thought was of the recapitulation of the creation in Christ: that in Christ the whole creation was taken up and restored to its proper place in God's being and God's love. Whatever she might say in deference to the teaching of the church, her own teaching on the unity of being in creation and in salvation left no explanation of the failure of salvation for any creature.

The difficulty in later spirituality was to keep this clear-eyed perception of love in the face of ever more complex descriptions of direct God-experience. Spirituality achieved its most complex exposition from St John of the Cross in Spain in the sixteenth century. Juan de Yepes was born in 1542 near Avila and became a member of the Carmelite order of friars, with the name of John of the Cross, in 1563. In 1567 he met St Teresa of Avila, who was already engaged in reforming the women's order of Carmelites, and helped her to found the first reformed house for men. In their early years the new foundations were of great simplicity and indeed severity, both in the physical conditions of the little houses and in the lives the friars led in them. The main work of the new houses was preaching the Gospel in the poverty-stricken countryside.

As the reform movement grew, St John, rather against his will, was drawn into administration within the order, and into deepening conflicts about the reform, which led to his imprisonment in a house of the order in 1577-1578. During this time, on the basis both of his own inner life and of his experience as a spiritual director of other monastics, he began to write the treatise in two parts known as *The Ascent of Mount Carmel* and *The Dark Night of the Soul*.

This work was an account of the way of purgation of the soul, in order to arrive at the experience of union with God. The purgation consisted of two 'nights'; the night or purgation of the senses and the night or purgation of the spirit. St John was writing for contemplatives, those committed to lives of prayer within religious orders, who had already gone beyond the stages of prayer which were possible for those in the active life of the world. In the active life it was possible to come to the lowest level of contemplative prayer, known as 'affective' prayer — a quiet 'being there' with God which needed no words to support it. In the monastic life it was possible to take the risk of passing beyond simple affectivity through a deeper knowledge of the self into a deeper knowledge of God.

The new thing was the stripping of the self of all concerns except the direct approach to God. This was purgation. Then came 'illumination', an experience of direct knowledge of God, and finally 'union', in which the soul was placed 'in' God and needed to make no further effort, being taken over and directed by God so that all that happened was joy. These were the final stages of the spiritual life.

In the first part of the purgation, the purgation of the senses, St John's text was full of images of delight. 'Wherefore, when it gives itself to prayer, the soul is like to one to whom water has been brought, so that he drinks peacefully, without labour, and is no longer forced to draw water through the aqueducts of past meditations and forms and figures' (*Ascent*, Book II xiv 8; 1935:112). He described the soul in this state as 'confused, loving, passive and tranquil'. The confusion arose because the very simplicity of this state of pure knowledge of God made it seem obscure: the soul was not used to being without occupations.

This state of simple understanding was not a place in which to rest. What had happened so far was that the distractions of the needs of the senses had been stripped away. The soul no longer needed to speak words of prayer, to look at physical objects, to imagine biblical scenes, to worry about its physical comfort or to hear words of wisdom from others. Now it must cease to hold on to the one thing that so far had been central to it — its own knowledge of God. Here the soul must not even be sure of the Godhead itself. St John emphasized that this second night was a work of God in the soul. It was the action of God's love, not something the human being could undertake for her or himself.

'Because however greatly the soul itself labours, it cannot actively purify itself so as to be in the least degree prepared for the Divine union of perfection of love, if God takes not its hand and purges it not in this dark fire' (*Dark Night* I iii 3; 1935:337-338). Because the soul which was beginning to achieve contemplation still had many imperfections in it, this last cleansing process was particularly painful, threatening the very centre of the self.

> And when the soul suffers the direct assault of this Divine light, its pain, which results from its impurity, is immense; because, when this pure light assails the soul, in order to expel its impurity, the soul feels itself to be so impure and miserable that it believes God to be against it, and thinks that it has set itself up against God . . . (*Dark Night* II v 5: 1933:383).

Yet the end of the process was joy in the union with the Beloved.

> In order to arrive at knowing everything,
> Desire to know nothing . . .
> For, in order to pass from the all to the all,
> Thou hast to deny thyself wholly in all.
> (*Ascent* I xiii 11; 1933:59)

What these contemplatives set out to show was that there was a path to the total experience of God, and that this path was part of the human experience of the reality of creation. Yet the problem with this level of contemplation was that it might seem to be too sharply restricted to those who could enter monastic life and who had a special gift for progress in this sort of prayer. What in Julian of Norwich was a radical opening of prayer to any Christian became in this post-Reformation spirituality once again a way of making the highest levels of prayer a closed book to the lay person. The simplicity of the Christian love ethic disappeared behind the institutional demands of the church.

(v) The Reformation

A fundamental social change occurred in Europe in the thirteenth and fourteenth centuries, from the early mediaeval world

123

centered on the church and the countryside, to the modern world centered on the towns and on the individual. C. M. Cippola remarks that the later mediaeval town was significantly different from the towns of the ancient world. 'The mediaeval city was dominated politically, socially, and culturally by the merchants and the moneychangers — as all textbooks of economic history teach — and also by the pharmacists, the notaries, the lawyers, the judges, the doctors and the like' (1972:18). These interests formed a cohesive social group and tended to develop a new political structure. 'Establishing the city as an independent corporate entity with well-differentiated administrative organs, the burgher actually gave birth to the modern state as we conceive it' (1972:19). The rise of the towns made a substantial difference to mediaeval society in two ways.

Ecclesiastically they shifted the centre of power from the monasteries to the cathedrals. Initially the cathedrals represented royal patronage, but increasingly they represented also the growing commercial power of the twelfth and thirteenth century towns. In this period feudalism in the narrowest sense was beginning to break down. Everywhere the rise of a money economy directly weakened the ties of feudal service through the practice of substituting money payments for actual military and other service. It is perhaps ironic that in this period 'wage-labour' represented a step into freedom rather than into the servitude of nineteenth and twentieth century industrialism.

In intellectual life the shift of education out of the monasteries into the cathedral schools, and in time into independent universities made possible the development of that questioning, creative style of mind which found its home in the experimental sciences. It is significant of the speed with which education became a secular cause that Cambridge, in 1209, and Padua, in 1222, were both founded without a basis in an existing ecclesiastical foundation, whether monastery or cathedral. The relative freedom of the towns, based on economic success, made them natural centres for the new learning, and the new teaching orders of the friars, the Dominicans and the Franciscans, were the instruments through which the church dealt with the new urban society.

Even the physical structures of the gothic cathedrals were a symptom of this change. Jacob Bronowski comments that 'Of all the monuments to human effrontery, there is none to match these towers of tracery and glass that burst into the light of Northern Europe before the year 1200' (1973:109). He also points out that 'The cathedrals were built by the common consent of townspeople, and for them by common masons'. But these people were also the bearers of technical, scientific and imaginative revolutions. The mathematics of the buildings were developed by experimenting in practice with the living force of the stone, but it was indeed mathematics that produced these buildings and with that mathematics came a new view of nature.

The Franciscan friar Roger Bacon (c.1214-c.1292) was one of the first to write on the importance of experiment in science. In France the cathedral of Saint-Denis was rebuilt by the monk Suger between 1134 and 1144 and 'for the first time in the history of any edifice, the plan had been drawn "with the help of geometrical and arithmetical instruments"' (Duby, 1981:117). The same minds that applied the logic of mathematics to buildings also represented nature in a logical order in the decoration within them. Decoration now represented creatures not as bearers of myth but as the eye saw them. 'The universe ceased to be a code that the imagination strove to decipher. It became a matter of logic, and the cathedrals were to restore the pattern of it by situating all visible creatures in their respective places' (Duby, 1981:117). René Huyghe suggests that the whole gothic style is the result of a change from having the basis of knowledge in ideas or universals to having the basis of knowledge in physical reality, in particulars. He comments, 'This was a profound revolution: for can there be a more far-reaching change in human affairs than a shift of the very concept of reality?' (1962:177).

What effect the great outpouring of human experience had on the mass of the population is not clear. Intellectual change is first of all the business of an élite, and most of what is recorded for us under the heading of 'religion' is also the business of an élite. Only someone educated in Latin could even follow the eucharistic rite — hence no doubt the success of the alternative devotion to the passion of Jesus which found its popular apex in the seventeenth century cult of the Sacred Heart. Both scholastic theology and spiritual experience filtered down to the people as best they could, But what was seen were the buildings, the frescoes, the windows and the statues, and the theatre of the Mass; and what was required was observance. Christina Larner remarks, 'Religion was about doing things. It was about observance. It was about attending mass, giving money to the church, genuflection, going on pilgrimage. Such performances could complement rather than compete with magical animist beliefs and practices' (1984:118). What was not yet necessarily demanded of the believer as an individual Christian was that intensity of commitment and knowledge of the faith which came with the Reformation.

The reformation of religion in the sixteenth century was part of a wider mental change. Jacob Bronowski identifies the symbolic year for this change as 1543, three years before the death of the reformer Martin Luther.

> In that year three books were published that changed the mind of Europe: the anatomical drawings of Andreas Vesalius; the first translation of the Greek mathematics and physics of Archimedes; and the book by Nicolaus Copernicus, *The Revolution of the Heavenly Orbs*, which put the sun at the centre of the heaven and created what is now called the Scientific Revolution. (1973:142)

At the same time in the arts the exploration of the potentialities of human life and of nature turned painting from religious iconography to a delight in landscape and the human body, even in pictures on religious themes. Architecture lost the tensions of the gothic and returned to classical form beyond its earlier limits. The new spirit of humanism also turned energetically to the study of the texts of the rediscovered classical writings and established a method of critical enquiry that was soon to be applied to the New Testament and the Hebrew Bible.

All of this was made possible by a new economic prosperity that had begun half a century before. The fourteenth century had been a time of economic disasters. 'An overburdening of population as a result of previous prosperity, harvest failures, the crushing fiscal policies and currency disturbances which the new endemic warfare imposed on rulers, and finally the Black Death of 1348 to 1350, all contributed to a long contraction in the economy, which lasted up to the middle of the fifteenth century' (Bernard, 1972:275). Nevertheless it was in this period that the financial mechanisms necessary for the development of early capitalism began to be formed in earnest and to provide the basis of venture capital by which the expansion of trade and the great voyages of exploration were financed. Nothing better symbolizes the new daring of mind than these voyages westwards to the Americas and round the southern tip of Africa, beyond the edges of the known world.

The religious changes of the Protestant Reformation were part of this new spirit of optimism and critical enquiry. There were few new ideas in the sixteenth century reformation, but there was a dramatically new context for old and tried ideas. William Langland in the late fourteenth century in *Piers Plowman* had a character 'Anima' who quoted from the Corpus Christi hymn the words *'Sola fides sufficit'*, 'faith alone is sufficient for salvation' (Book XV; 1959:228). This phrase was the key to Martin Luther's revolution in theology, but Langland used it only to explain that simple people could receive the grace of the Mass even when ill-educated or lazy priests left out some of the text. Although *Piers Plowman* was a catalogue of all possible complaints against the clergy and other professions, Langland was nowhere near to drawing Luther's practical conclusion that faith alone was sufficient for the salvation of all persons under all conditions.

Neither was Martin Luther himself, in the beginning, near to this conclusion. Luther's problem was the personal one that however faithfully, as a good monk, he used the sacraments of the church as a means of grace, never did he feel in his own spirit liberated and forgiven. Being a determined man, this caused him to work even harder at the means the church provided. Roland Bainton records that 'Without confession, he testified, the Devil would have devoured him long ago. He confessed frequently, often daily, and for as long as six hours on a single occasion' (Bainton, 1950:41). In Luther's own words, 'The more I tried to remedy an uncertain, weak and afflicted conscience with the traditions of men, the more each day I found it more uncertain, weaker, more troubled' (Rupp, 1970:4).

Relief came when, in meditating on the 'righteousness' or 'justice' of God, which he understood as the quality of God by which God condemned the sinner, it came to him that righteousness was rather the quality by which God invited sinners to be forgiven. The words of St Paul in Romans 1.17 took on new meaning, *'The upright man finds life through faith'*. In an 'Autobiographical Fragment' written at the end of his life Luther said that on understanding these words, 'At this I felt myself straightaway born afresh and to have entered through the open gates into paradise itself' (Rupp, 1970:6). From this release it followed that many of the works which the church required of Christians, such as the necessity of regular confession to a priest, fasting, going on pilgrimages and buying indulgences to release the soul from so much time in purgatory, were unnecessary. 'For if by our own efforts we are to attain peace of conscience, why then did Christ die?' (Rupp, 1970:8).

In the first instance this was all that Luther asked, that the church be cleansed from these accretions of history and returned to the original simplicity of the New Testament. But the church's interpretation of the Gospel was deeply corrupted by a system in which the call for reform threatened both episcopal authority and ecclesiastical income. Moreover many people had not experienced Luther's tension, but found in the sacraments and authority of the church a true means of grace. The political authorities were divided. On the one hand the princes derived their authority from God through the church, so that the issue of power tended to line them up with the papacy. On the other hand the possibility of reducing the taxes paid to the church and perhaps increasing their own revenues was attractive. In the

German territories moreover there was the beginning of a national feeling which demanded expression in local autonomy from the rule of both the church and the Holy Roman Empire.

Under these pressures the questions of faith and conscience escalated into an attack upon and defence of the whole structure of church and state in Europe. It was Luther's genius that provided the spark for a great bonfire of the past. A conservative in the simplest sense of wishing the church to be true to its origins, coming from a rural background and serving a largely peasant people who were easily aroused and to whom he was devoted, he ended by destroying the one thing that held the mediaeval world together, the concept of a hierarchy from God and the angels down to the meanest serf, with the Catholic Church as the central organ of the hierarchy, holding the power of interpretation and the keys which symbolized the power to excommunicate and the power to forgive. By placing the purity of faith before obedience to the church, the Reformation left this conceptual system in tatters. It was to be replaced in time by the concept of an autonomous individual in a world almost wholly determined by the causalities of natural science.

So far as ethics were concerned, Luther was on the whole a reactionary, trying, but in vain, to stem the rising tide of commercial capitalism. On political authority he set his followers on the second of the two dangerous paths indicated by St Augustine's division of the two cities. Where Aquinas had chosen to make the temporal city subordinate to the heavenly city in the form of the earthly institution of the church, Luther used the same doctrine of the two swords to teach a submission by the church to the state in temporal matters. When the German peasants pressed their demands for an alleviation of their economic disadvantages to the point of armed revolt, Luther supported the restoration of law and order in words which after the terror and counter-terror were over, seem too strong. 'The rulers, then, should go on unconcerned, and with a good conscience lay about them as long as their hearts still beat', he wrote *Against the Robbing and Murdering Hordes of Peasants*, in May 1525 (Rupp, 1970:124). But in those times of the shaking of civilization, nobody was talking about half-measures on either side.

What Luther provided most importantly was not a discourse on social ethics but a theological foundation for an ethic of freedom. In 1520 he issued three manifestos. The first was an appeal *To the Christian Nobility of the German Nation Respecting the Reformation of the Christian Estate,* which asked for the support of the politically powerful classes for the ideas of the reform in the German territories. This treatise drew particularly on the argument that the priestly authority of the church was to be found in all Christians in virtue of their baptism, citing I Peter 2.9 and Revelation 5.10. The second was *On the Babylonian Captivity of the Church,* in which Luther recognized only three sacraments, 'baptism, penance and the bread' (Rupp, 1970:47-48).

The third, *The Freedom of a Christian,* gave an exposition of the double principle of Christian responsibility: 'A Christian is a perfectly free lord of all, subject to none. A Christian is a perfectly dutiful servant of all, subject to all' (Dillenberger, 1961:53). These two claims encompassed the whole teaching of the Reformation on ethics.

The freedom of the Christian came from the fact that the promises of God had been given and fulfilled in Jesus. The freedom of the new life of the risen Jesus was open to everyone who believed the promises. No amount of good works could produce this effect. But once the promises were freely accepted, good works would flow naturally from the changed nature of the Christian. 'Just as the heated iron glows like fire because of the union of fire with it, so the Word imparts its qualities to the soul' (1961:60). It was this exchange which made human beings priests and kings in the kingdom of Christ, and so subject to none in their inner nature, though not free of suffering in their outward experience. 'As a matter of fact, the more Christian a man is, the more evils, sufferings and deaths he must endure, as we see in Christ the first-born prince himself, and in all his brethren, the saints' (1961:63).

The other half of the principle of freedom was the responsibility for service. The fact of being justified by the saving action of Christ did not relieve the Christian of the obligation to further action. On the contrary, there was now work to be done in faith. 'As long as we live in the flesh we only begin to make some progress in that which shall be perfected in the future life' (1961:67). The main necessity for Luther was to acquire control of one's own body, for though the spirit had accepted Christ, the outer man still put up a resistance of various kinds. There was a place, therefore, for 'works' to make the outer nature obedient to the inner nature and to purify it of its fierce desires. 'We do not, therefore, reject good works; on the contrary we cherish and teach them as much as possible' (1961:72). These works were the personal discipline of the individual in the church, consisting of 'penitence, confession and satisfaction', together with 'the word of grace and the promise of forgiveness' (1961:72-73).

Finally Luther came to the responsibility of the Christian towards the neighbour. Here he expressed himself briefly but strongly. 'A man does not live for himself alone in this mortal body to work for it alone, but he lives also for all men on earth; rather he lives only for others and not for himself' (1961:73). And again, 'I will therefore give myself as a Christ to my neighbour, just as Christ offered himself to me' (1961:75). The love to the neighbour did not require so much attention as the works of self-discipline; firstly because it was the works of self-discipline which carried the greatest danger of misleading the Christian into thinking that she or he could earn salvation by these efforts; secondly because action towards the neighbour was a result of faith, not a means of training in it. 'Behold, from faith thus flow forth love and joy in the Lord, and from love a joyful, willing and free mind that serves one's neighbour willingly and takes no account of gratitude or ingratitude, of praise or blame, of gain or loss' (1961:75-76). Luther nowhere in this argument considered the possibility that a secular person, ignorant of Christ, might still do loving actions towards the neighbour which would be acceptable to God (Matt. 25.31-46). The question of the status of the secular humanist had not yet arisen.

Although Luther drew his standard of Christian behaviour from the sense of union with Christ that came with the conversion of the heart, nevertheless he and other reformers were aware of a need for more precise indications. These were to be found in scripture. The law, meaning all the moral teaching of the Bible, but chiefly the Ten Commandments, had for Luther two functions.

The first was the use of the law of God in the form of the secular law to restrain by force all those who were not willing to act in Christian fashion towards their neighbours. In *Secular Authority: To what extent it should be obeyed*, Luther agreed that 'All who are not Christians belong to the kingdom of the world and are under the law' (Dillenberger, 1961:370). Such restraints made ordinary life tolerable, for Christians and non-Christians alike, but did nothing towards the salvation of those who were not converted. The second use of the law of God was to convict each person of being a sinner. The sheer impossibility of doing God's will, once recognized, began the process of conversion to Christ. 'It is to teach men to recognize sin, that they may be made humble unto grace and unto faith in Christ' (1961:370).

Luther summarised this position in his *Commentary on the Epistle to the Galatians*:

> And forasmuch as we teach these things both diligently and faithfully, we do thereby plainly testify that we reject not the law and works, as our adversaries do falsely accuse us: but we do altogether stablish the law, and require works thereof, and we say that the law is good and profitable, but in his own proper use: which is, first to bridle civil transgressions, and then to reveal and to increase spiritual transgressions. (Dillenberger, 1961:144)

After the bruising effect of the law came the Gospel of imputed righteousness, the simple acceptance of the sinner by God through the sufferings of Jesus on the cross. The hidden majesty of the Creator could be seen only in and through the suffering of Jesus, in the scandal of the humiliation of God for the sake of the repentance of human beings. However, to repent and be accepted by God was not to be made perfect in this life. Christians still had a remnant of sin dwelling in them, which needed purging. 'We therefore do make this definition of a Christian, that a Christian is not he which hath no sin, or feeleth no sin, but he to whom God imputeth not his sin because of his faith in Christ' (1961:112).

It was for this reason that Luther's friend Philip Melancthon began to write of a third use of the law, as a guide to the life of the Christian after repentance and acceptance. It is a matter for argument now how much damage this may have done subsequently to Luther's fundamental distinction of 'Law' and 'Gospel'. Franz Hildebrandt comments that 'The dilemma in introducing the "tertius usus" lies in the paradox that it can only apply to the "reborn" inasmuch as he is not "reborn"' (1946:42). Certainly it introduced a danger of once again relying on fulfilling a law, and so on 'works', rather than on the Gospel. On the other hand, it was a response to another dilemma, that some followers of the reformed church were claiming to need no guidance at all. How could the guidance of Christ in the heart be expressed and written down for those still weak in faith?

Melancthon's choice was inevitable once the Reformation had produced a new church, with its own institutions and its own need of an educational programme. In Geneva John Calvin settled the matter by making the 'third use' a part of his teaching. The problem then was to keep Luther's sense of 'Gospel' alive at all.

When the second generation of the reformation came under the leadership of Calvin, the individual conscience of the believer came face to face with the unbearable sovereignty of God in a new way. In an address to the reader at the beginning of the 1559 edition of his *Institutes of the Christian Religion*, Calvin said, 'God has filled my mind with zeal to spread his Kingdom and to further the public good. I am also duly clear in my own conscience, and have God and the angels to witness, that since I undertook the office of teacher in the church, I have had no other purpose than to benefit the church by maintaining the pure doctrine of godliness' (1960:4). The change in language and in purpose was dramatic. From an outpouring of the Spirit in the heart, the reformation had become a matter of comprehensive training in perfected and unchangeable doctrine, set out clearly by the learned for the sake of the ignorant.

The *Institutes* began in Book One with 'The knowledge of God and the Creator'. The sovereignty of God could not be denied. Every human being was aware of it, both in his or her own conscience and in looking at the glories of created things. At the same time this knowledge was no help to human beings in guiding their behaviour, for all human beings since the fall of Eve and Adam were deeply corrupted. 'First, we are so vitiated and perverted in every part of our nature that by this great corruption we stand justly condemned and convicted before God, to whom nothing is acceptable but righteousness, innocence and purity' (1.1.8; 1960:251). Secondly this perversity never ceased to produce new evils in us.

Even so, the corruption was the human being's own fault, in the sense that the inheritance of the first sin from Eve and Adam was really present in each person — it was, as it were, their own possession. But nothing that the human being could do could remove the original problem. Only God's action in the crucifixion of Jesus of Nazareth, the Son of God, could lift the guilt of being human. 'The Father destroyed the force of sin when the curse of sin was transferred to Christ's flesh' (2.16.6; 1960:510). The benefits which Jesus won were given to the believer by Christ dwelling in her or him through faith. And faith could not be demanded but must be received as a gift.

At this point Calvin raised the ancient problem of 'double predestination'. Because the human being could do nothing towards salvation except receive the gift of faith, salvation could come about only as an action of God towards each specific human being who became a believer. But it remained a mystery why God should give justifying faith to one person and not to another. Such action by God was beyond all human considerations of justice: nothing that God did bore any relation to human merit. 'For the pious mind realizes that the punishment of the impious and wicked and the reward of life eternal for the righteous equally pertain to God's glory' (1.3.2; 1960:43).

Luther had agonized over this question, but had left it in the hiddenness of God, accepting predestination to salvation but not attempting to explain it. Calvin accepted calmly the double predestination to salvation and to damnation as incomprehensible but just. 'We assert that, with respect to the elect, this plan was founded upon his freely given mercy, without regard to human worth; but by his just and irreprehensible but incomprehensible judgment he has barred the door of life to those whom he has given over to damnation' (3.21.7; 1960:931).

In practice, of course, Calvin dealt mainly with those who were called to salvation. It was the glory of this election, and the necessity of humility before it, which was the mainspring of Reformed theology. For this reason the overall feeling of the *Institutes of the Christian Religion* was a sure, if restrained, warmth and joy. It was the certainty of God's action in creation and in redemption, and the certainty of faith in those who were awake to God's call, which was the basis of the Christian life. Attention to this calling meant separating oneself from wickedness and uncleanness by spiritual discipline.

> Now this Scriptural instruction of which we speak has two main aspects. The first is that the love of righteousness, to which we are otherwise not at all inclined by nature, may be instilled and established in our hearts; the second, that a rule be set forth for us that does not let us wander about in our zeal for righteousness. (3.6.2; 1960:685)

The Reformed church in Geneva, under Calvin's leadership, attempted to control every aspect of daily life. Though there was conflict between the clergy and the lay magistrates about areas of responsibility, there was no argument about the fact that commitment to Christ involved discipline and that the moral life of the individual was a matter for public concern. Not only were the social controls more effective than those of the mediaeval church, they were also more wide-reaching. With the abolition of the monasteries the high level of virtue theoretically demanded of the monk by the 'counsel of perfection' was now the level at which secular life must aim. In consequence the ordinary activities of daily life, marriage, the family and work became subject to a scrutiny they had not previously received. As R. H. Tawney describes it, 'The essence of the system was not preaching or propaganda, though it was prolific of both, but the attempt to crystallize a moral ideal in the daily life of a visible society, which should be at once a church and a state' (Tawney, 1938:123).

(vi) Ethics and the Reformation

The Reformers had three major effects on Christian ethics. The first was that with the abolition of the monastic system the married state became the normative way of obedience to God. The second was that a movement that spread mainly among the urban commercial class necessarily accepted urban economic values with respect to profit and accumulation of property. The third was that the need to establish the reformed version of Christian faith by political means broke the notion of a single theological political system, which was a Christian ideal from the time of Constantine, and contributed to the formation eventually of the western liberal ideal of democratic pluralism. This in time led to the relativization and even privatization of the churches themselves.

From this point onwards Christian ethics is no more than a detailed development of what has already been laid down. In the Roman Catholic Church the practice of auricular confession with pastoral counselling led to the development of a complex moral theology (Mahoney, 1987). Some Protestants drew up similarly detailed patterns of counsel on practical matters, but Protestants also remained aware that any system of ethics or moral theology remained subordinate to direct obedience to the word of God by the individual conscience. In this sense Christian ethics was abolished in Protestantism almost before it began (Gustafson, 1978).

Sexuality

In the Middle Ages the church made a serious attempt to take control of the institution of marriage. Still essentially an arrangement between families, marriage had consisted of the betrothal, which was the initial arrangement, and the contract, the final signing of the documents containing consent of the parties, followed by the physical consummation of the sexual act. All of this was a domestic matter. By the thirteenth century the church had imposed itself on this domestic institution in various ways. One was to move the institution from the private to the public sphere, first by requiring a nuptial blessing on the agreement by the priest and secondly by moving the ceremony from the house to the church door, a common place of business. Needless to say, the actual practice varied. 'Wealthy and prominent persons usually had their marital consent witnessed by a notary; their humbler neighbours were much more likely to exchange consent in the presence of a priest' (Brundage, 1987:502-503). In the Orthodox Church it appears that the interest of the state in marriage led to the separation of the ceremony from the nuptial eucharist in the ninth century (Chryssavigis, 1989:21-23). In the west 'the practice of gathering in one formulary the blessing of the gifts, the exchange of promises, the blessing and handing over of the ring, the priest's benediction of the parties, the nuptial mass — and the series of prayers which culminated in the bridal chamber — is first found in the service books of England and Normandy of the late eleventh and early twelfth centuries' (Brooke, 1978:24).

Another concern from the eleventh century onwards was for consent from the betrothed persons as well as from their families; this also was applied increasingly to the sending of children into monastic institutions (Brooke, 1978:25). The church also exerted pressure for an acceptance of the indissolubility of marriage. The pressure was resisted by the aristocracy, who saw marriage primarily in terms of alliances and property deals; in the middle social strata, it has been argued, the need to preserve alliances may have tended in the reverse direction, providing a need for stability in order not to lose the goodwill of close neighbours. Either way, the view of the church gradually prevailed. 'After the twelfth century indissolubility ceased to be a problem. It was grudgingly accepted by the aristocracy and certainly more spontaneously adopted by rural communities' (Ariès, 1985:53).

Equally successful was the development of the teaching that marriage was a sacrament of the church in the same sense as baptism or the eucharist. This had no clear basis in the New

Testament or in patristic practice. The fact that indissolubility was not enforced until the twelfth century was witness to that. James Brundage remarks of the emperor Justinian in the sixth century, 'His divorce legislation, in general, tended to increase restrictions upon divorce, but there is no evidence that he considered marriage indissoluble or that he believed that marriage was a sacrament' (1987:114-115). By the thirteenth century this question, like others, was in process of settlement.

> The teaching of Aquinas and others in this period, however, affirmed that marriage was a sacrament and that the exchange of consent itself conferred grace in the same way that other sacraments did. This view was adopted as a dogmatic truth by the Council of Florence; the Council of Trent ultimately condemned contrary views as heresy. (Brundage, 1987:433)

At the same time that the church was tightening its control over the institution of marriage, the authorities were also hardening their attitude to homosexuality. John Boswell notes that after a long period of suppression of homosexuality at the end of the Roman empire, the rise of the towns in the eleventh century 'was accompanied by the reappearance of gay literature and other evidence of a substantial gay minority', but that in the second half of the twelfth century the approach became more hostile (1980:334). This may have been connected with the attempt to work out in moral theology the new concept of natural law and to give it effect in canon law. On the other hand James Brundage suggests that 'For reasons that may be linked to concern over the population crisis following the Black Death, lawmakers in the generation after 1348 suddenly seem to have perceived sodomy as a grave threat to society and visited upon those convicted of deviant sexual practices severe and gruesome punishments' (1987:533); these punishments included burning alive. No relief was offered from this situation after the Reformation, though the application of the law no doubt varied in different times and places.

The great change that the Reformation brought to the history of marriage was the reaffirmation of the Old Testament belief in the goodness of sexuality, a goodness not confined to the purpose of procreation. The abolition of the monasteries and of clerical celibacy restored marriage to the primacy in human relationships. Equally, from an Old Testament basis, the reformers rejected the idea that marriage was a sacrament of the church and consequently accepted the possibility of divorce and remarriage, under various limitations.

Finally, the reformers, while still seeing women as in some ways the weaker sex, no longer held the misogynistic views of many patristic and mediaeval theologians. Luther's loving, teasing letters to his wife are a clear indication of the benefit to theology of the practice of clerical marriage.

Property

From the classical world to the beginning of modern times the moral theory of economic life was based upon the precept that only labour was worthy of reward. Profit and interest were consequently immoral. A trader might be remunerated for bringing goods from one place to another, but it would, for example, be immoral for a trader to charge a higher price because goods were in short supply. St Thomas Aquinas, drawing on Aristotle, commented that the profit made from trading did not in itself imply honesty or dishonesty. What was permissible was simply that a trader should enjoy a modest life-style and be able to be charitable 'as a reward for his labour' (*Summa Theologica*, Secunda Secundae, Qu. 78, Art. 1; D'Entrèves, 1948:173).

Much more difficult was the question of the payment of interest. It was obvious that where something was lent to be consumed, like a loaf of bread, another loaf should be given back. Similarly, if someone occupied another's house, this was a use which prevented the owner enjoying the same use and compensation should be paid in rent.

The problem came when the object which was lent was money. For money was not fruitful: it could not be eaten and it could not be sown in the ground to grow and give more money. According to classical economic theory, only labour could add value to a product so that a higher price could be charged for it. If

139

wood were fashioned into a chair, the wood in the form of the chair had a higher value than the wood on the ground because of the labour put into it. But if someone lent money to the craftsman to buy the wood to make the chair, this required little labour and put no value into the chair.

What was needed in the community was the chair, to be exchanged for some other necessary object or service. The inert money, on the other hand, should simply be given back to the lender once the chair was sold. Any payment of interest beyond a reward for the labour of the lender was usury, a sinful charge for the sake of gaining money alone. So Aquinas ruled, 'To accept usury for the loan of money is in itself unjust; because this is selling what does not exist, and must obviously give rise to inequality, which is contrary to justice' (*Summa Theologica*, Secunda Secundae, Qu. 78, Art. 1; 1948:173).

In the later Middle Ages this theory weakened in the face of an increasingly complex and active economy. R. H. Tawney cites St Antonino in the fifteenth century, writing on the notion of a just price for goods, as one who gave more play to purely economic motives. But Tawney also comments that this was not a modern economic theory of the priority of market forces, 'the characteristic doctrine was different. It was that which insisted on the just price as the safeguard against extortion' (1938:53).

It was in the economically advanced city of Geneva that the decisive step was taken of recognizing the payment of a moderate rate of profit on trade and of interest on loans as a reward for a legitimate service. As Calvin wrote, 'Whence do the merchant's profits come, except from his own diligence and industry?' (*De Usuris*; Tawney, 1938:113). Similarly Calvin rejected the total condemnation of the charging of interest — or usury — and looked instead for the government to set a fair rate of return on monies lent. The significance of this was that, as Ernst Troeltsch puts it, 'Calvin abandoned the purely consumer's standpoint of the previous Christian ethic, and recognized the productive power of money and of credit' (1931:643). The crucial change made by the Reformation in the area of economic ethics came, not between the mediaeval Catholic Church and the Reformers, but between Luther and Calvin. As Troeltsch again comments,

> Unlike Lutheranism in similar circumstances, Calvin did not hark back to the agrarian patriarchal form of life as the ideal with its closely knit self-contained family life, based as far as possible on primitive methods of production, but he recognized industrial production based on a money economy as the natural foundation and form of professional work alongside of agrarian labour. (1931:642)

The one obedience to God the sovereign Lord meant that the work of the elect was to live out their own salvation by bringing as much as possible of human life under that rule. The work of caring for the sick and the poor was taken over from the monasteries by the state or by the parishes, using the endowments and taxes released by the institutional break from Rome and dissolution of the monasteries. The calling to monastic life was replaced by a doctrine of work itself as a calling from God, and the heirs of Calvin proved to be willing supporters of the capitalist virtues of thrift and rational organization in business. R. H. Tawney comments on early Calvinism that 'it is perhaps the first systematic body of religious teaching which can be said to recognize and applaud the economic virtues' (1938:114).

Luther had already seen not only the state but all daily activities as ordained by God. To those who argued that Christians should not serve as soldiers or as magistrates, he said 'Be not so wicked, my friend, as to say, A Christian may not do that which is God's peculiar work, ordinance and creation. Else you must also say, A Christian must not eat, drink or be married, for these are also God's work and ordinances' (*Secular Authority: To what extent it should be obeyed*; Dillenberger, 1961:377). These ordinances created opportunities for service to God and to fellow human beings, but there was no one rule which everyone must follow.

Calvin took the point further, arguing that every person needed a position in society and a work to be done in order to protect them against idleness or folly. 'Therefore, lest through our stupidity and rashness everything be turned topsy-turvy, he has

141

appointed duties for every man in his particular way of life' (3.10.6; 1960:724). The ethic of the calling, combined with the acceptance of the rapidly growing new economic order of commercial capitalism, led to a new understanding of human nature. As Troeltsch says once again, 'It laid the foundation of a world of specialized labour which taught men to work for work's sake, and in so doing it produced our present-day bourgeois way of life, the fundamental psychological principles which gave it birth' (1931:643).

Yet this was far from Calvin's own intention. The following of a secular calling was not to be seen as a means to prosperity. The main theme of Christian action for Calvin was self-denial. 'We are not our own: let us therefore not set it as our goal to seek what is expedient for us according to the flesh' (*Institutes*, 3.7.1; 1960:690). To love the neighbour was to give up the self. This was a most difficult thing to do, both because of the tendency to self-love and because of the unlovableness of the neighbour. 'But Scripture, to lead us by the hand to this, warns that whatever benefits we obtain from the Lord have been entrusted to us on this condition: that they be applied to the common good of the church' (3.7.5; 1960:695). A general duty to the whole of humanity as being originally created by God was concentrated more specifically on the household of faith, in whom the original image of God had been restored, but it must be remembered here that this church encompassed in principle the whole of society. It was not the reformers' intention to preside over a situation of economic individualism, although this was the eventual result of combining the Calvinist doctrine of work with the rationalist philosophies of the late eighteenth and early nineteenth centuries.

Political Power

It was also not the intention of either Luther or Calvin to reform society in any broad political sense. Luther held that the church needed freedom to preach the pure Gospel, and had an interest in the working of the ordinances of the family and daily labour, but that the organisation of everything in secular life was a matter for the secular power. The tendency of this doctrine of the two powers, temporal and spiritual, in later Lutheran teaching was to render the church passive before the secular power. In return the church received the privilege of the protection and financial support of the state for its ministry.

Calvin also separated the two sorts of obedience. He was concerned for liberty of conscience, but he was also concerned that individual liberty from sin and from the Law of Moses should not be construed as freedom from political obedience, as the more radical leaders of the Reformation movement tended to demand. Calvin laid down clear rules to guide political governors, including 'the duty of rightly establishing religion' (4.20.3; 1960:1488), and he showed from scripture the necessity of obeying an unjust ruler, since the power to rule was still given by God. Only when a constitution included officers whose duty was to moderate the actions of a ruler could such officers resist a prince.

There was, however, one crucial exception to this policy of obedience. If a legitimate ruler ordered something which required disobedience to God, then disobedience to the ruler became not a right but a duty. 'And how absurd would it be that in satisfying men you should incur the displeasure of him for whose sake you obey men themselves!' (4.20.32; 1960:1520). This was the final instruction of the *Institutes of the Christian Religion* and it proved in time to be the straw that broke the back of the notion of a unitary society based on a unitary church. The freedom of conscience of a Christian in religious matters could not in the end be contained in the framework of an establishment of religion.

The limits of this Christian idea of religious freedom were shown by the treatment of the Jews, both before and after the Reformation. Whereas the Roman empire, even under the Christian emperors, had recognized itself as a collection of races and religions, the theory of Christendom in the Middle Ages had become exclusive. 'There were always indeed some outsiders, even within the geographical area of western Christendom, but at best they were people with very limited rights, and at worst they had no right even to live. At best they were Jews' (Southern, 1970:17). St Thomas Aquinas applied his mind to the question of the Jews in a letter to the Duchess of Brabant, 'On the Government of the Jews'. Here he argued that the Jews, because of their sins in rejecting Jesus, 'are or were destined to perpetual slavery' (D'Entrèves, 1948:85). To this he added the economic charge that the Jews in the Duchess's territories lived solely by lending money at interest, and that it was legitimate for a ruler to relieve them of the sinful profits of this usury, which should be restored to the Christians from whom it had been extorted, where they could be identified, or otherwise put to pious or public use. The same rule applied to other money lenders who were not Jews.

In the *Summa Theologica* he noted that the Jews, who had never been Christians, were not to be converted by force to the Christian faith. 'The faithful may, however, if they wish, use force to prevent them from impeding the faith by blasphemy or by evil persuasion or even by open persecution' (Secunda Secundae, Qu. 10, Art. 8; D'Entrèves, 1948:153). For economic and ideological reasons the Jews were expelled from England in 1209, from France in 1182 and 1306, and from the Low Countries in 1370. Here again the Reformation offered no relief; it was the rational humanism of the late eighteenth century which eventually overcame the mediaeval distortion of Christian doctrine which regarded the Jews as having sole responsibility for killing Christ. Revolutionary France was the first European state to offer Jews equal citizenship.

One other ethical problem in the area of political action was settled in broad principle in the Middle Ages. This was the question of justice in warfare. When Christians were committed by the formation of the Christian empire under Constantine to accept responsibility for military service, it became possible and even essential to debate under what circumstances a war could be considered to be just. There were two sources for this debate in Roman law, the principles of *jus ad bellum*, the right to go to war, and of *jus in bello*, proper behaviour once war began.

On the first set of questions, the right to go to war, the

classical Christian expression has been that of St Thomas Aquinas, following the teaching of St Augustine. In the *Summa Theologica* Aquinas laid down that

> For a war to be just three conditions are necessary. First, the authority of the ruler within whose competence it lies to declare war . . . Secondly, there is required a just cause: that is that those who are attacked for some offence merit such treatment . . . Thirdly, there is required a right intention on the part of the belligerents: either of achieving some good object or of avoiding some evil. (Secunda Secundae, Qu. 40, Art. 1; D'Entrèves, 1948:159)

The first of these conditions meant that war must be declared by a political body generally recognized as a legitimate government, not begun as an act of private revenge by a subordinate power. The second meant that the reason for beginning military action should be a genuine wrong such as the imprisonment of a citizen or the seizure of property. The third meant that the intention behind the action should be genuinely to seek justice, not merely revenge or gain. Desirable as these criteria were in theory, their practical application was never free of controversy.

On the question of justice within warfare, the mediaeval church, again following Roman law, made valiant attempts to restrict the kinds of weaponry that might be used and to protect non-combatants. The argument that the use of force should be proportionate to the end desired staked a moral claim for the church to have a voice in this area and won a broad theoretical acceptance, both before and after the Reformation. What effect it had upon the practice of warfare is more doubtful: here as so often the relationship between general moral principles and practical possibilities offered scope for letting the practical determine the moral end. Yet even to have set up a moral aim in the area of warfare was a substantial achievement. It reaffirmed once again that in Christian ethics the political order could never claim exemption from moral scrutiny.

4
The Challenge from the Modern World

From the sixteenth century onwards, any attempt to talk about Christian ethics has faced not only the claims of other kinds of knowledge, in particular the knowledge obtained through the natural sciences, but also the claim that the fundamental values of human life could now be established in only one way — by the exercise of human reason, free of any question of revelation. The notion of human rationality eliminated almost all that Christianity had sought to establish as knowledge about God and human existence, as being in principle unknowable and therefore effectively untrue.

In the eighteenth century Christian ethics seems to have gone into a sort of doldrums, giving way to the apparent primacy of human rationality and seeking a harmony in society that would appeal to all reasonable 'men'. Meanwhile, those who had the task of running western societies were beginning to produce a political and economic system that had less respect for the human being than almost any previous form of human society.

The nineteenth and twentieth centuries were fruitful in the development of theories for every human contingency, from the organization of drains to the origins of religion, but the harvest of the twentieth century has been a bitter one. In practice we have proved much better at analysing and guiding physical systems than political and spiritual ones. Today our knowledge of physical systems is vast and ever-growing, our ability to destroy ourselves and our planet is undeniable, and our sense of direction is less and less clear. The challenge of modern thought to Christian faith and action has been both severe and salutary, but it has not clearly removed the need for a religious ethic of some sort.

(i) The Harmony of Nature
In 1652 Gerrard Winstanley, the leader of the 'Diggers', one of the radical groups in the English Civil War, wrote about those

who were to be allowed to make speeches in the Commonwealth, that they were not to be allowed to go beyond what could be known through the creation.

> To know the secrets of nature is to know the works of God; and to know the works of God within the creation is to know God himself, for God dwells in every visible work or body . . . And if a man should go to imagine what God is beyond the creation, or what he will be in a spiritual demonstration after a man is dead, he doth (as the proverb saith) build castles in the air, or tells of a world beyond the moon and beyond the sun merely to blind the reason of man . . . God manifests himself in actual knowledge, not in imagination . . .
> (1973:348-349)

Winstanley's desire to restrict the range of the imagination had ancient roots. Plato desired to banish artists from the republic because they were a possible source of subversion. But in Winstanley's voice there was a new note, the appreciation of nature as something to be worked-on. 'To know the secrets of nature is to know the works of God'. It is difficult for anyone today to sense just how new this note was.

Before the seventeenth century nature was largely seen as a force that could dominate the human being. Although early philosophers were willing to make a theoretical exploration of nature, nevertheless the ultimate force in the universe, which expressed itself through the physical world, was to be treated with respect. Wayne Meeks writes of the major philosophical traditions of Greece and Rome,

> All agree, too, that the rational and therefore happy life is a life in accord with nature, although their conceptions of nature, including human nature, differ. Because what is natural has been obscured by error and by social conventions, all require an austere reasoning process and a strict discipline in order to carry out the maxim, live in harmony with nature.
> (1987:60)

This 'nature' was a power that was encountered, not a personal God. If indeed there were gods within nature, they would be busy mainly with their own affairs.

147

The Jewish tradition, by contrast, placed the creator God in the dominant role as one who sees and answers human beings. When God answers the complaints of Job, the passage begins,

> Who is this obscuring my design
> with his empty-headed words? (Job 38.2)

Then comes the challenge,

> Where were you when I laid the earth's foundations?
> Tell me, since you are so well-informed!
> Who decided the dimensions of it, do you know?
> Or who stretched the measuring line across it?
> What supports its pillars at their bases?
> Who laid its cornerstone
> when all the stars of the morning were singing with joy
> and the Sons of God in chorus were chanting praise?
> (Job 38.4-7)

Yahweh claims responsibility for the snow and the rain, for feeding the lioness's cubs and for keeping stars in their place. Job's only remaining response is submission

> I retract all I have said,
> and in dust and ashes I repent. (Job 42.6)

For the Old Testament 'nature' could not be an independent force over against the human being. The crucial distinction was between the whole creation, of which the human formed a part, and the uncreated God. The human might be the high point of the creation, but the human was still created and as nothing in the sight of God.

In the first thousand years of Christianity this Jewish teaching was considerably modified by the use in Jewish and Christian philosophy of Neo-Platonism, which propounded a theory of the ultimate unreality of the material world as a limited embodiment of Divine form. In the human being the spark of the Divine sought to free itself from the prison of the material and to return to its origin in God.

Only in the late middle ages did this theology begin to break down. In the movement from the authority of Plato to the authority of Aristotle, of which St Thomas Aquinas stands at the centre, there was a movement from the assumption of Divine forms behind reality to the assumption that objects were simply what they were and not the bearers of universal form. The doctrine of nominalism reduced the notion of universals to single acts of the human mind. For Aquinas the form of any object or living being was not exhausted by any particular existence, so that each particular always had reference to the form which shaped it, and so to the mind of God. For William of Ockham, in the next generation, there was nothing but the existence of each particular object or being, which could be known by experimental proofs, but not in any other way. There was no inwardness to be looked for in the world. As Etienne Gilson comments, 'Since creatures are pure singulars, there can be between them no intrinsically necessary relations of causality' (1955:497).

In Ockham's theory, God could be shown to exist as the cause of the conservation of the world, but within philosophical theology the word 'God' had no other content. Ockham's work led directly into the modern world in which the experimental way of western science would claim primacy in the understanding of the world. This philosophical revolution of the fourteenth and fifteenth centuries prepared the ground for what happened in the seventeenth century, when the scientific way of defining knowledge came to be seen as the primary or even the only form of knowledge. By the time of Gerrard Winstanley it had already become a general assumption that the creation could be understood as basically a mechanism. It appears to have been the French philosopher René Descartes who first used the term 'laws of nature' in the sense of 'observed regularities', and his view of the human body as a very complex machine already had a practical grounding in William Harvey's description of the process of the circulation of the blood, published in 1628. From here on the pace of change increased rapidly.

As part of the increasing success of the practical investigation and practical innovation of the seventeenth century, and the

149

success of the combination of abstract thought and experiment in penetrating the mysteries of physical science, there was now a shift in the focus of thought from universal explanations centered on the nature of 'being', and so on the nature of God, to explanations centered on the nature of human thought and its capacity to explain. The Reformation was the last moment in European history when the work of theologians had a major impact on the structures of society. Its most crucial effect was to open the way to a new plurality of thinking, and so to a certain scepticism about what thinking itself could do.

(ii) Knowledge of the Self

It was an interest in the sciences of optics and of anatomy, and in geometry, which stimulated René Descartes to write an introduction to his work in these areas setting out his method of inquiry, the *Discourse on Method*, published in 1637. Although he recognized the need for practical experiments, Descartes was not primarily interested in the investigation of the universe through scientific work. Rather, given that experimental knowledge existed, he wished to establish what kind of knowledge this might be.

For the distinction between 'true' and 'false' was not altogether obvious. Sensory information about the real world could be imitated in dreams. Common sense assumptions about the way the world worked could be invalidated by scientific arguments. Even a fact known by everybody, that the sun moved round the earth, had turned out to be false, though Galileo was condemned by the Roman Catholic church for saying so in 1633.

Consequently, both in the *Discourse* and in the later *Meditations on the First Philosophy*, published in 1641, Descartes very cautiously made a case for a certain scepticism as the preliminary to philosophical statements. He proposed that investigation should proceed by a method of systematic doubt, accepting only what was evidently true, proceeding from that by way of successive deductions to a complete knowledge of the universe. In the *Meditations* he wrote that in order to destroy his former opinions it was not necessary for him to show that every individual thought was false, only that there could be doubt about whole classes of thought: 'the slightest ground for doubt that I find in any, will suffice for me to reject all of them' ('First Meditation', 1968:95). In this way he could show that all the experimental sciences admitted of doubt about their findings, but that the propositions of mathematics seemed always to be true. 'For whether I am awake or sleeping, two and three added together always make five, and a square never has more than four sides; and it does not seem possible that truths so apparent can be suspected of any falsity or uncertainty' (1968:98).

But then the possibility had to be considered that even these truths might be an illusion, created not by God but by 'some evil demon'. The simple possibility of this hypothesis deprived Descartes of absolute certainty about all sensory inputs and mental axioms, including the sense of his own body.

What was left out of this radical doubt? Descartes needed one fixed point of absolutely certain knowledge, on which all other knowledge could be based. In the 'Second Meditation' he looked at the possibility of his own non-existence. 'But I had persuaded myself that there was nothing at all in the world; no sky, no earth, no minds or bodies; was I not, therefore, also persuaded that I did not exist? No indeed; I existed without doubt, by the fact that I was persuaded, or indeed by the mere fact that I thought at all' (1968:103). In the words he had used earlier in the *Discourse on Method*, the one indubitable fact was that *'I think, therefore I am'* (1968:53).

But how could he get back from this basic discovery to the rest of the world? The word 'think' for Descartes covered not merely reasoning but everything that today would be described as 'consciousness'. In the 'Third Meditation' he wrote 'I am a thing which thinks, that is to say, which doubts, affirms, denies, knows a few things, is ignorant of many, which loves, hates, wills, does not will, which also imagines, and which perceives' (1968:113). The certain existence of this centre of consciousness could lead back into a knowledge of the objective world only through some link, some objective existence in the world that could be established as being as certain as Descartes's own thought.

He noted first that any perception of the world required not only a sensory input but also an act of judgment. It required an exercise of reason to know that the solid wax from which the honey had just been extracted was the same wax when melted, even though it was different in every outward appearance. It required an act of judgment to know that the figures passing on the street were men and not simply 'hats and cloaks which can cover ghosts or dummies who move only by means of springs' (1968:110).

In general such acts of perception were reliable. In the 'Third Meditation' Descartes asserted, 'And consequently it seems to me that I can already establish as a general rule that all the things we conceive very clearly and distinctly are true' (1968:113). There were two possible senses to this claim. Primarily it was a claim that mental operations were really taking place — to think of a goat or a chimera was truly to think of a goat or a chimera; to feel love or hate was truly to feel love or hate.

But in the area of judgment there was a further consideration, that some input seemed to come from the outside. Descartes found in himself two reasons for accepting such inputs as true. The first was simply 'nature', the existence of an inborn inclination to rely on the objective reality so reported. The other was the experience that such inputs could come unbidden by the conscious mind, as with the sudden feeling of heat or cold on coming unawares on fire or ice. But though these inputs were generally reliable, there was no guarantee that the judgments the human being made were always exact representations of objective reality; nor was there any guarantee that such a representation was never created wholly within the perceiver's own mind.

So far as nature was concerned, Descartes meant 'nothing other than God himself, or the order and disposition that God had established in created things' ('Sixth Meditation'; 1968:159). His ability to move from the 'I think' to certainty about the world clearly rested on the theological proposition that God 'cannot be a deceiver' ('Third Meditation'; 1968:131). But in order to bring this point about the nature of God into the philosophical argument it was necessary to demonstrate the existence of God.

One route to this end was by a consideration of degrees of reality in experience. Descartes argued that an impression received from outside the self could never have more reality than the object which caused it. Any perception of an object which conveyed a greater content of reality than the thinker's own reality must necessarily exist outside the thinker. One perception always had this quality, the perception of God. 'By the name of God I understand an infinite substance, eternal, immutable, independent, omniscient, omnipotent, and by which I and all the other things which exist (if it be true that any such exist) have been created and produced' (1968:123-124). Because this idea of God was a clear and distinct idea, it was not produced merely by negation — 'God is not-Descartes'; nor was it produced by extension from the present reality of the thinker, as a 'better-Descartes', since such a notion of improvement could not realistically stretch a human being to infinity.

The problem about this argument was that it still began from a thinking in Descartes's own mind. Only by adding to this experience some further principle about degrees of 'realness' could the argument begin to work, and even then it would come up against Descartes's initial principle of systematic doubt. For either Descartes had already successfully doubted the realness of God, or there was another and equally compelling starting point alongside the 'I think'.

The other route was the argument in the 'Fifth Meditation' that one of the qualities implied by the concept 'God' was that of perfection and that perfection was not perfect unless it included actual existence. Real existence must always be more perfect than possible existence. There is a complex philosophical debate around this argument for the necessary existence of God; but the simple practical fact is that Descartes did not, from his time to ours, compel assent from philosophers to the proposition that the existence of God is a logical necessity. Again the problem was the nature of the bridge from a thought in a human mind to any kind of reality 'out there'. As Bernard Williams comments, 'Descartes at least offered his argument to readers who shared with him a world of which the existence of God was a formative and virtually unquestioned feature; moreover he thought that the premises of the argument were exceedingly straightforward. Modern advocates have neither excuse' (1978:162).

Once the climate of acceptance of God broke down, there proved to be no sure way back from the 'I think' to an objective reality that had been demonstrated to exist by an absolute proof. The eighteenth century saw a gradual shift from the question of absolute knowledge to the question of sufficient knowledge for particular purposes. By the end of the century the shift had been accomplished, although the idea of God had not been formally abandoned.

Throughout this time the appeal to reason continued to be made within the assumption of an orderly universe, but it became increasingly difficult to see what sort of a connection might be made between the reality of such a universe and the working of human reason. The Scottish philosopher David Hume published in 1748 *An Enquiry Concerning Human Understanding*, in which he presented himself as a reasonable and friendly fellow who merely wanted to know what grounds there were for accepting the products of his thought as being in some sense secure knowledge. He rejected the method of radical doubt used by Descartes on the grounds that no single, wholly-convincing original principle existed, and that even if it did exist there would be no way forward from it except by the same methods of reasoning that had just been shown to be inferior to it. 'The Cartesian doubt, therefore, were it ever possible to be attained by an human creature (as it plainly is not) would be entirely incurable; and no reasoning could ever bring us to a state of assurance and conviction upon any subject' (Section XII, Part I; 1975:150).

Recognizing with gentle irony that most moral philosophy was properly concerned with moving people to action by the simplest means possible, Hume nevertheless put forward a case for the usefulness of abstract thought as a means of clarifying ideas and bringing greater accuracy into practical operations. At the beginning of the *Enquiry* he depicted human nature as being concerned now with science, now with society, now with business and now with relaxation. 'It seems, then, that nature has pointed out a mixed kind of life as most suitable to the human race . . .' (Section I; 1975:8). A reference to 'the cold reception' proper to 'pretended discoveries' in abstruse thought hints at his disappointment at the lack of interest shown in his own earlier work, *A Treatise of Human Nature*, published in 1739-1740.

Turning to the serious business of abstract thought, Hume considered it possible for philosophy to make progress; professed an open mind about how far general principles of reason could be established; disavowed the possibility of solving easily the problems which had puzzled philosophers through the ages; and proceeded to undermine the greater part of existing metaphysics and science.

For Hume had a very simple key with which to open the rusty lock of metaphysics and let air and daylight in. This key was the claim that all ideas were dependent upon either immediate sensation or the memory of sensation. Memory and imagination could copy or mimic the perceptions of the sense, but always in a weaker form. 'All the colours of poetry, however splendid, can never paint natural objects in such a manner as to make the description be taken for a real landskip' (*Enquiry*, Section II; 1976:17). Thoughts, however complicated, could always be analysed into such simple ideas as were 'copied from a precedent feeling or sentiment' (1976:19). So ideas about the nature of God were necessarily built up from our own human experience of wisdom and goodness.

Just what Hume meant by 'impressions' or 'sensations' is a little complicated to decide, since he included in the term both direct sense-impressions of objects such as the heat of a fire, and also the inner 'passions' such as envy and friendship. One problem of his theory is the lack of detailed analysis of perception and of the relationship between perception and feeling. To go further in this direction the discussion would have to pass over into the psychology of perception and leave aside the philosophical argument about the nature of knowledge. Alternatively the philosophical theory would have to inquire further into the

155

relationship between external object, sense-impression and the organization of consciousness. Hume did not go deeply into the question of the nature of the self: some of his expressions suggest that the self exists apart from the sensations, other passages would allow of the view that the self comprises nothing but the present experience of sensations. Either way, it is clear that the practical point was that morality and religion could not be shown to be anything other than what was built up on the basis of sensations.

What was constant in the human being was the operation of natural instincts. An instinct was a response to a sensation or the memory of a sensation. There was only a small number of these instincts and they were sufficiently uniform in the human race to make possible a science of human behaviour. Norman Kemp Smith suggests that in this Hume was influenced by the argument of Isaac Newton in his discussion of mechanics that principles such as mass, gravity and cohesion in bodies are ultimate properties as far as we are concerned, 'learned directly from sense experience' (*The Philosophy of David Hume*, 1941:55). For Hume the existence of such principles in human nature was equally universal and equally open to the test of experience. Any apparent variation of human behaviour from these principles could always be traced to local causes.

This system included the principles by which people made moral decisions. Moral judgments occurred immediately like sensations; they were immediate reactions of praise or blame. 'The mind of man is so formed by nature that, upon the appearance of certain characters, dispositions, and actions, it immediately feels the sentiment of approbation or blame; nor are there any emotions more essential to its frame and constitution' (*Enquiry Concerning Human Understanding*, Section VIII, Part II; 1975:102). These moral sensations always had a location in social needs, such as the need for peace and security.

Some addition to this theory was required to account for our reactions to the experiences of others. Hume settled for a principle of sympathy as part of the basic human equipment. In the *Treatise* he had suggested that this worked by some form of psychological association, but by the time of the *Enquiry Concerning the Principles of Morals*, which was published in 1777, after his death, he rejected this attempt at explanation. 'It is needless to push our researches so far as to ask why we have humanity or a fellow-feeling with others. It is sufficient, that this is experienced to be a principle in human nature' (Section V, Part II,178; 1975:219, note 1). Investigations into cause and effect had to stop somewhere, and Hume doubted if this principle would ever be analysed into more simple elements.

It was clear that in this framework there could be no theory of general moral obligation. For Hume the obligation arose from the response of the passion to the input from the other person, whether immediately present or reported from a distance. Reason by itself could not move a person to action; only feeling could do that. The work of reason was to assist the work of these fundamental principles of human nature, not to direct them. The *Treatise* put this provocatively. 'Reason is, and ought only to be the slave of the passions, and can never pretend to any other office than to serve and obey them' (Book II, Section III; 1978:415). This, of course, was based on Hume's practical observation of what moved people, not on any theory about what ought to move them. With this he was content.

Such an empirical approach also posed a problem for the theory of natural science. The highly successful progress of science and technology in the seventeenth and eighteenth centuries depended fundamentally upon the observation of laws of cause and effect. Hume argued that no amount of observation of events which were called 'effects' following upon events which were called 'causes' could prove that the effect necessarily followed from the cause. The status of the proof given by the one hundredth observation was the same as that given by the first observation — namely that this had happened in the past. Past events contained no absolute guarantee about what would happen in the future.

The experience of one hundred observations merely built up a habit of mind which expected the effect always to follow the cause — for example that a kettle of water would boil when put upon the fire. The impression of laws of cause and effect arose from custom alone. Consequently those forecasts about the outcome of the next experience of the 'causal' event which were the basis of science could not be guaranteed by pure reason. 'The mind can never possibly find the effect in the supposed cause, by the most accurate scrutiny and examination. For the effect is totally different from the cause, and consequently can never be discovered in it' (*An Enquiry Concerning Human Understanding*, Section IV, Part I; 1975:29). So what could be known by a baby, or by an ignorant peasant, that fire burns, or that water in a kettle boils on a fire, could not be shown by philosophy to be necessarily so. The mind responded always to a present object, such as a fire, and did so more efficiently than could be done by deductive reasoning.

It is clear that Hume was not greatly interested in practical scientific experiment and did not expect great increases of human knowledge from it in the future. In particular, as J. R. Lucas points out, he underestimated the importance of the active process of trial and error in producing scientific certainty. 'Hume's account of human nature is that of a very passive participant, not that of an active agent who learns a lot in the course of doing things. But it is chiefly by doing things that we discover causal connexions in the world around us, and in particular obtain a sense of what is possible and what is not' (1984:35). Moreover, Hume did not appreciate the epistemological power of interconnected explanations or theories. He failed to see that science is not a matter of isolated observations but the building up of a pattern of theories and experiments that increasingly move towards giving a coherent explanation of the whole of physical experience. The argument was, however, sufficient to establish once and for all that no practical reasoning about the world can give absolute certainty about any claim of science, much less any claim of morality or of religion. In this sense Hume set out once and for all the relativity of the modern mind, which works without the assumption of a God-ordered world. But in pressing this point home against the philosophers of his own day, he understressed some of the work that the reasoning mind has to do. As

Norman Kemp Smith remarks, Hume failed to investigate adequately the problems of the way we structure experience, or in Hume's terms 'sensation', so as to arrive at an idea or belief about the world. Since there is for him a real distinction between the occurrence of a causal event in the world, the experience of sensation in the human being and an idea or belief about this experience, it is clear that the belief depends to some extent on a judgment of reason. 'And the way is thus opened for the distinctively Kantian thesis that even the *minimum* consciousness . . . is inherently complex, its possibility being conditioned by the manifold factors, sensible, intuitional and categorical, which are required to constitute it' (Smith, 1941:553). In other words, sensation is not enough to account for thought: where there is not a postulate of God, there must be other postulates to do an equivalent work.

(iii) **The Autonomy of Reason**
This radical scepticism was not the last word of the eighteenth century. In the latter half of the century Immanuel Kant laid down the modern theory of reason as the basis of human knowledge. Kant wanted to know what must be the principles already present in human reason for human beings to have any knowledge about the world. Like Hume, he began with the fact that human beings deal with their own sense-impressions received from objects, not the objects themselves. In the *Critique of Pure Reason*, first published in 1781, he wrote, 'What may be the nature of objects considered as things in themselves and without reference to the receptivity of our sensibility is quite unknown to us' (Part I, Section II, 9; 1934:54). But unlike Hume, Kant insisted that human reason had an ability to deal with the contents of experience, and that this existed in itself and was not given as part of the sense-impressions. Human reason organized experience and transcended it. 'For reason is the faculty which furnishes us with the principles of knowledge *a priori* . Hence, pure reason is the faculty which contains the principles of cognizing anything absolutely *a priori* (Introduction VII; 1934:37-38).

The fundamental revolution which Kant effected by this distinction was to give reason itself the primacy in determining what the world is. Only reason reflecting upon experience could make legitimate judgments about the world. If reason did not supply the basic rules of understanding, there would be no possibility of conceiving 'nature' or of asking questions about what would then be haphazard occurrences of singular events. Kant was not arguing that reason created the objective world, nor that it stood entirely apart from it. As he had written to Marcus Hertz on 21 February 1777, 'The pure concepts of the understanding must not be abstracted from sense perceptions, nor must they express the reception of representations through the senses; but though they must have their origin in the nature of the soul, they are neither caused by the object nor bring the object itself into being' (Cassirer, 1981:128).

This 'transcendental philosophy' required only that human beings recognize within themselves that they have a capacity for processes of judgment. This capacity contained certain necessary rules of understanding. The highest state of human nature was the knowledge of the universal laws of human reason.

This highest capacity of human nature was as near as human knowledge could get to anything that could be called 'God'. Kant, in reaction against the German Pietist environment of his childhood, had a contempt for anything remotely mystical or emotive as a basis for judgment, or for any suggestion that feeling or enthusiasm could give real knowledge of a Godhead. The only transcendence open to human knowledge was the transcendence of reason over sense-experiences, and that was strictly limited to the kind of organizing ability shown in mathematics and in the basic principles of the natural sciences. Behind Newton's account of the physical universe could be found not God but the given capacities of the human mind.

Consequently the 'soul' was not an objective entity. The self was simply an act of 'transcendental apperception'. To say the word 'I' was to state the unity of perception and reasoning in the 'I think', but this was a pure condition of knowing. To regard this mental unity as a substance or soul added nothing to human knowledge.

For Kant the physical world, the world of science, was brutally determinate. The physical universe followed rigid laws of cause and effect and reason allowed no exemption from this causality for human beings. Yet Kant needed one exception from these laws. In the area of morality, he asserted the possibility of free decisions. Kant had no basis for this assertion except the requirement of his own argument, that 'freedom' was a basic intuition of the mind. Morality was a matter of practical reason, of action in the world, but decisions could not be based on feelings alone, in the manner of Hume, because in comparison with the certainties of cause and effect in the natural world feelings were simply illusory; nor could it be directed to the pursuit of one's own interests, since this could not lead to happiness — Kant stated this as an empirical fact — nor could the pursuit of any other interest.

What could be demanded universally, and sometimes attained, was a right disposition of the will. In the *Groundwork of the Metaphysic of Morals*, published in 1785, he defined the ethical aim for human beings as the production of a will that willed the good. The good meant not a complex of values but the single value of accepting a universal duty. 'A good will is not good because of what it effects or accomplishes — because of its fitness for attaining some proposed end: it is good through its willing alone — that is, good in itself' (Chapter 1; 1953:62). This pure willing, without reference to the content, was the point at which reason exercised moral autonomy. In spite of living in a determinate universe, the human will could always do one thing freely, to will to be itself. It was this autonomy which constituted the moral good, not the effecting of a particular purpose.

The pure moral act was the act which was done out of reverence for the law of reason. As soon as the human being wanted to do something for some other purpose — to preserve her or his own life or to help a neighbour — she or he had moved out of the realm of the universal and the moral act became determined by particular needs and desires. Once given the recognition of the possibility of the state of the good will, however, two

161

things followed.

The first was that any action which proceeded from the good will must be such that the agent could, with equal reason, require all other rational agents to follow the same course in the same circumstances, 'that is to say, I ought never to act except in such a way *that I can also will that my maxim should become a universal law*' (1953:70). This 'categorical imperative' was not itself a moral rule, but a test for any particular moral rule that might be proposed, such as 'Love your enemies' or 'always tell the truth'. A rational agent could only act in such a way that the action could be made a rule for all rational agents.

The second step was to notice that all human beings consider themselves to be 'persons', that is to say rational moral agents. The existence of the capacity for moral freedom differentiated human beings from the rest of life and created an objective basis for an ethic. Consequently each human being, as a potential source of the good will, was to be treated only as a moral end. A human being could not be used for another's purposes; the only rational moral use for a human being was to fulfil her or his own purpose. 'The ground of this principle is: *Rational nature exists as an end in itself*' (Chapter II; 1953:96). Rational moral action by one human being required recognition of the existence of a universal community of rational beings, each acting in freedom as a law-maker both for her or his self and for the whole community. 'A rational being belongs to the kingdom of ends as a *member*, when, although he makes its universal laws, he is also himself subject to these laws. He belongs to it as its *head*, when as the maker of laws he is himself subject to the will of no other' (1953:101).

There is a strong echo here of Luther's dictum that 'A Christian is a perfectly free lord of all, subject to none. A Christian is a perfectly dutiful servant of all, subject to all'. The difference, of course, is that Luther's saying was given content by the teaching, life, death and resurrection of Jesus, while Kant's principle was deliberately devoid of content. Kant did not give any grounds for obeying the law of reason except its existence as a universal fact. The primacy of the law of rational understanding in the area of pure reason was the fundamental assumption of the critical philosophy, and in practical reason, or moral philosophy, the reverence for reason followed from the assumption of the possibility of freedom. If moral freedom were not possible at all, then what was called moral action would be subject to the same causality as the physical universe, though mediated through emotion and desire, and screened by the human capacity for self-delusion. But to accept the existence of human reason was to accept the existence of human freedom and the possibility of making responsible choices.

The categorical imperative provided, not a body of moral principles derived from it by pure deduction, but a critical question that could always be asked about any particular moral case: Is this proposed action something that can be universalized within the notion of humanity as a kingdom of ends? All human beings as members of the intelligible world, the world of reason, could recognize the value of moral action when they saw it in others. Only the fact that human beings inhabited the sensible world, the world of desires and impulses, prevented them from invariably making their actions accord with the autonomy of the will. The path from desire to autonomy lay in transferring oneself to the intelligible world and seeing that the sensible world was only the appearance of which the intelligible world was the reality. That pure reason could in this way overcome necessity Kant regarded as a fact inexplicable by reason itself. Here the mind defined one of its own boundaries.

It is impossible not to admire Kant's honesty and purity of thought. The critical philosophy pursued reason to its limits and recognized its bounds. Beyond these boundaries Kant admitted the possibility of a harmony of understanding which might be described as infinite, but the possibility of this harmony constituted a task for the future work of reason rather than a present fact. Nothing could be added to the intuition of such harmony by giving it the name 'God' or considering it to constitute an entity of some sort. Even the work of natural science was no more than a report from the current operations of reason, about a universe which was in a continuous state of becoming. The

163

religious conservatives who today attack Darwin and the theory of evolution for excluding God from human experience mistake their target. Half a century before Darwin, Kant had effectively displaced God from all forms of rational explanation.

(iv) The Individual in the Market Place

While the sixteenth and seventeenth centuries were a time of great advance in philosophy and in the basic theory of science, industrially they were a period of consolidation. 'Around 1700 industrial technology, in spite of some significant innovations, was still very much what it had been in the late mediaeval period, with its limited array of power-driven machines — fulling mills and paper mills, mechanical bellows and tilt hammers — and its dependence on manual effort at the loom and the anvil, in the glassmaker's workshops and the shipyard' (Sella, 1970:354-355). Most work still centered on the household, with women playing an equal part with men in manual labour, and what manufacturing there was outside the home was still in small units.

One vital innovation had already taken place in economic organization in the late sixteenth century. The system of subscribing capital *ad hoc* for each venture by merchants was replaced by a system of permanent subscriptions of working capital for enterprises. In this way an individual subscriber could withdraw capital by selling 'shares' in the enterprise on the public exchange without business being interrupted. This invention of a reliable permanent capital base in combination with flexibility for the individual subscriber laid the financial ground for modern industrial capitalism.

Two further changes in the seventeenth and eighteenth centuries laid the foundations of modern industry.

The first was the revolution in agriculture. The enclosures of common land in the seventeenth century had been for the extension of sheep farming, less labour-intensive than individual peasant production and highly profitable in domestic and in export markets. In the eighteenth century the enclosures also enabled landowners to take advantage of a series of technical innovations in arable farming. New varieties of crops and new systems of crop rotation meant that the new large fields could be used profitably to produce food surpluses which could feed larger numbers of people living away from the land. For the first time in human history the food supply was not a check on the growth of population.

The new method of organizing industry was to require precisely this ability to build up a concentrated population away from the land. A surplus population would have been of no value without a means to employ it more effectively than in the old manorial and domestic workshops. The second change put the people to work by the method of the division of labour.

At the beginning of Adam Smith's *An Inquiry into the Nature and Causes of the Wealth of Nations*, published in 1776, there is a dramatic account of the difference that could be made in the business of manufacturing pins by dividing the process into separate operations, each the responsibility of a different employee. In the old style of work, in which one person did everything, 'a workman . . . could scarce, perhaps, with his utmost industry, make one pin in a day, and certainly could not make twenty'. But in a small factory organized on the principles of the division of labour, even ten men, performing two or three operations each, could hugely exceed this output. Smith recorded of such a factory that he had visited, 'These ten persons, therefore, could make among them upwards of forty-eight thousand pins in a day' (1950:5).

Smith commented that the division of labour had three advantages: by concentrating on only one or two operations each worker increased his or her dexterity in that part of the work; no time was lost in passing from one kind of operation to another; and the simplifying of the manufacturing process by sub-dividing the operations made it easier to invent and apply machines 'which facilitate and abridge labour, and enable one man to do the work of many' (1950:7). In the long run it was to be this last which was the most important. Man was now to be bound to the machine.

At a personal level the results were dire. Agricultural life for the poor had been no golden age and industrialization did in the very long run bring about increased economic prosperity for the majority in industrial populations. But industrialism also brought in a new kind of labour discipline.

> By the 1840s the term 'factory system' had ceased to be an objective description of a certain type of economic and social organization and had become a slogan or a convenient label for a complex of social attitudes and assumptions. This is not hard to appreciate, for the changes demanded by the new order were terrifyingly fundamental and aroused men's deepest responses. The factory integrated men and machines in a way that had never before been attempted. 'Whilst the engine runs, the people must work — men, women and children are yoked together with iron and steam. The animal machine . . . is chained fast to the iron machine, which knows no suffering and no weariness', wrote James Kay Shuttleworth in 1832 (Harrison, 1984:221)

The industrial revolution involved a change not only in working conditions but also in the ethic of work. In a subsistence economy the equation between work and life was simple. The sixteenth century still held the view expressed by William Langland in Book IV of *Piers Plowman* through the figure of 'Hunger', that the main problem was to deal with shirkers and sturdy beggars, whose ailments were only a pretence. 'It is common sense that every man must work, either by ditching and digging, or by travailing in prayer — the active or the contemplative life — for such is God's will' (1959:126).

The Reformation had swept away the contemplative life in the countries where it ruled. In centres of growing prosperity it put all its weight on obedience in secular callings, which were ordained by God. John Calvin, working in a flourishing urban centre, was the first Christian teacher to accept economic progress whole-heartedly as given by God — though he warned also that economic failure was equally to be accepted as coming from God. Later generations of Calvinism tended more directly to equate economic progress with God's own blessing on an individual. The result of this change was revolutionary. Having removed both the sacramental system of discipline of the Catholic Church and the outlet for the expression of religious hopes through participation in or support of the contemplative life, the Reformation left the believer with the two concerns of individual salvation and worldly success.

The two concerns came together in the practice of hard work by a conscientious people. Since the profit that was reaped could not in such a society be spent on conspicuous consumption, it was available for reinvestment in business. What Max Weber called the 'elective affinity' between Calvinism and capitalism cannot be proved to be causal in either direction. But there is no doubt that the Puritan spirit was helpful to the initial process of capital accumulation that gave the financial base for investment in the new machinery demanded by the division of labour. There were to be no more monasteries or cathedrals. Instead the Protestant people worked hard to build the cathedrals of capitalism.

Why was the surplus nevertheless not spent on works of piety towards the poor? The answer may be that, at least in the early days of industrialism, what were regarded as the genuine poor were reasonably well cared for. The system of parish poor relief set up by the Reformers everywhere to replace monastic charity worked well enough so long as parishes had populations they could cope with. The Reformers did not regard assistance to the poor as being meritorious in itself, since in their view no human action was meritorious. Nor was the situation of being poor regarded as carrying any special merit in itself. To help the genuine poor was simply a duty, adequately carried out by parish officials. There was no call for anything more.

In its social aspects the religion of the Reformation was on the whole an employers' religion. It is true that the radical party of the English Puritans during the Commonwealth period advocated a free and equal collectivity, based on the family as a labour unit. Gerrard Winstanley wrote that 'Every freeman shall have a freedom in the earth, to plant or build, to fetch from the store-houses any thing he wants, and shall enjoy the fruits of his

167

labours without restraint from any . . .' (*The Law of Freedom in a Platform*, or *The Magistracy Restored*, 1652, Chapter 6; 1973:385-386). But capitalism was not to be built on the free agricultural labour of the family: in this Winstanley was hopelessly conservative. The new industrial methods would require to be run 'by the book' under the economic whip of wages paid or withheld.

What Protestant ethics failed to pick up at this stage in the development of industrialism was the fact that work itself was becoming oppression.

In fact the mechanical universe of natural science was matched by a mechanical view of political economy in which any interference to improve conditions could only make things worse. In *The Wealth of Nations* Adam Smith had argued that by each person applying his or her capital and labour to the best personal advantage the maximum output would be achieved for society as a whole, even though that was not the individual's intention. 'He generally, indeed, neither intends to promote the public interest, nor knows how much he is promoting it'. By simply pursuing profit, the individual is 'led by an invisible hand to promote an end which was no part of his intention' (Vol. I, Book IV, Chapter II; 1950:400). Smith was here arguing simply against restraining the import of goods from abroad, but he was also expressing a general confidence in the ability of a market economy to produce the best attainable economic result, so long as it was left at liberty to do so.

In practice neither governments nor merchants nor manufacturers were likely to leave markets at liberty for very long. Civil government was necessary to check vice, but had not much chance with the commercial vice which was the distortion of markets, because government always tended to fall into the hands of particular interests, be they landowners or merchants or manufacturers. Smith's economic theory was by no means a picture of inevitable progress.

Furthermore he recognized that the processes of industrialization through the division of labour would tend to produce a less healthy and vigorous populace whose work, being so specialized, offered less opportunity for initiative, and so made them less suitable, for example, for military service. Even though freedom of trade and the division of labour could bring a general economic improvement in the sense of making the best use of land and capital to have more goods available more cheaply, it would not increase the happiness of everyone. There is in *The Wealth of Nations* the beginning of that economic treatment of human labour which sees it as units of production, important to the industrial process only as 'labour costs'. Though Smith himself was a deeply humane man, he was too committed to economic processes as something natural and given to look for more fundamental change.

This tendency was strengthened by the argument which soon developed about the size of the British population and the importance of the relationship of population to food supply. The view which came to prevail was that set out by Thomas Robert Malthus in successive editions of *An Essay on the Principle of Population*, first published in 1798. Malthus argued that the power of human population to increase was so great that it would always tend to outrun the available food supply. Any measures to alleviate the suffering of the poor in the long run would be self-defeating unless they also included means to check the tendency to reproduce.

Unfortunately for the poor, this led Malthus and others to argue that the making of cash payments by way of Poor Relief was detrimental to the well-being of the economic community as a whole. Where the food supply could not be increased, as in a year of bad harvest, the 'Relief' simply forced up prices, without giving the starving more food; where food supply could respond to higher prices in the long run with increased production, the poor would also increase their production of children and so reduce themselves to misery again.

Malthus's biographer Patricia James points out that in this stage of his argument he was not fully aware of the complexities of a modern monetary economy, which could cause suffering to the poor for other reasons than crop failure or the loss of ships at sea. But she also points out that Malthus was talking about a real problem of public policy.

In 1803 nearly one-seventh of the population of England and
Wales was receiving some parish relief (there were 15,000
parishes), at a total annual cost of £4½ million, raised from
local rates on the value of land. This was a large sum of
money for a country at war, when the gross national revenue
from taxation and the Post Office was only about £41.2 million. (James, 1979:135-136)

The cry of the poor was not going unheard, but there were
formidable intellectual defences being put up against doing very
much for them.

In the rising tide of industrialism in the nineteenth century
the necessary questions were asked not by Christian leaders but
by Karl Marx and Friedrich Engels. The intellectual success of
Marxism can be directly related to the failure of Christians to
pick up and use two very simple ideas which came together with
tremendous force as industrialization gathered speed in Europe
and North America.

The first idea had a long pedigree. It was the classical judgment that value was created by human labour. What made goods
and services worth having was that human beings worked on
them. As a cry of the poor, this had been heard through the
centuries.

> When Adam delved and Eve span,
> Who was then the gentleman?

John Ball's text for the sermon which signalled the start of the
Peasants' Revolt in England in 1381 echoed not only the social
conditions of his own time, but also the memory in Israel of the
comparative equality of the time in the wilderness, the primitive
communism set up as a model for the church in the Acts of the
Apostles and the early monastic emphasis on physical labour as
well as prayer. It continued after Ball in the German Peasants'
Revolt of the sixteenth century, and in the claims of the English
Levellers in the seventeenth century. It can be found in a modern form in the statement of the Second Vatican Council that
'Human labour, employed in the production and exchange of

goods and in supplying economic services, is the chief element in economic life — all else is instrumental' ('Pastoral Constitution on the Church in the Modern World', Art. 67, 1966).

The second simple idea was that human societies were not static but were involved in processes of change. Eighteenth century writers, including Montesquieu, Adam Smith and Malthus, believed that they could identify stages of development, without necessarily implying an inevitable progression. What Marx did was to add the suggestion that once human beings took conscious control of this change, the result would be a kind of Utopia. Marxism began with a profoundly moral statement, that the form of production in contemporary capitalism prevented the worker from being a fully human person. It refused him access to the product of his labours, it treated him as a machine, it set him in competition against his fellow workers and it had no concern for his status as a human being. 'The more wealth the worker produces, the more his production increases in power and scope, the poorer he becomes. The more commodities the worker produces, the cheaper a commodity he becomes' ('Alienated Labour', 1844; Kamenka, 1983:133).

Marx did not stop at moral indignation but went on to give what he claimed to be a precise economic analysis of how the worker, who theoretically held the power of creating value, was forced to surrender all that she or he created, above the bare minimum required to sustain life and reproduce the labour force. The trick lay in the control of all political power by those who owned the means of production. Those who collected the surplus were the masters, the owners of 'capital', who had the power to turn on or off the tap of employment at will.

Because the workers had no comparable power of organization the owners could always squeeze wages down to the minimum. The only thing driving the capitalist was profit. Competition from other capitalists would always tend to drive the rate of profit down, so that owners would always be trying to reduce wage costs and looking for new markets, by force if necessary, through war or through colonial expansion.

The labour theory of value and its outcome, the notion of

171

'surplus value' is not a widely accepted economic theory today. Indeed, R. H. Tawney remarks that 'The true descendant of the doctrine of Aquinas is the labour theory of value. The last of the Schoolmen was Karl Marx' (1938:48). But the validity of the economic theory was largely irrelevant to the appeal of Marxism. What it did, and did brilliantly, was to put at the heart of a complex economic theory an eminently graspable fact — that you work and do not get back all that you produce. This was true even when all allowance had been made for payment for the organizational skills of management, for depreciation of machinery and for the replacement of raw materials. The payment of profit to the owner of the means of production was as unjustifiable in labour value terms as the payment of rent for land. It was enough to set the worker thinking hard about the way society was organized.

Even so, it would not have been a revolutionary theory without the addition of the claim that society must inevitably change. Marx took the theory of historical development and gave it a twist to show that while capitalism was the latest development in a historical series, it must in its turn be overcome by something new.

The inevitability of change came from the fact that in the long run the capitalist system could not work. The competition for profit would inevitably drive down wages and erode distinctions of skill and status among workers. The result would be a society increasingly divided between those who profited from the ownership of the means of production and an increasingly brutalized and suffering mass of wage labourers and unemployed workers. This 'proletariat' must eventually have revolutionary tendencies, because nothing else was left for it.

In the *Manifesto of the Communist Party*, published in 1848, the year of attempted revolution all across Europe, Marx and Engels proclaimed that 'The history of all hitherto existing society is the history of class struggles' (Kamenka, 1983:203). But the modern bourgeoisie, by creating a world market, had brought expansion to its limits within the capitalist system. It was itself a revolutionary force. 'The bourgeoisie, during its rule of scarce one hundred years, has created more massive and more colossal productive forces than have all the preceding generations together' (Kamenka, 1983:209). These forces were now beyond the control of the bourgeoisie and must pass to the proletariat. All that remained was for leaders to arise among the proletariat to lead the way to a Communist society.

While the moral appeal of the Communist claim was clear, Marx was concerned to stress that Communism was a scientific theory rather than a moral theory. The present situation of capitalism was not an accidental event, but the result of clear laws of historical development. The key to the various stages was the nature of the organization of production. How the means of production were owned and how labour was organized governed everything else in society. From ancient slavery through feudalism to capitalism, the stages were marked by the gradual development of wage labour. Consequently the final stage of the historical process must be the coming into its own of labour, when labour and ownership would be fused into a single entity, and distinctions based on property would drop away, because all property would be held in common. Eventually, in the stage after socialism, even the state itself would drop away.

What Marx and Engels thus did was to invest the notion of historical development with an eschatological hope. Academic criticism of Marxism can be formidable, but it is in a sense beside the point. As Marx wrote, 'Philosophers have only *interpreted* the world in various ways; the point is to *change* it' ('Theses on Feuerbach', XI; Kamenka, 1983:158). What was given to the labourer in Communist theory was not only a deeper historical knowledge but a new way of thinking about society. For the first time in history it could be seen that human beings had made the world and that human beings could change it.

(v) The Christian Vision

Meanwhile, Christian theology appeared to be largely marking time. In the mid-seventeenth century Thomas Traherne wrote for his friend Mrs Susanna Hopton a treatise on 'felicity', with a description of his own spiritual experience as a child in which innocence made all marvellous to him. 'The corn was orient and immortal wheat, which never should be reaped, nor was ever sown. I thought it had stood from everlasting to everlasting. The dust and stones of the street were as precious as gold: the gates were at first the end of the world. The people also were objects of wonder . . . Boys and girls tumbling in the street, and playing, were moving jewels. I knew not that they were born or should die; But all things abided eternally in their proper places' (*Centuries* III 3;1960:110). And he comments: 'So that with much ado I was corrupted, and made to learn the dirty devices of this world'.

This remembrance of his childhood vision captured definitively the best of the spirit of seventeenth century Anglicanism: the quiet confidence in God and the deep sense of abiding values, rural and conservative, that bound human beings to one another and to nature. Though the childhood vision was inadequate and had to die, the struggle of the rest of life was to attain to a new innocence, the new childhood in the Kingdom of God.

For Traherne a simple affirmation of the unity of all things in the creation was the starting point for the experience of reconciliation. Nature was still the key.

> You never enjoy the world aright, till the Sea itself floweth in your veins, till you are clothed with the heavens, and crowned with the stars: and perceive yourself to be the sole heir of the whole world, and more than so, because men are in it who are every one sole heirs as well as you. Till you can sing and rejoice and delight in God, as misers do in gold, and Kings in sceptres, you never enjoy the world.
> (*Centuries* I 2; 1960:3)

The satisfaction did not arise from a simple enjoyment of nature, but from the discovery that the true human enjoyment was the enjoyment of God, and therefore the enjoyment of the creator in what was created. 'The image of God implanted in us, guided me to the manner wherein we were to enjoy. For since we were made in the similitude of God, we were made to enjoy after His similitude' (*Centuries*, III 59; 1960:142). Once this discovery was made it seemed easy, because the initiative came from God, who loved human creatures and drew them to perfection. Sin began with the failure to see God in all things. At the same time, only the seeing of God in all things could teach the nature of sin. 'Till you see that the world is yours, you cannot weigh the greatness of sin, nor the misery of your fall, nor prize your Redeemer's love' (*Centuries*, II 3; 1960:58).

Only the knowledge of what had been lost by the Fall could make human beings appreciate what had been gained by the restoration in Christ. Human miseries were caused more by human actions to one another than by the kind of world God had given. Even the hiddenness of God was a gift, lest the human being be overwhelmed by the divine power. Neither this view of nature nor this view of humanity depended simply on the arousal of feelings. The perception which Traherne demanded was the theological perception that both nature and humanity were created by God for specific purposes — nature in order to fulfil in each part its own functions, and human beings as the image of God returning the creator's love with praise.

This very strongly affirmative theology raised a problem about the nature of sin. Traherne seems to have regarded sin primarily as a failure of knowledge, since his chief concern was with the perception of God's goodness. Yet he had a theology of redemption which he clearly regarded as being entirely orthodox — indeed he took some pains to justify the action of God the Father in accepting the sacrifice of the Son, saying: 'Nor yet was it forced or imposed upon Him, but He voluntarily undertook it' (*Centuries* II 33; 1960:73). The knowledge of this redemptive activity stirred the human being to love, and love was the power of the Holy Spirit.

Consequently the freedom of humanity, by which it was possible to sin, must have been necessary in order to obtain a greater benefit. This benefit was the joy and dignity of attaining salvation through the co-operation of free will. Indeed the liberty of the human creature could be said to have increased the liberty of God. 'When all that could be wrought by the use of His own liberty were attained, by man's liberty he attained more'

(*Centuries* IV 46; 1960:187-188).

Traherne wrote his meditations as a poet rather than a theologian. But the *Centuries* represent very well the predominant cast of mind of England as it emerged from the Civil War, vigorous, tolerant, optimistic and believing in a fundamentally harmonious universe. In this world God was seen primarily as creator, benevolent but remote. Theology became concerned chiefly with the recognition of the existing moral order. Nearly a hundred years later, in 1726, Joseph Butler, later to become bishop of Bristol and of Durham, preached a series of sermons in the Rolls Chapel in London. The first three of these sermons had the title 'Upon Human Nature', and they set out in a classic form the theological ethics of the English church in this period.

Butler had an enemy in view, which was the theory of human nature put forward in Thomas Hobbes' *Of Human Nature* and *Leviathan* in the seventeenth century, and continued in Bernard de Mandeville's *Fable of the Bees*, in his own time. Hobbes had argued that the ultimate self-gratification was the exercise of power, even compassion being a subtle exercise of power over another human being. Society was an attempt at self-preservation by handing over authority to the strongest in return for some limited protection. Mandeville added that people were moved only by their own self-interest but that it just so happened that the pursuit of private interest also produced the most favourable economic and political results. More people than Butler were stung by *The Fable of the Bees*, but it was chiefly to Hobbes' theory of self-interest that Butler addressed himself.

Since these were sermons, he began with a biblical text, 'For as we have many members in one body, and all members have not the same office; so we, being many, are one body in Christ, and every one members one of another' (Rom. 12.4,5). The second and third sermons began with another text, 'For when the Gentiles, which have not the law, do by nature the things contained in the law, these, having not the law, are a law unto themselves' (Rom. 2.14). From these passages Butler argued that there was in human nature under God a sense of moral obligation that came before the specific revelation in Jesus.

176

He began by considering St Paul's analogy of the body and remarking that it must have had more force in the earliest years when Christians were conscious of themselves as a small, persecuted group guided by charismatic gifts which had quite ceased in the later church. Nevertheless, the analogy of the body still had a certain force, particularly when it was understood that by the body and its members St Paul meant *'the whole nature of man* and *all the variety of internal principles which belong to it'* (1953:32). The internal principles of the soul were as much an indication of the moral nature and purpose of the human being as the external features of the eye were an indication of its function in the body.

The problem was that the internal principles, the passions and reasonings, were more varied and less constant than the external features. Recognizing this, Butler argued that if a survey were made of the generality of human beings, rather than referring to a single individual, a general nature would be discerned which would show both self-love and benevolence. Self-love regulated the feelings concerned with self-preservation, from hunger to the desire for public esteem. It necessarily considered long-run effects as well as short-run satisfactions, for even a very thirsty person would not knowingly drink tainted water. Benevolence was the love of other human beings for their own sake, and sufficient evidence existed in human society of the reality of compassion, family affection, and friendship to establish this principle.

The appeal was to general human experience. Against Hobbes' claim that all such affections were merely forms of the exercise of power, Butler looked to the ordinary use of language. Asking of the arguments of a hypothetical philosopher who asserted that what was called 'benevolence' was 'only the love of power', Butler demanded, 'Would not everybody think that here was a mistake of one word for another?' (1953:33, note 1).

He then set out to show that the principles of self-love and of benevolence were not mutually exclusive but on the contrary tended towards one another, since many private satisfactions could only be obtained in a public context. More importantly he argued that among the many varied, sometimes conflicting and sometimes misdirected human passions there was one regulative principle of reason by which human beings made judgments about their own actions. This principle was 'conscience', which Butler supposed to be a specific faculty of the human mind. Because of this faculty it was impossible to do good and not approve it, or to do wrong in the heat of the moment and not disapprove it on reflection.

The function of conscience was to regulate the desires not according to their strength but according to a hierarchy which would be proportionate to the nature of the agent. In this scheme there was no place for a general principle of self-hatred, or for a principled desire to do harm to others; evil arose only from too-hasty or mistaken judgments, or from unconsidered desires for particular objects.

The only alternative to following this inner law of human nature would be to follow every passion according to its strength, but this would be absurd because it would mean that every person was to be defined by his or her strongest passion, without any moral distinction. Such a conclusion would be contrary to the general moral sense of human beings, for one would be known only as 'a murderer' and another only as 'a mother'.

Butler here had two different claims which were to some extent contradictory. The first was that human beings through the faculty of conscience had a natural sense of morality. In this sense he said that the moralist had no need to enunciate a general rule of morality. All that was necessary was for 'any plain honest man' to ask himself about any planned course of action, whether it was right or wrong, good or evil. 'I do not in the least doubt but that this question would be answered agreeably to truth and virtue, by almost any fair man in almost any circumstances' (1953:63). This was more a tribute to the coherence of educated society in Butler's time than to the moral sense of the human race as a whole.

The second claim emerged only indirectly at the end of the third sermon. Where earlier he had talked as if rational self-love and benevolence could be understood and followed by a simple process of introspection, here he began to speak of the need to acquire a habit of virtue through self-discipline. 'To this is to be added, that when virtue is become habitual, when the temper of it is acquired, what was before confinement ceases to be so, by becoming choice and delight' (1953:67).

This is an echo of Traherne's cleansing away of 'the dirty devices of this world' to arrive at a new and adult version of childhood's innocence. The 'plain honest man' was not any man, but the practitioner of Butler's own version of virtue. Virtue required a kind of submission in advance to conditions which were defined but not yet experienced. Happiness was not what a person first set out to seek under the pressure of desire, but what proved to be happiness as experienced by those who followed the law of conscience. So the inner law of human nature moved imperceptibly but unavoidably into that religious practice of virtue which the Book of Common Prayer defines in the Second Collect for Morning Prayer: 'O God, who art the author of peace and lover of concord, in knowledge of whom standeth our eternal life, whose service is perfect freedom . . .' Indeed, how could any Anglican preacher conclude otherwise?

It was an ethic for a world that was passing away. The interesting thing about Butler is that his work shows no hint of the cataclysm that was about to come upon his people. The prosperous élite of the eighteenth century, educated in the Greek and Latin classics, was attached to the Gospel as an ethic of duty, mediated through the sober Calvinist worship of the Church of England and the Church of Scotland. Through the actions of the law, the landowner and the church, the concepts of duty and hierarchy, honesty and sobriety, respect for superiors and care for the well-being of inferiors, dominated rural life. When properly practised, it was not an ignoble ideal. It embodied the feudal idea of a society of mutual obligation and its death came in parts of rural Britain only at the very end of the nineteenth century.

One voice which recognized intuitively the tensions of the new industrialism was William Blake, himself outside the recognized boundaries of Christian theology. Blake is probably best known as the sweet poet of the *Songs of Innocence*, published in 1789, and the *Songs of Experience*, published in 1794. The poet of 'The Lamb' and 'The Chimney Sweeper' and 'The Little Boy Found' expressed the victory of innocence and the presence of God in human actions;

> For Mercy has a human heart,
> Pity a human face,
> And Love, the human form divine,
> And Peace, the human dress.
> ('The Divine Image' in *Songs of Innocence*, 1974:117)

Yet the same human form contains all that is wrong with the world.

> Cruelty has a Human Heart,
> And Jealousy a Human Face;
> Terror the Human Form divine;
> And Secrecy the Human Dress.
> ('A Divine Image' in *Songs of Experience*, 1974:221)

Blake was writing not only at the beginning of the change to industrial society, but also at a time of political hope and frustration arising from the French Revolution. In *The Marriage of Heaven and Hell*, written in 1793, he celebrated the liberation of energy from the restraints of rationality in such aphorisms as 'The tygers of wrath are wiser than the horses of instruction' (1974:152). Certainly he himself had a revolutionary intention in the years 1790-1793, seeing a new age dawning for Europe and for the New World. Yet even at this time his celebration was as much of the energy of creatures in their own kind as of political change. The poem ends with the words 'For everything that lives is holy' (1974:160).

After 1793 Blake moved away from this political zest. There is room for argument about the nature of Blake's later writings. Jacob Bronowski sees the prophetic writings as a retreat into fantasy by a defeated man. Kathleen Raine, more sympathetic to the background of the western esoteric tradition, judges that 'Blake gradually renounced politics for something more radical: not religion, in the sense of a system of beliefs and observances, but a transformation of the inner life, a rebirth of "the true man"' (1970:56).

In the vast poem *Jerusalem*, written between 1804 and 1820, Blake recognized the vigour and in a sense the irresistibility of the new industrial system. As Los, the demon of the furnaces, affirms

"I must Create a System or be enslav'd by another Man's.
"I will not Reason & Compare: my business is to Create."
(Chapter 1, Plate 10:20,21; 1974:629)

It is a very different world from the quiet certainties of Traherne, but Blake had an eschatological hope that was still a Christian hope.

Jesus replied: "Fear not Albion; unless I die thou canst not live;
"But if I die I shall arise again & thou with me.
"This is Friendship & Brotherhood: without it Man is Not".
(Chapter 4, Plate 96:14,15; 1974:743)

In this Blake was at the end of one tradition and some way from the beginning of another. Jacob Bronowski recognizes the significance of the religious element in the later writings. 'We are no longer used to linking radicalism with religious fervour: in this, Blake was at the end of a Puritan tradition which we have lost. Yet unless we can see as one the revolutionary idealism of Blake's politics and the Gnostic heresy in his religion, we simply do not see Blake' (1972:15).

Certainly Protestantism had a concern for social issues. The impulse to social reform in Britain came first from the Quakers and the Methodists. In the nineteenth century individuals within the churches took an interest in the harsh conditions of industrialism with some success, although it should be noted that adult male workers achieved the reduction of the working day to ten hours only in 1874, a change first introduced by law for children in textile mills in 1833.

These individual initiatives did not, however, amount to a general social analysis. The great failure of Christianity in nineteenth century Europe was that nowhere in the areas of developing industrialism did the churches, Protestant or Catholic, create a reasoned criticism of what was happening to the people. Only in the 1870's, with the rise of the Christian Socialist movement in Britain, the Social Gospel movement in the USA, and in the Catholic Church the publication of the encyclical letter of Leo XIII, *Rerum Novarum* in 1881, did general attention begin to be paid to 'the social question'.

There were several reasons for this absence of mind.

The first was that the industrial populations grew up outside the parochial systems which had served the pre-industrial populations. E. R. Wickham has shown for Sheffield that even in the most energetic periods of church building, all the churches in the town together could not have seated more than one in six of the population, and even so, most of the seats that were available had to be paid for. 'There had always been the poor, but until the early part of the eighteenth century they were recognizably within and part of the community of township and hamlet, but with the rapid growth of population they became an undifferentiated group, lost to view except as a mass' (1957:215). When the poor moved from their rural communities to the slums of the towns they became non-persons and nobody noticed their absence.

Another reason was that at the beginning of the nineteenth century the attention of the churches shifted to mission overseas. European colonial expansion drew attention to the fact that the Gospel had not been effectively preached in vast areas of the world. The success of the missionary movement of the nineteenth century was immense, but it did tend to distract attention from affairs at home.

But the most formidable reason of all was probably the moral one. Out of the combination of Calvinism and capitalism there emerged the 'Protestant work ethic', which said in its crudest form that hard work and honest trading would necessarily lead to worldly success as a sign of the blessing of God. Calvin's stress on duty to God was replaced by Benjamin Franklin's *Advice to a Young Tradesman*, in 1748, 'Remember that TIME is money' (1961:306). In the immortal words of William Lawrence, the Bishop of Massachusetts from 1893 to 1926, 'Put ten thousand immoral men to live and work in one fertile valley and ten thousand moral men to live and work in the next valley, and the question is soon answered as to who wins the material wealth. Godliness is in league with riches' (*The Relation of Wealth to Morals*, Forell, 1966:331). Unfortunately there was just enough truth in this theory to distract the attention of Christians from the fact that the industrial masses of Europe — and increasingly of the United States also — had no such life chances.

(vi) The New Concept of Nature

After the revolution in thought of the eighteenth century committed human affairs to wholly human processes of interpretation, there lingered for a time a sense of 'Nature' as a directing power, but it soon became clear that this amounted to no more than saying that there was a certain observable order in the physical world. The universe had a physical structure which seemed to guarantee that the same conditions would always produce the same results. What was clear about physical science was that the reliability of observation and experiment had produced an enormous power to transform nature. If human affairs were no longer considered to be ruled by God, might there not be other principles which could be discovered and manipulated in the same way to produce a human society closer to some desirable norm?

The rationality which Kant had been exploring in philosophy was also becoming an increasingly important part of the running of practical affairs. The change cannot be better illustrated than by the fact that in Scotland the last trial for witchcraft that came to the High Court in Edinburgh was in 1682 while just over a century later, in 1799, Sir John Sinclair presented to the General Assembly of the Church of Scotland the first complete statistical account of the whole nation, based upon returns from all the

938 parishes of the kirk. In 1801 came the first population census of Britain. The age of social measurement had arrived. Indeed the completion of the movement from the mediaeval to the modern mind lies in that hundred-year journey from the fear of witches to trust in figures. In this transition theology was bound to suffer from new competition.

The greatest change came in natural science. Many of the early geologists and collectors of fossils were clergymen, interested in the history of God's creation and hoping to establish a supportive relationship between theology and natural science. Their work helped to establish a definitive order for the laying down of the various strata of the earth's crust. Many strands of investigation were drawn together when Charles Lyell in 1830 began the publication of his *Principles of Geology*. John Maynard Smith remarks that 'Lyell's great achievement was to explain the past history of the rocks of the earth's crust in terms of processes such as erosion, sedimentation, and volcanic activity which can be observed at the present time' (1975:31). If the physical structure of the planet had been formed by a series of intelligible physical processes, which acted uniformly under similar conditions, and which were still in action at the present time, then creation could no longer be understood to have happened in a moment, in response to God's *Fiat*.

The period of time over which the earth had been created was now seen to be vast. The period which had to be counted as 'time' was suddenly increased from the few thousand years of biblical history to more than four billion years of physical process. It was not yet apparent that even this measurement applied only to this planet and that other parts of the universe might be older still.

Once geological time was established, the presence of fossils in the strata had a further significance, pointing not only to the laying down of physical structures but also to changes over time in the species of living creatures. It so happened that the eighteenth century's admiration for God as the supreme technician of the universe depended in part on the perception of the perfection of each creature in its own environment, and hence on the stability of species in environments. The suggestion that species might change over time was deeply shocking to such sentiments.

What was lacking at this stage was a key to the way such change might have come about without a succession of creative acts by God. Various people had begun to speculate about some form of 'evolution', but without a biological explanation this remained speculation. Once again the answer came from the observation of present-day processes. Charles Darwin and Alfred Wallace, working independently, came to the conclusion that the methods by which plant and animal breeders reproduced new varieties might have a parallel in natural processes.

The key was provided by Malthus's work on human populations. If populations of all species could be assumed to expand to the limits of the environment that supported them and if there were sufficient random variations among individuals within a species over a sufficiently long period of time, then individuals carrying advantageous variations would tend to predominate within the species, so changing the species or replacing it. The advantage of random change would operate more readily when the environment itself was changing and the species needed to adapt to it afresh in order to survive.

When Darwin and Wallace presented this argument to the Linnaean Society in 1858 they were not able to explain the genetic mechanism for the transmission of advantageous changes through successive generations, but the experience of breeders had already shown that such transmission did in fact take place.

Most mutations would render the individuals concerned less fit rather than more fit to survive in their environments. But over a long enough period of time — and geology now provided ample time — there could be enough beneficial variation to account for the processes of change that were indicated sketchily by the fossil record. The honour of establishing this theory of development of species falls to Darwin rather than Wallace because of the sheer weight of evidence which he accumulated in his breeding experiments with pigeons, in his travels with H.M.S. Beagle, and in his studies of the work of other observers, all of

185

which were brought into play in *The Origin of Species*, published in 1859.

'Fitness to survive in a given environment' was the criterion by which an evolutionary process could be defined. Basically species were very stable, and some continued unchanged over millions of years. Random genetic change was not fully understood until the mid-twentieth century, when Crick and Watson helped to unlock the genetic code in the double helix structure of DNA. Since then molecular biology has amply confirmed the theory of evolution. But in 1858 it was already clear that such change occurred and that over geological time change in such factors as climate and food supply could impose 'change or die' pressures on species. In these circumstances the ability to compete was the clue to survival.

The intellectual shock of this discovery was severe. If evolution was the outcome of an interaction between genetic change and food supply, it was no longer possible to talk about 'design' in the universe. God could be seen at best as the initiator of a multi-million year process which was as unfeeling in the creation of species as in the destruction of them. Worst of all, human beings themselves had to be included in the process. As Jürgen Moltmann comments, 'The theory of evolution shook the self-interpretation of Christians and the self-understanding of civic society alike — the self-understanding of the European who, in the name of God, had made himself the lord of nature. It rocked the whole modern, anthropocentric view of the world: the species human being is no more than one small line in an evolutionary sequence whose end cannot be foreseen' (1985:193).

This intellectual shock in some ways made the work of the theologians easier. For theology had been having its own problems. The methods of critical analysis of texts, which had been applied to the Bible since the time of Jerome, but had been used most extensively since the early seventeenth century on the writings of classical antiquity, now began to be applied in earnest to the Biblical texts. It was becoming obvious that the documents which made up the Hebrew Bible and the New Testament showed signs of composite authorship and mixed literary forms. Some had little or no relation to the person to whom they were ascribed and in some cases the person to whom they were ascribed was also of dubious historicity. That the first five books of the Old Testament might not have been written by Moses was one problem, and that Moses might not be a real person was another.

The historical accuracy of the Bible became the central question largely because some people now began to defend it by claiming for it literal inerrancy. Partly, no doubt, this was a legacy of the Reformation, since the move from the authority of the Catholic Church, which could in practice be a fairly flexible authority, to the authority of the Word of God in the written word tended to become an authority of the written word itself. Partly also the believers, without noticing what they were doing, adopted the same rationalism that the eighteenth century had bequeathed to the nineteenth century as the main problem for Christian faith, squeezing out the poetic, the intuitive and the personal as real means of human knowledge, and making a rationalistic factuality the sole basis of authority.

It was therefore a considerable relief to the intelligent liberal theologians to be able to work with the theory of evolution to place the Biblical stories in a new frame of reference. By the end of the century writers such as Henry Drummond and F. R. Tennant in Britain had begun to argue that human beings could be seen as the crowning achievement of the evolutionary process, in which the physical evolution of the biosphere developed into the moral and spiritual evolution of human consciousness. In this case the 'problems' of the Bible could be seen to be the result of its having been written at an earlier stage of human development.

But the nineteenth century did not return to being an age of faith. As Sir Leslie Stephen wrote, 'The ordinary Briton persists in thinking that the words "I believe" are to be interpreted in the same sense in a creed or a scientific statement. His appetite wants something more than "theosophic moonshine"' (1873:59). Stephen went on to argue that calling religion an 'art' rather than a 'science' would not solve the problem for believers.

Let us give up the question of fact, and admit that the demand for truth in a creed is utterly unreasonable, so far as its influence upon our lives is concerned. Still there remains an aesthetic perplexity. Can even an art — if religion is to be definitely an art — be noble and genuine when entirely divorced from reality? (1873:61, 62)

On this basis the freethinkers were bound to have the best of the argument.

Many sensitive critics simply gave up on the battle for some spiritual understanding that would impose an order on the sheer physical ebullience of the century. Not all believed in the inevitability of progress. Matthew Arnold, one of the most alert cultural critics of the period, wrote in 'Dover Beach' of the 'melancholy, long, withdrawing roar' of the Sea of Faith. In a move that was to become characteristic of theology in the twentieth century, he turned to the consolation of the personal.

Ah, love, let us be true
To one another! for the world, which seems
To lie before us like a land of dreams,
So various, so beautiful, so new,
Hath really neither joy, nor love, nor light,
Nor certitude, nor peace, nor help for pain;
And we are here as on a darkling plain
Swept with confused alarms of struggle and flight,
Where ignorant armies clash by night. (1939:111)

Some theologians, however, took these scientific developments as an opportunity rather than a threat. In the winter of 1901-1902 F. R.Tennant delivered the Hulsean Lectures in the University of Cambridge on the theme of *The Origin and Propagation of Sin*. Tennant had an unusual background for a theologian in having a science degree and his lectures constituted the first major attempt to integrate the theory of evolution into Christian ethics by starting from the premise of evolution rather than from the premise of the fall and original sin. Of the scientific side of evolution he said very little, for his first concern was with the doctrine of original sin. 'This corruption of human nature has generally been represented since Augustine as consisting in a diminution of the freedom of the will and in an acquired, ingrained bias or inclination to evil; and the universal appearance of sinfulness in the lives of men is ascribed to its hereditary transmission by means of natural generation' (1902:5).

Tennant pointed out that the existence of actual sin was not in itself a proof of the doctrines of the fall and of original sin. So long as thought about man was dominated by the idea of an original state of innocence, it was a natural mistake to identify the historical universality of sin with the idea of a fall and original sin, but now we had the possibility of an alternative explanation, that human beings were flesh before they were spirit. 'On such a view, man's moral evil would be the consequence of no defection from his endowment, natural or miraculous, at the start: it would bespeak rather the present non-attainment of his final goal' (1902:11).

There was something to be said for the Augustinian position, as could be seen by looking at his adversary Pelagius. The weakness of Pelagius was his atomistic conception of sin: 'the view, that is, which regards the will as equally unfettered for the choice of good after any number of surrenders to the side of evil', which ignored the effect of habit in building up character. On the other hand Pelagius' strength was in his emphasis on the concept of individual responsibility, to which Augustine did not give sufficient recognition. The positive contribution of Augustine was to take seriously the universality of sin and the social and historical solidarity of humankind.

The solidarity of humankind lay in the fact that all shared in the sin of Adam. But this strength of the theory was also its greatest weakness — for how could this sharing in the sin of Adam work? For the later individual did not personally take part in Eve and Adam's act of disobedience. So how could a person's state at birth now be considered sinful? The traditonal answer had been to regard original sin as a deformity of nature rather than as a sin actually committed by an individual. But Tennant argued that this position broke down at four points.

The first was on the necessary assumption of an original unfallen moral state ('original righteousness'). Even if the theory of evolution were not accepted, the history of the development of the theological concept showed that it had no sure base in scripture (the argument was given in full in *The Sources of the Doctrines of the Fall and Original Sin* in 1903).

The second point was the difficulty of conceiving the transition from an original implanted goodness to the actual sin of the first human beings: 'If actual sin, in us, presupposes a sinful state, it is hard to see why the same inference should not equally apply to the case of the first man, whose *peccatum originans* has been held to be the cause of our *peccatum originatum*' (1902:28).

The third point was the difficulty of conceiving 'how one act of sin, however momentous, could serve to dislocate at once the whole nature of man and to destroy the balance of all his faculties'. He commented 'Human experience furnishes no analogy to such disturbing action' (1902:28). This of course, was not a conclusive argument, but it did point to the problem of the arbitrariness of the concept of a single act of original sin.

The fourth point was the difficulty of conceiving the means of transmission of the results of the fall to posterity, for biology and psychology did not offer any way in which the transmission of sin could be understood apart from the influence of the social environment. He concluded that the doctrine was largely the result of theological speculation.

Finally Tennant came to the question of sin in evolutionary theory and empirical science. Here he placed the origin of sin in the conflict between the characteristics of the human being as an evolving animal and the growing moral consciousness which pertained only to human beings. It was the evolutionary inheritance which accounted for the universality of sin, and the moral consciousness of each individual human being which accounted for personal responsibility. In this way the two strands of Augustinianism and Pelagianism could be held together satisfactorily.

Tennant himself, of course, was now working within certain presuppositions. In the first place he accepted the Augustinian assumption that sin was so universal that it required 'a real, physical, organic race-solidarity' to explain it and he accepted the Pelagian principle that only a personal act could carry personal guilt. In the second place he accepted an assumption, beyond the biological account of evolution, that there had been a general human progress in society up to his own day and that the psychological development of the individual paralleled the development of law in society.

The second point would need to be put more cautiously today. The history of the twentieth century has made it more difficult to think in terms of a simple line of progress in human society and the increasing knowledge of 'primitive' societies has led to recognition of their complexity and, for their own purposes, of the adequacy of their law and custom, and indeed their superiority in terms of their relation to the environment. Similarly, a present-day understanding of child development would see the relation between 'nature' and 'nurture' as much more complex than this simple account, and the early life of the infant as more differentiated and responsive than Tennant's account of simple egotism.

Nevertheless, Tennant's basic point, that a developing sense of sin is related to a developing consciousness, has some value as a working hypothesis. What does become clear in the course of his argument is that this developmental standard was strictly relative, both for society and for the individual. It could not provide an absolute standard of 'sin'. He paid very little attention to this point, since his main concern was to develop a theodicy — an account of the relationship of sin, free will and the creation of the world by God.

The practical origin of sin in the human race Tennant had to admit was largely a matter of 'theory and speculation' because of the thinness of the evidence about prehistoric human beings. He began by assuming 'continuity between the physical constitution of man and that of the lower animals', but refused to commit himself as to the possibility of moral sentiments in animals lower than ourselves. 'The question whether the moral has been developed out of the non-moral would seem to be largely a

191

matter of words, and to depend on the definition we assign to the term "moral"' (1902:86).

His main argument was that morality was a social creation, arising 'through the prolonged intercourse of individuals'. Within this context the development of sin in the individual must be the result of the development of the individual conscience. The basic fact about the individual was the same as the basic fact about the human race, that we were natural beings before we were moral beings. The infant recapitulated the moral history of the race. She or he was at the start 'simply a non-moral animal', with those impulses and propensities that were essential to her or his nature. Only with the appearance of will and reason did morality — and therefore sin — become a possibility.

The development of the moral will was the result of a process of education, by which the race transmitted to the individual the morality it had slowly learned, and this imposition from without was assisted by processes within the child's own nature, as the external command was internalized and made a matter of relationship, first to a human other, and then to God. 'The newborn moral agent, therefore, has much to unlearn and much to subdue, as he enters on the task of moralising his organic nature' (1902:106-107). It followed that the universality of actual sin resulted from a continual failure to make perfect the self-moralisation process: 'It is simply the general failure to effect on all occasions the moralisation of inevitable impulses and to choose the end of higher worth rather than that which, of lower value, appeals with the more clamorous intensity' (1902:107).

Consequently the theological problem of how sin arose in a universe designed for unity and harmony rested on a false assumption. 'Empirical science asserts that the discord in us is not sin until we make it so, and unity and harmony, in the sense of freedom from effort to avoid evil, never has had actual existence' (1902:107). This satisfied the two parts of the problem of sin: the fact that sin was universal and arose out of human solidarity corresponded to our common biological and social heritage, and the fact that the moral nature of sin was derived solely from the action of an individual will in a social relationship corresponded to the facts of individual child development. Tennant claimed that his argument was strictly empirical, but the relationship of this kind of moral claim to biological science was more problematical than he supposed. So long as the evolutionary account of the development of life on earth is accepted, it is clear that either biological life is in itself non-moral (which is Tennant's position) or that there is an inter-relationship between the biological and the moral which requires further investigation. Some modern biological study tends towards the latter position.

As a minimum it seems reasonable to say that natural selection sets one of the limits which any account of human behaviour has to observe. N. G. Blurton Jones remarks that 'No general theory of human behaviour can be *incompatible* with the implications of natural selection' (1976:441). Theodosius Dobzhansky defines the present understanding of natural selection as follows:

> Classical evolutionists used to say that natural selection makes the fittest survive and the rest die off. We prefer less dramatic language; natural selection favours the perpetuation of adaptively more efficient, and decreases the chances of perpetuation of less efficient, genotypes. Natural selection was often compared to a sieve which retains the fit and lets the unfit be swept away. We prefer a less mechanical analogy: environment presents challenges to living populations, to which the latter may, through natural selection, respond by retention or by improvement of their adaptedness to the conditions of their existence. (1958:24-25)

J. M. Thoday, in an article on 'Natural Selection and Biological Progress', argues that a biological concept of 'progress' can be developed from the initial principle of reproductive success. Since the environment in which living beings reproduce changes over time, survival over a long period requires change as well as stability. The possibility of change comes from genetic mutation. A species requires genetic stability, so that it may remain recognizably the same species, but it requires also genetic variability, so that it always has the possibility of producing individuals more suited to new environments, both in the sense of adaptation to changes in an environment through time and in the sense of the capacity to adapt to other environments available at the same time. Consequently, versatility in the individuals of a species increases the possibility of reproductive success for the species as a whole.

In this sense human beings can be claimed to be the most successful of species. The human ability, not only to control the environment but also to communicate what has been learned to future generations, has moved the species from biological evolution to social evolution. This increased human possibility of control of a local environment carries with it an increased possibility of the species getting out of balance with its total environment in such a way as to threaten its chances of survival. Thoday concludes: 'Biological progress, therefore, not only involves increasing versatility of individual species, but also increasing diversity of species *harmoniously adapted to one another*' (1958:333).

Here biology arrives at a requirement that affects the social life of human beings and therefore potentially has moral implications. Some biologists argue that in some species altruism may have a biological cause, since in some environments an individual that cares for the offspring of a close relative may increase the chances of reproduction of their common genetic inheritance more than it could do by producing more offspring itself. But it is not clear at present how far the arguments of sociobiology lead into human moral concepts. Indeed the main effect of sociobiology so far seems to have been to shift the locus of evolutionary success from the individual to the kinship group (Kitcher, 1985).

After Darwin, the theological problem for those who remained within the Christian faith was about the special nature of the Atonement. If paradise and the fall no longer have the status of history, a very simple but very important problem arises, that without the fall the concept of restoration must also undergo some change. The problem lies in the parallelism: if the fall of Adam is myth, so also must be the restoration in Christ. It is the need to protect an historical atonement that creates the need to establish an historical fall. But myth is a tricky tool to work with.

It is perfectly fair to say that the myths of the origins of humanity in various religions deal with matters about which human beings need to have an understanding in order to achieve a coherent view of their universe and that such accounts, which are 'untrue' in relation to the scientific account of the physical universe, may still be 'true' as telling that the universe is in the hands of God, in the same way that the story of Hansel and Gretel or The Snow Queen may help children to come to grips with their own feelings before they can articulate their real experiences of separation and loss in other ways. But the explanations given through myth are not singular: I can read both 'The Snow Queen' and Genesis with profit. The demand placed upon the myth of the fall, however, is that it should be singular in order to support a singular atonement. For Jung myth is that which speaks directly out of the collective, archaic but still present experience of the human race: it is that which cannot be dealt with simply as history. But the Christian claim is that the faith is rooted in a specific historical moment. This historical claim is created by the historicity of Jesus, not by the historicity of Eve and Adam. If there is a problem created by the realization that the fall is myth, it can be answered only by looking again at the conditions requiring reconciliation that are established by human history and pre-history. This requires attention to a further development in scientific theory.

In the twentieth century the problem for theology has shifted from the effect of evolutionary theory in biology on the theory of the Fall to the effect of the study of the cosmos on the theology of the Atonement. One of the two great changes in the way of envisaging the physical world came about in the seventeenth century, with the victory of the mechanistic model. Theology coped with this — though not well — by developing the notion of God as the great artificer who designed the physical universe as if it were a clock and then left it to run under its own laws with an occasional miraculous intervention where necessary. These interventions were mainly in the past and the whole theory made the creator a somewhat distant figure. The benevolent originator of the eighteenth century may indeed have been part of the reason why the churches defaulted so spectacularly on the moral needs of the poor in the nineteenth century.

The other great change in the way of envisaging the world came in the twentieth century with the discovery of quantum mechanics. Newtonian mechanics remained valid for most of the phenomena in daily life, but as scientific investigation moved outwards into the cosmos and inwards into sub-atomic physics, new descriptions of physical reality became necessary. In 1905 Albert Einstein put forward the theory of special relativity and in 1915 the theory of general relativity. The most interesting effect of these theories has been on the notion of time. Stephen Hawking explains that 'The fundamental postulate of the theory of relativity, as it was called, was that the laws of science should be the same for all freely moving observers' (1988:20). While this made little or no difference to most human beings, who continued to keep time by seventeenth century clocks, for observers who could theoretically approach the speed of light it made a dramatic difference. The speed of light is one of the limits of the known universe. As observers approach that speed the energy required for the motion, which is very large, increases their mass until at the speed of light it becomes impossible to move faster. Since the speed of light is a constant, observers looking at light from a given source will judge the distance it has travelled relative to their own motion, and so will have a different idea of 'time'. As Hawking comments, 'In other words, the theory of relativity put an end to the idea of absolute time! It appeared that each observer must have his own measure of time, as recorded by a clock carried with him, and that identical clocks carried by different observers would not necessarily agree' (1988:21).

Meanwhile in the study of extremely small phenomena another problem arose, that it became impossible in principle to define both the position and the speed of the smallest particles of matter, because the attempt to observe a particle would interfere with either its speed or its direction. The observer was somewhat in the position of a commander firing a cannonball into an

advancing army in order to find out where the individual soldiers were. At the most fundamental level of matter it meant that
all that could be established was a degree of probability about
the path that a particle was travelling. This was not a trivial
matter. As Hawking again comments, 'Heisenberg's uncertainty
principle is a fundamental, inescapable property of the world'
(1988:55).

The third major change in modern physics was the observation of Edwin Hubble in 1929 that the galaxies which compose
the universe seemed to be moving away from each other. The
theory that the universe was expanding like a balloon being
blown up suggested also that at the beginning it was in a col-
lapsed state, with all available matter compressed with unimagin-
able density in a very small space. Such a condition would be
unstable and would result in a 'big bang' which produced the
expansion we now observe. This theory gave a possible age for
the universe, from the original explosion to the present day, of
between ten billion and twenty billion years.

These latest steps in physical science have posed two general
questions. The first is whether it still makes sense to talk about
order in the universe and the second whether it still makes sense
to talk of the universe as being in some sense personal.

The first question appears to have a simple affirmative answer.
The uncertainty principle has not made the universe less ordered, though it may prevent human beings from giving a complete account of that order. It has frequently been noted that
there are in some respects very narrow limits, relating to the
original conditions in the first moments of the expansion, within
which intelligent life is possible (Lovell, 1979:122-123). As Stephen
Hawking again explains, 'The laws of science, as we know them
at present, contain many fundamental numbers, like the size of
the electric charge of the electron and the ratio of the masses of
the proton and the electron . . . The remarkable fact is that the
values of these numbers seem to have been very finely adjusted
to make possible the development of life' (1988:125).

The order in the universe is complex and beautiful. As D. J.
Bartholomew has pointed out, there are two principles at work

197

(Bartholomew, 1984). The first is chance, which is strict random-ness. The second is order, which is apparent whenever the number of individual movements becomes large enough to be statistically significant. Whether we are looking at the movements of molecules in a gas or the votes of electors in a democratic election, our inability to trace the movements of all the individuals does not prevent us from making predictions within quite narrow limits about the movements of the whole. Consequently, Bartholomew argues, the combination of random movements and statistical probability in the universe as a whole provides the essential scope for free will and for intelligent co-operation with a creator. In spite of the apparent indeterminacy of the process of evolution, the creation of intelligent life is a likely result of these processes. It is therefore not illegitimate within theology to regard human life as being intended by a creative power to be the culmination of these processes, though the physical science should certainly not be taken as *proving* such a hypothesis.

If the present knowledge of the physical universe is compatible with the idea of intelligent creatures freely co-operating with the creative process, what sort of God does this imply? Does it still make sense to talk of the universe as being in some sense personal? One theologian who thinks not is James M. Gustafson, who after a life-time devoted to theological ethics has come to the conclusion that we have taken too lightly what is known about the nature of the universe. He argues that 'God' is simply a term for the powers encountered in the universe which sustain and limit human existence. The fact that human beings, seeing themselves as agents forming purposes and attempting to carry them out, can by analogy apply the concept of agency to God does not mean that God can or should be conceived of as a human agent. 'Insofar as the analogy leads us to assert that God has intelligence, like but superior to our own, and that God has a will, a capacity to control events comparable to the more radical claims made for human beings, the claims are excessive' (1981:270). In these words Gustafson returns us to the Greek and Roman philosophers of nature.

Consequently the ultimate power of the cosmos as it is now

understood cannot plausibly be seen as seeking human good as its primary activity. The ultimate good can only be good for the cosmos as a whole and for those relationships within it which enable it to maintain itself and to proceed as cosmos in every detail. The ethical good for human beings is to observe the proper relationships within nature thus understood, and Gustafson asserts that human beings have the capacities to discern something of these relationships and of what appropriate action would be.

In this austere vision the task of ethics is to undertake this discernment and to respect the proper relations between all things and the governing and sustaining powers, included among which relations, but only as part of the whole, are the needs and possibilities of human beings. If asked why human beings positively aspire to perfection and hope for that which is truly beyond them, Gustafson would reply that human beings do not yet properly understand their finitude, or accept the limits of their place in the universe.

The question that might be put in return is why Gustafson wishes to speak of 'Christian' ethics at all. For he regards Jesus as simply a symbol of what is already within every human being. This is certainly one of the possible choices. But another possible choice is to take a much more radical view of the inter-relationship of God and the universe, abandoning what remains of the divine watchmaker and asserting that not merely some but all events in the universe are the direct result of the will of God — that the universe only exists because it is directly willed, from micro-second to micro-second, by the love of God. So every unit of energy from our point of view moves by its own laws, but the whole matrix, including the laws, is continuously sustained by the creative will. This does not imply determinism, if part of the willing is the willing of freedom to intelligent creatures. Nor does it imply that the Godhead is co-terminous with the creation, but rather that the creation exists within the Godhead.

What is the point of making such a claim? It is that the purposiveness of creatures can only be understood if the whole creation is purposive, or in more theological language, if the whole

199

creation is in process of being saved. The claim cannot be established from within natural theology. It can only be established from within the theology of salvation, that is to say, as part of the personal experience of God by human beings. The claim that the divine creative purpose wills that the entire cosmos should be brought to conscious knowledge of the creator and should freely choose to align itself with that purpose arises only out of our knowledge of Jesus Christ. Only the experience that salvation works in the lives of persons can justify the claim that salvation is the purpose of the cosmos.

5

Vision and Discipline:
Christian Ethics in the Twenty-First Century

'The human person is a created icon of the uncreated God'. With these words Kallistos Ware states the Orthodox view of the potentiality of the human being (1987:178). Made of the earth in the image of the triune God, it is the human being who links the created and the uncreated into a single whole. It is the human being who links the self and the other with God. In this also we represent the Holy Trinity. 'As love, God is not self-love but mutual love' (1987:206). Why, then, do we not think about ourselves like this?

Modern western society has clearly lost the ability to integrate the intellectual, the affective and the spiritual life of human beings into an effective image of the self that can place the self in the cosmos and can convey a sense of status and responsibility. The cost of the freedoms given by the Enlightenment has been very high. The support systems for the person have been removed one by one. The intellectual understanding of the unity of being, the single church-based structure of social institutions and the prophetic sense of creation have all been removed without anything coherent appearing to replace them.

Once these support systems for the self-understanding of the human being have disappeared, the notion of a 'person', itself the product of Christian faith, seems bound to disintegrate. Marcel Mauss, beginning his discussion of the notion of a person in 1938, was able to put aside the ordinary knowledge of the self as not in question. 'Let me merely say that it is plain, particularly to us, that there has never existed a human being who has not been aware, not only of his body, but also at the same time of his individuality, both spiritual and physical' (1985:2). For many daily practical operations, this continues to be true. But when the question is posed reflectively — Who am I? — western consciousness seems to have no answer. So Jerome Bruner, as a psychologist interested in educational development, admits that 'It is a topic that makes me acutely uncomfortable' (1986:129). For Bruner the self is a project, but a project in inter-action: 'just as I believe that we construct or constitute the world, I believe too that self is a construction, a result of action and symbolization' (1986:130). He describes the self as 'a canonical text', about the powers and skills and dispositions that are available from past experience. 'The interpretation of this text *in situ* by an individual *is* his sense of self in that situation' (1986:130).

All this means that the adoption of the model of the person by Christian ethics involves more complications than the old problem whether the human term 'person' could be applied to God. The problem now is that Christian ethics has to structure for itself the model of 'person' that it wishes to use. In Greek thought *persona* was first a representation upon a stage, then a legal concept. In Christian civilization the person became defined as the indivisible rational soul. Marcel Mauss comments, 'It is the Christians who have made a metaphysical entity of the "moral person" (*personne morale*), after they became aware of its religious power. Our own notion of the human person is still basically the Christian one' (1985:19). But the Christian notion itself is now in need of reconstruction.

(i) The Self as the Experience of Relationship

The difficulty seems to have begun with the Romantic Movement. In letters *On the Aesthetic Education of Man*, published in 1795, Friedrich Schiller addressed the problem of the fragmentation of the image of the human being into different specializations, as a result of which no one human being could be fully human. This fragmentation was the inevitable result of intellectual and material progress. 'Once the increase of empirical knowledge, and more exact modes of thought, made sharper divisions between the sciences inevitable, and once the increasingly complex machinery of State necessitated a more rigorous separation of ranks and occupations, then the inner unity of human nature was severed too, and a disastrous conflict set its harmonious powers at variance' (6.6; 1967:33).

For Schiller human nature was divided between its potentiality and its historical condition. The 'person' was the capacity for absolute, unchanging being. 'The Person therefore must be its own ground; for what persists cannot proceed from what changes' (11.4; 1967:73). This absolute being was a state of freedom, not determined by any details of the historical, sensual world. On the other hand the historical condition of being was the actual experience of changingness. 'We pass from rest to activity, from passion to indifference, from agreement to contradiction; but *we* remain, and what proceeds directly from us remains too' (11.2; 1967:73). Without this existence in time, absolute being could have no content.

Schiller argued that the solution lay in aesthetic education, in bringing about the harmony of intellect and feeling through the experience of beauty, which was also the experience of free play. In the world of the developed imagination, the aesthetic state, 'none may appear to the other except as form, or confront him except as the object of free play' (27.9; 1967:215). In fact, since the end of the eighteenth century, the concept of the self has become more and more unplayable.

Schiller's argument was based on the theory of an evolution from a natural, sensuous condition of human beings to a consciousness of the power of the human being rationally to control and organize the self and the world; from this it was necessary to move to the recognition of the possibility of artistic creation, which was the only true expression of both sides of human nature, the only form of expression which could combine the reality of both freedom and restraint. Schiller believed — and it could only be an act of faith — that the human being had the capacity for self-creation. 'By means of aesthetic culture, therefore, the personal worth of a man, or his dignity, inasmuch as this can depend solely upon himself, remains completely indeterminate . . . the freedom to be what he ought to be is completely restored to him' (21.4; 1967:147).

In theology the pressures experienced by Schiller led to a new emphasis on the personal. The influence of Søren Kierkegaard, the Danish philosopher and theologian, is greater in the twentieth century than it was in his own period of the early nineteenth century. Kierkegaard's insistence that only inner, personal knowledge of the self and of God could validate doctrine and ethics led in one direction, after the experience of the 'death of God' in European culture, to the attempt at a new humanism, in the movement broadly called 'existentialism' (Macquarrie, 1973). Indeed, it might be claimed that Kierkegaard's work gave a much stronger impulse to secular thought than to Christian thought.

Three developments, however, led to new possibilities of Christian thought about the nature of persons, all of them initially from outside the Christian faith. The first was a continued positive evaluation of the work of natural science. Here, the leading figure was the Jewish philosopher, Henri Bergson, whose book *Creative Evolution*, first published in Paris in 1907, set a new level of debate by seeing almost mystical possibilities in the idea of a dynamic of evolution. Bergson's mystical side was continued in the work of the Jesuit scholar Pierre Teilhard de Chardin; more soberly the movements known as 'process philosophy' and 'process theology' continued to work at the notion that the evolutionary cosmos was itself, in some sense, a participator in the nature of God.

The second element in the changes in Christian thought in the twentieth century was the anxiety created by the destruction of the material and philosophical hopes of European civilization by the successive blows of the war of 1914-1918, the Russian revolution of 1917 and the rise of fascism in Italy and Germany in the 1920's and 1930's, leading eventually to the war of 1939-1945. Paul Tillich, in *The Courage to Be*, which first appeared in 1952, claimed that the twentieth century was predominantly an age of anxiety, and drew together existentialism and depth psychology to argue that the word of God could now be spoken only by passing through the accepted structures of Christian doctrine and ethics to find the 'God beyond God' who was known to every human being who tried to treat the world with moral seriousness. From these very modern bases, Tillich indeed returned to the God of Meister Eckhart, the God beyond God who was to be known in the most profound moments of personal experience. Process theology was a search for a new public theology, based on a scientific view of the universe. Tillich's search for the God beyond God aimed eventually at a new public theology, but only by passing through the most intensely personal questions. Martin Buber, a Jewish philosopher from the same German background as Tillich, provided the third element of challenge to Christian thought with the publication in 1921 of *I and Thou*. In this work Buber picked up the idea of personal encounter as the foundation of knowledge and turned it into a complex theology. For Buber there were two possible forms of encounter with an other. In the 'I and Thou', the other, whether another person or an animal or a tree or a fragment of rock, was known as itself alone. The 'I' stood before the other in mutual communion. In the 'I and It', the other became an object to be used or analysed or ignored.

Buber pointed out that the mode in which one chose to encounter the other also determined the nature of the I that entered the encounter. Not only the other changed, but also the self.

> If *Thou* is said, the *I* of the combination *I-Thou* is said along with it.
> If *It* is said, the *I* of the combination *I-It* is said along with it.
> The primary word *I-Thou* can only be spoken with the whole being. The primary word *I-It* can never be spoken with the whole being. (1959:3)

There are consequently two modes of being.

> As EXPERIENCE, the world belongs to the primary word *I-It*.
> The primary word *I-Thou* establishes the world of relation. (1959:6)

It is important to note that Buber is not talking about the basic word 'I-It' as necessarily improper. When clearing a forest it is not necessary or possible to encounter each tree as 'Thou'. Yet the work of forestry will be destructive unless it is undertaken in a context of knowing the 'Thou' of trees as the gift of creation, and therefore even the use of trees as needing to be held within the purpose of the whole creation.

Even the closest of personal relations may at times be properly in the basic word 'I-It' — that is, at a low level of attentiveness. Yet any relation can be transformed into the basic word 'I-Thou'. The break-through is not into a different world, but into a re-ordering of present experience. As Buber wrote in *Dialogue* in 1929, the break-through is 'Into nothing exalted, heroic or holy, into no Either and no Or, only into this tiny strictness and grace of every day, where I have to do with just the very same "reality" with whose duty and business I am taken up in such a way, glance to glance, look to look, word to word, that I experience it as reached to me and myself to it, it as spoken to me and myself to it'. In the middle of this reality, 'there appears to me, homely and glorious, the effective reality, creaturely and given to me in trust and responsibility'. He comments, 'We do not find meaning lying in things, nor do we put it into things, but between us and things it can happen' (1961:55-56).

The basic word 'I-Thou' is the quality of attentiveness. Consequently it can be a reality even where the other is not equally attentive. It is always possible to speak the basic word 'I-Thou' and so to create the other as a gift. It might also be said that this creative speaking of the basic word 'I-Thou' is the whole task of ethics. This transcendent act is possible because the relationship of I and Thou touches on the inner reality of the whole universe.

Buber resisted any notion of mysticism as a way of escape from the world. But he insisted that in encountering the reality of another person in the world, the inner reality of the world was also present. Behind the human possibility of 'I-Thou' was the ultimate Thou which was both hidden and always present. Only through the human 'Thou' could God be known, but God was present in every encounter of I and Thou. 'Only one *Thou* never ceases by its nature to be *Thou* for us. He who knows God knows also very well remoteness from God, and the anguish of barrenness in a tormented heart; but he does not know the absence of God; it is only we who are not always there' (1959:99).

There are two possible weaknesses in Buber's position from the point of view of Christian theology. The first is that it risks being simply a polarity between 'I and Thou' and 'I and It', with no continuing centre for the self. The second is that it perhaps underestimates the importance of sin.

Buber's polarity, in which the self swings between the I of the 'I-Thou' and the I of the 'I-It' has its centre guaranteed, not by the self's own experience, but by God. It is God's search for the self and God's intention towards the self that creates the person. Even so, the argument needs extending, for Christian ethics, by some notion of development, and it needs some explicit treatment of the immense power of resistance that is sin.

(ii) The Self as an Experience of Development

Recent studies in child development suggest that the young child from the beginning comes into the world in order to act. From the moment of birth the child creates a world in co-operation with others. Drawing on the work of the Russian psychologist Lev Vygotsky on the development of consciousness, Jerome Bruner has noted that the conscious control of a function comes only after the function has been used. 'This suggests that prior to the development of self-directed, conscious control, action is, so to speak, a more direct or less mediated response to the world' (1986:73). Vygotsky suggested that in the process of acquiring conscious control, adults around the child could 'lend' their consciousness temporarily to the child so that the child could discover in action what it could not master entirely by itself nor follow simply from being told. This creation of learning situations Vygotsky called 'a zone of proximal development'.

Bruner comments on a particular learning situation which he himself observed, 'In general, what the tutor did was what the child could *not* do. For the rest, she made things such that the child could do *with* her what he plainly could not do *without* her' (1986:76). The task of the tutor was then gradually to hand over more parts of the task to the child. The process was a transaction in which the co-operation of both parties was necessary.

Bruner also refers to the finding of Barbara Tizard on learning in families. 'The more likely parents are to give good answers, the more likely are children to ask interesting questions. But, on the other hand, given the nature of correlations, the finding can be stated in the reverse direction: the more likely children are to ask interesting questions, the more likely parents are to give good answers' (1986:76). The acquisition of language thus requires both an innate ability for language use and also a social support system that allows the acquisition to take place in regular steps; the development of consciousness is essentially a co-operative process.

It might then be argued that the co-operation which is necessary in the acquisition of language or motor skills is also necessary in the development of emotional skills. This is a process which it is less easy to plot, since it depends on feeling as well as action. Psychology on the whole, as Bruno Bettelheim has noted, has been better at negative definitions than at positive ones, perhaps because it began by investigating situations of emotional damage (Bettelheim, 1986:24-25). But it seems reasonable to assume that there is a dynamic of emotional development and that it begins very early. Jerome Bruner remarks that in a game of exchanging objects which he observed, 'Very young children had something clearly in mind about what others had in mind, and organized their actions accordingly. I thought of it as the child achieving mastery of one of the precursors of language use: a sense of mutuality in action' (Bruner, 1986:59).

The task for which the child is preparing is extremely complex. As A.R. Radcliffe-Brown remarks,

> Every human being living in society is two things: he is an individual and also a person. As an individual, he is a biological organism, a collection of a vast number of molecules organised in a complex structure, within which, as long as it persists, there occur physiological and psychological actions and reactions, processes and changes. Human beings as individuals are objects of study for physiologists and

psychologists. The human being as a person is a complex of social relationships. (1952:193-194)

The self as intuited cannot be separated from this social personality, for the structural differences between societies delimit the possibilities of person-hood. Francis Hsu claims, for example, that different patterns of relationship, different ways of conceiving what it is to be 'a human being', in China and Japan compared with Europe and North America account for the low penetration by Christianity into these societies. 'Given the westerner's attraction to one God and one absolute truth, he was bound to suffer disappointments elsewhere' (1985:47). The physical basis of personality must also be recognized as having its own spontaneity and autonomy. The autonomy of the body is a source of wonder, for example in the ever-growing knowledge of the processes of foetal development. It is also a source of moral problems, from abortion to euthanasia. The sheer physical possibilities of the human body raise problems about the concept of human identity.

If a definition of the self is to be attempted from the point of view of the human sciences, some or all of the following claims may be made.

(i) *The self is bodily.* No account which concentrates solely on mental features can approach the basic operational sense of the self which carries the human being through the day and night. This means that the self is structured by actions as much as by words.

(ii) *The self is reflective.* Michael Lockwood, seeking a definition to use in medical ethics, lays down the criterion of reflection. 'A person is a being that is conscious, in the sense of having the capacity for conscious thought and experiences, but not only that: it must have the capacity for reflective consciousness and self-consciousness' (1985:10). It is not clear that this entirely solves the problem of the boundary cases about when there is or is not a 'human being' in relation to such issues as abortion and euthanasia. But it does provide a marker for the broad sense of what is meant by a self. To think about the world and the self

209

must be part of any general definition of a self.

(iii) *The self has persistence over time.* It is at least arguable that the sense of continuity through memory is an illusion, that the self has no existence except the present moment of sensation. But Bruner's use of the analogy of the 'canonical text' makes the point that what persists is more than memory; what persists is skill and the power to act. The bodily part of this persistence is more than an image in the brain. The mental part of this persistence is also more than memory, since it involves also the use of the power to control. The practical experience of the building-up of 'character', the expectation of consistency in action and of change of character along a consistent line, all indicate something at work other than simple reminiscence. Frank Johnson, reviewing different descriptions of the self in different disciplines remarks that 'Self is seen as situational, and yet as something which transcends the ebb and flow of transitory encounters and reflections' (1985:95). This persistence is a kind of transcendence of the immediate phenomenological aspect of the self.

(iv) *The self exists only in relation to other selves.* As Frank Johnson comments again, 'Within many of these conceptual systems, *the self is no longer regarded as a unitary phenomenon* — that is, as an encapsulated, individual variable. Instead, the self is accepted as an *interpersonal*, i.e., as an *intersubjective* unit — even in terms of the self's interaction with its own self' (1985:129). What constitutes the self at any particular moment is the outcome of an inner and outer dynamic of relationships both personal and cultural, which result from the individual's past history and present location.

The problem is that there is a cost in all this. Experiences are negative as well as positive. To respect the other as an agent, a doer, a centre of consciousness like myself demands both restraint and commitment. It is always possible for the gift of the 'I-Thou' not to be made. Children are particularly vulnerable because the infant, though active in transactions with the adult, is nevertheless in a state of recipience, dependent on others for the most basic care. The demand on the caring adult is heavy: to create possibilities for the infant's sake. Though there are satisfactions in this, it is not surprising that the process breaks down, to some extent, for every human being.

Consequently the dynamic of growth as a 'person' requires a situation in which the experiences that have gone wrong can be healed. That which is not examined, accepted and forgiven is not under the control of the whole personality. Jack Dominian has analysed this dynamic in terms of three key words: sustaining, healing and growth. Sustaining is the giving of security in a relationship. 'Security in turn means that we need to have meaning, recognition, acceptance and significance for another person who is in touch with our inner world through sensitive, empathetic communication and reacts to our needs with increasing accuracy' (1977:38).

Healing begins when confidence is sustained long enough for deeper self-revelation to begin. The self which is hurt, frustrated, angry or empty needs to be shown to another. To a large extent the revealing is the healing, since it is growth in self-knowledge. The defeats of the past, which give the shadow within us its particular form, begin to lose their hold. The energies which have been taken up with repression and anger become available for new life. This is not done without pain and indeed some risk of damage to the other who receives the revelation — and again to the self if the revelation is rejected.

Growth follows healing in the sense that no one can say in advance what the potentialities of another person may be, nor can the self define in advance what its potentiality may be, until the dynamic of healing and growth has begun. In this dynamic the fundamental offer of sustaining is the beginning of salvation. Without this offer, no process can begin.

The process may be long in working. Dominian comments, 'It hardly needs saying that healing cannot easily occur under circumstances of transient relationships. If we are going to take the risk of exposing our painful wounds, we need to trust the other sufficiently to feel that he or she can take our pain and handle it with care and effectiveness. This needs time, continuity, reliability and predictability' (1977:39). The fundamental Christian teaching of marriage as a life-long process may be seen as one

211

expression of this understanding of relationships, though it would be wrong to press this as the only model. Other kinds of relationship may also be healing, both long-term and short-term.

(iii) The Self as Destructive

The alternative to the understanding of salvation as a process of growth is the doctrine of total annihilation, in thought, word and deed. The experience of the rule of terror by the National Socialists in Germany and in the occupied territories of Europe has been analysed by Bruno Bettelheim, who was himself imprisoned in a concentration camp for two years. Bettelheim sees the terror as the final form of the application of the principles of industrial capitalism in a situation that is completely devoid of moral restraint. When the direction of power passed from private capitalism to the totalitarian state, even the profit motive disappeared: there remained only the desire for total control. 'Both the concentration camps and the death camps, and what happened in them, were an application beyond reason of the concept of labor as a commodity. In the camps not only human labor but the total person became a commodity' (1986:243).

The ultimate aim of Nazism was to have only one point of decision-making, the leader, to whom all else was subordinate. From this point of view the aim of the camps was not so much to control those who were in them as to create a source of terror for those who were not in them, so that no decision made by anyone anywhere could be considered 'safe'. It was fundamental to the system that there could be no claims of 'right' or 'wrong', in or out of the camps. Only the absolute power of the state remained. Of course the National Socialist ideology did not penetrate every part of life in the territories it occupied. But in the fifteen years from 1930 to 1945 it destabilised every major social institution, including education, the law and the churches.

Bettelheim's study is concerned chiefly with the psychological factors which enabled some inmates to survive the experience of the camps. Sheer physical survival depended on positive mental organization, a will to survive, but this in turn depended on the possibility of some form of outside support. This could be

attachment to others or attachment to some idea or cause. Both
Communists and Jehovah's Witnesses survived better than the
average. 'One of the lessons of the camps was that, contrary to
what I expected and thought Darwinism taught, the will to live
— the life drive, the élan vital, or whatever other name it is given
— provided little support unless it could attach itself to some
loved person or all-important idea, such as communism or religious conviction' (1986:xvi).

From this experience Bettelheim came to reflect on the importance of environment as well as of the inner psychological
forces which in Freud's analysis were the foundation of psychology. A healthy environment had to provide both enough security
for inner integration and enough variety for some real freedom
of choice. Bettelheim wrote as a survivor of a system which aimed
to reduce choice to zero. Can one speak of morality at all in the
face of those who did not survive? Survival, after all, was arbitrary. George Steiner described the reality he did not himself
see.

> Often the children went alone, or held the hands of strangers.
> Sometimes parents saw them pass and did not dare call out
> their names. And they went, of course, not for anything they
> had done or said. But because their parents existed before
> them. The crime of being one's children. During the Nazi
> period it knew no absolution, no end. Does it now? (1979:164)

The intellectual and artistic brilliance of Central European Jewish humanism did not save it from the Holocaust. There was no
weighing of advantage or disadvantage. Both European capitalism and Russian communism emerge without credit from the
story. 'The French delivered to the Gestapo those who had fled
from Spain and Germany. Himmler and the G.P.U. exchanged
anti-Stalinist and anti-Nazi Jews for further torture and elimina-
tion' (1979:172). The British and American air forces did little
or nothing to break the supply lines to the camps.

Steiner asks if there are perhaps two different kinds of time,
ordinary time and inhuman time, which co-exist?

213

If we reject some such module, it becomes exceedingly difficult to grasp the continuity between normal existence and
the hour at which hell starts (on the city square when the
Germans begin the deportations, or in the office of the *Juden-
rat* or where-ever), an hour marking men, women, children
off from any precedent of life, from any voice 'outside', in
that other time of sleep and food and human speech.
(1979:181)

For Steiner there is no possibility of forgiveness, except by those
who entered into the experience. 'What the Nazis did in the
camps and torture chambers is wholly unforgivable, it is branded
on the image of man and will last; each of us has been dimin-
ished by the enactment of a potential sub-humanity latent in all
of us' (1979:188). But there is a specific responsibility for Christian faith. He refers to Chaim Kaplan, who left a diary of the life
of the Warsaw ghetto.

He knew what not very many, as yet, are prepared to see
plainly: that Nazi anti-Semitism is the logical culmination of
the millennial Christian vision and teaching of the Jew as
killer of God. Commenting on the murderous beatings of
Jews by German and Polish gangs at Easter 1940, Kaplan adds:
'Christian "ethics" became conspicuous in life. And then —
woe to us'. (1979:187)

Various qualifications could be put around this statement.
National Socialism was a more complex phenomenon than
just anti-Semitism, though anti-Semitism was a substantial
part of it. The extermination policy was aimed not only at
Jews; there were other ethnic groups regarded as inferior such as
Poles, Russians and Gypsies; there were also the mentally ill and
homosexuals, as well as political opponents such as Socialists
and Communists. Moreover, the atrocity of the camps and the
whole ethnic policy is only part of a long list of such atrocities in
human history, including, for example, the British settlers'
extermination of the Tasmanian people in the late nineteenth century and the Turkish massacre of a substantial

proportion of the Armenian people in 1915.

But the Jewish accusation remains true, that this particular atrocity, the Holocaust, in its grossness, in its single-minded and deliberate intent, and in its cold selectivity, was the peculiar product of western European civilization, shaped by more than a thousand years of Christian culture.

It is equally clear that a prophetic voice which speaks to the tension of guilt and forgiveness need not necessarily be a Christian voice. In the years of the Stalinist terror in Russia between 1935 and 1940, the poet Anna Akhmatova spent many hours trying to find out something about the fate of her friend Nikolai Punin and her son Lev Gumilev. In *Requiem* in 1957 she wrote:

> In the fearful years of the Yezhov terror I spent seventeen months in prison queues in Leningrad. One day somebody 'identified' me. Beside me, in the queue, there was a woman with blue lips. She had, of course, never heard of me; but she suddenly came out of that trance so common to us all and whispered in my ear (everyone spoke in whispers there): 'Can you describe this?' And I said 'Yes, I can'. And then something like the shadow of a smile crossed what had once been her face. (1976:23)

Akhmatova's husband, Nikolai Gumilev, was shot as a 'counterrevolutionary' in August 1921 (a move to 'rehabilitate' him was begun in April 1986); Nikolai Punin and Lev Gumilev were arrested in the purges of the 1930's. Punin was released quickly , but Lev Gumilev was arrested twice more and was not finally released till 1956. Akhmatova saw the beginnings of the great siege of Leningrad before she and other writers were evacuated to safer territory. Through the years of the terror and the war and the post-war purges the greatest burden for those who waited was the not knowing, the records withheld, the parcels returned to the senders, the sense of being in a world deliberately turned to disorder.

The power of the human spirit to resist disorder, to express the inexpressible, is, among others, the work of the poet. The power of the poet is to assert being, love, memory, against all that the false orders of the world can do. In *Requiem* she says that if the Russian state should ever put up a memorial to her, 'I consent to that honour', but only on the condition that the monument should not be in any of the places where she had been happy.

> But here, where I stood for three hundred hours
> And where they never, never opened the doors for me.
> (1976:32)

How far is it possible to speak specifically of 'Christian' ethics, in the light of these experiences? The experience of suffering and the response of outrage and of hope has been common to all human beings, as also has the guilt of what has been done. Would it not be more satisfactory to talk of human ethics and of human responsibility?

The answer is both a 'yes' and a 'no'.

It is a 'yes' in so far as the whole history of the putting into context of Christian ethics shows the need to acknowledge a common human base. The Christian faith has to be seen today as one claim among others to discern the needs of persons within a wider knowledge of order and of disorder. What may be specific to the Christian version of this claim is the sense of an empowerment which penetrates the cosmic order itself, through the sign of the crucified man, which asserts that the being of God both suffers with and redeems the suffering of every created being. To say that the whole cosmos can be experienced as suffering and directing and personal is a strange claim. Moreover, it leads to strange demands for the exercise of forgiveness and caring love, even for those who are enemies. Kim Malthe-Bruun, a young Danish seaman who was arrested in April 1945, and tortured for being part of a resistance communications link with Sweden, wrote before his death that the waiting was worse than the torture itself. 'One other strange thing', he wrote, 'I felt absolutely no hatred. Something happened to my body: it was only the body of a boy, and it reacted as such. But my soul was occupied with something completely different'. In a later letter he reflected, 'Since then I have often thought of Jesus. I can well understand the measureless love he felt for all men, and especially for those who took part in driving the nails into his hands. From the moment when he left Gethsemane, he stood high above all passion . . .' (Gollwitzer, 1958:80-81).

The experience of the extreme moment stands as a challenge to consider the possibilities of all moments. Christian faith does not claim a complete set of answers to all ethical problems. It claims only the presence of Spirit to enlighten and empower those who are open to such power. Such a claim needs the critical context of a community to keep it steady. But if Christian ethics forgets the power of Spirit in persons, it loses spiritual vision and is too much at the mercy of historical circumstances. Without the vision, the church itself becomes part of the problem.

(iv) **The Spiritual Vision**

The radical tradition of Christian spirituality, which asserts the direct knowledge of God in the soul, resurfaced in a new form in Protestantism. The radicals of the Reformation were feared because they showed that the rejection of the authority of Rome could lead to the rejection of all authority, both spiritual and political. Yet the radicals' revolt was a direct descendant of the challenge to authority inherent in mediaeval mysticism. As Steven Ozment comments, 'It fed on the de facto possibility of the exceptional, on God's freedom to communicate immediately with men, to speak more conclusively in the depths of the individual heart than through all the official writings and ceremonies of even the most holy institution' (1973:1).

Though the older texts such as the *Theologia Deutsch*, edited by Luther, never entirely disappeared, this radical Protestant tradition resurfaced in new writers, such as John Bunyan in England, whose work *The Pilgrim's Progress* became a classic text for almost everyone who could read. The foundation of the most influential new movement in spirituality, however, was laid by Jacob Boehme. Boehme was born in Silesia in 1575 and trained as a

217

shoemaker. As a result of visionary experiences he began to write a mixture of philosophy and theology not unlike the writing of Meister Eckhart but in the context of a dynamic, though strangely-expressed, theology of the relationship between the individual, the natural cosmos and the wisdom of God. In the language of alchemists and astrologers he rediscovered and described the divine spark in a humanity called to be united to the uncreated God. Within the strangeness of Boehme's thought there was a profoundly democratic ideal.

Boehme influenced the Quakers and other movements, but the most dramatic effect he had was on the English writer, William Law. Law was a priest and a Fellow of Emmanuel College, Cambridge, and was sufficiently stiff in his principles to refuse to conform to the oath of allegiance to the Hanoverian succession required in 1714. His early writing on personal piety was greatly admired by John Wesley. When Law came to read Boehme's *Aurora* it changed his life. In two works, *The Spirit of Prayer*, published in 1749-1750, and *The Spirit of Love*, published in 1752-1754, Law expounded Boehme's doctrine of universal love. In *The Spirit of Prayer* he argued that the individual human being had the possibility of direct union with God, because there was already a spark of the divine in every human being. The significance of the divine within the human was primarily that it set a spiritual task for the individual. What mattered was first of all to recognize the divine within the self and then to submit the self increasingly to it. This recognition required a work on the part of the human being to make it effective.

Law was convinced of the necessity of discipline or mortification. The way of union with God was not an escape, a fantasy or an easy alternative. The light and spirit of God which was within the person desired union with the eternal Light and Spirit which was the Divine Nature, but the woman or man must change for this to be possible. A grain of wheat must die in order that the plant might grow from it. 'I shall only observe, that we may here see the true Ground, and absolute Necessity, of that dying to ourselves, and to the World, to which our Blessed Lord so constantly calls all his followers' (Part One II; 1969:48).

As with the sixteenth century radicals, this was no simple individualism: a change in the relation of the self to God was the way of bringing about the whole kingdom of God. 'This is Christianity, a spiritual Society, not because it has no worldly Concerns, but because all its Members, as such, are born of the Spirit, kept alive, animated and governed by the Spirit of God' (Part One II; 1969:55). Only this way of recognition, mortification and union could show what true love of neighbour was. It was only by giving up of the self and by union with the love of God that human beings could become in any way effective in this world. Renunciation of the self committed the person deeply to this world, for now it could be seen as it truly was, creation in the image of God.

So far this teaching, which was also the teaching of the Quakers, was not very different from the nature mysticism expressed a century before by Thomas Traherne. But Traherne, though he gave verbal recognition to the fact of redemption, seemed to regard sin as a failure of knowledge rather than a failure of will. Law recognized evil as an act of will, 'the great Apostasy from the Life of God in the soul' (Part One II; 1969:55). He recognized also the theoretical possibility of a choice for hell instead of heaven, 'to become either an eternal partaker of a Divine Life with God, or to have an hellish Eternity among fallen angels!' (Part One I; 1969:17); but his overwhelming impression was that there was no wrath in God. Wrath dwelt only in the created order. 'Nature and Creature is the only *Source* from whence, and the *Seat* in which, Wrath, Pain, and Vexation can dwell' (Part One I; 1969:29). The Holy Trinity, being all goodness and light, could will no ill to any existence. Only the human will to be separate from that Light could create harm, and only for as long as it maintained that stance. 'For the Love which God bears to the Soul, his eternal, never-ceasing Desire to enter into it, to dwell in it, and open the Birth of his Holy Word, and Spirit in it, stays no longer, than till the Door of the Heart opens for him' (Part Two Second Dialogue; 1969:120).

What Law affirmed was neither the total depravity nor the total goodness of the human being, but the presence in the human being of both an inherent spark of divinity and an inherent depravity or selfishness. The task of being human was the task of willing the one to take over from the other, so that each part of the cosmos could take its proper place in the Kingdom of God. The satisfaction given by Jesus was the wiping-out of sin in the human being by union with himself. The atonement was not a satisfaction given to God but a renewing of the human being. As he wrote in *The Spirit of Love*, 'The whole Truth therefore of the Matter is plainly this, Christ given *for us*, is neither more nor less, than Christ given *into us* '(Part Two Second Dialogue; 1969:235). As Law's biographer, J. H. Overton, remarked, 'Law's views on the Atonement were more obnoxious to his contemporaries than any other of his peculiar sentiments' (1881:266).

Yet Law was reaffirming the discovery of Julian of Norwich, that the primary fact about the existence of the universe was the overwhelming love of God rather than the barrier created by sin. In a complex way the tradition passed into the work of William Blake, who discovered Boehme through Law's work of translation. Blake, however, was almost overwhelmed by the harshness of the social conditions in which he lived. In the twentieth century the voice of Christian spirituality has become the voice of freedom. Steve Biko's claim that 'Freedom is the ability to define oneself with one's possibilities held back not by the power of other people over one but only by one's relationship to God and to natural surroundings' (1973:41) is a claim not only for Black liberation but for all human liberation. The affirmation of the individual requires also the affirmation of the whole human race. The American Cistercian monk Thomas Merton described his own change of consciousness when the monastic world first opened out for him.

> In Louisville, at the corner of Fourth and Walnut, in the center of the shopping district, I was suddenly overwhelmed with the realization that I loved all those people, that they were mine and I theirs, that we could not be alien to one another even though we were total strangers . . . It was like waking from a dream of separateness, of spurious self-isolation in a special world, the world of renunciation and

supposed holiness . . . This sense of liberation from an illusory difference was such a relief and such a joy to me that I almost laughed aloud. And I suppose my happiness could have taken form in the words: "Thank God, thank God that I *am* like other men, that I am only a man among others". (1977:153-154)

He commented further, 'But you cannot tell people that they are all going around shining like the sun'.

Twentieth century spirituality has come to understand that the Kingdom of God is addressed first to the oppressed, not first to those who would do something for them. Each person must face the challenge of that kingdom to become a self before God in a specific cultural and religious context. The challenge of the sign of the resurrection is to live with God's power within the conditions that afflict the human race. The rescue of society as a whole must begin from the creation of the free person within the present conditions. The worst state of the human race is self-oppression, which is not to think oneself capable of this liberating power.

It is in spirituality that the tension of love and guilt is resolved. Not intellectual argument, but the affirmation of the presence of God in all experiences gives the power to make ethical decisions in order to change experience itself. In this there is an element of 'substitution'. But it is now not a once-for-all act of substitution by the Son of God, overruling all human misdeeds, but an action by the man Jesus of Nazareth in which all human beings can participate. Christian ethics is and must be deeply rooted in this personal act, however far outward it reaches into social institutions.

The notions of wrath, of judgment and of hell, which have played so large a part in Christian imagery over the centuries, and which have distressed such thinkers as Julian of Norwich and William Law, have no place in a theology of atonement in their crude form, as punishments for disobedience to the church on earth, or as judgments of an inscrutable God on those 'elected' to damnation.

Yet the images in all their crudeness portray an ineluctable fact. The gift of love is given to be used. To refuse to use it must affect who I am. If the task is to explore my human potential, the refusal of this task must hamper, limit or destroy that potential. The unmaking of the self may truly be the punishment given by love. Such a possibility is the price that must be paid for the possibility of freely joining in the act of creation. The emptying of the self must come, either as a free act towards another person, creating growth, or as a refusal to give. The negative self-emptying is its own sufficient punishment.

At the same time it is also possible that nothing created will be lost for ever. The reason for this is the imbalance between the effects of good and the effects of evil. What is done well is always a permanent gain. What is done out of evil can still be recovered in the future though not in the same form, and perhaps at a higher price. It is not death or pain that hamper the process. All of us must die, and all pain passes when life in the material creation is over. What hampers the process is only one thing — the refusal to forgive. And for that infinite time may perhaps be given. What is certain is the offer, at every moment, of the freedom to forgive. It is the judgment by *potential* that is the characteristic of Christian ethical judgment. This is not a claim about what Christians have in fact done, but a claim about what the sign of Jesus commits us to do, whether we are currently capable of it or not.

The divine power is a mercy without end, but it always waits upon the human decision. This is the terrible responsibility of ethics. The key to what happens in 'salvation' must lie in what happens at the individual level as well as at the cosmic level. The act of love that was the crucifixion implies that the one who accepts the love must go through the same gate.

The conclusion can only be, therefore, that theology has been wrong about the direction in which the price of atonement was paid. The death of Jesus was not a satisfaction paid to God, but a price paid to human beings for their inability to love. Human violence, rage and repression demanded the cross. The lesson of Christian spirituality is that the unchanging love of God has been ready from before the creation to pay that price, because the good of the human race, as of any part of the cosmos, is the good of the whole cosmos. As Wolfhart Pannenberg has remarked, 'It was not so much God who had to be reconciled, but the world' (1983:42).

(v) The Paradox of Grace

Western theology has concentrated too much on sin and on atonement for sin. It has even been suspicious of its own spirituality because of the possible tension between the affirmation of love and the recognition of the reality of sin. The western tradition is deeply rooted in the recognition of the death of Jesus as the basis of all knowledge and action. Augustine of Hippo wrote that 'It was by a divine justice that the human race was delivered into the devil's power; the sin of the first man was passed on from the very beginning to everyone born as a result of intercourse between the sexes and the debt of the first parents became binding on all their posterity' (*On the Trinity* XIII; Wiles and Santer, 1975:115). Human beings belonged appropriately to the devil because of their sin — with Augustine's own addition that the first sin of Eve and Adam was passed on to their descendants through sexual intercourse.

What rescued the human race was an act of justice. The devil killed Jesus, though no sin could be found in him. 'So it is unquestionably just that the debtors whom he was holding should be allowed to go free on the strength of their believing in the one whom he killed despite his having no debt' (1975:117). In choosing to catch the devil on a point of justice, and not simply overcoming evil with power, God preserved the priority of justice over power, 'so that men too in imitation of Christ should seek to conquer the devil by justice and not by power' (1975:116). Even the devil was to be treated with justice as a person.

This 'ransom' theory of the sign of the crucified and risen man was the predominant explanation for a thousand years. Other theories lived alongside it: that the death of Jesus was a sacrifice on the analogy of Jewish liturgical sacrifice; and that Christ was the leader of the angelic forces of justice in a cosmic battle against the demonic forces of disorder. These were and are still powerful images.

At the beginning of the new millennium Anselm of Canterbury, in *Cur Deus Homo?* presented a subtler view of Augustine's theory. Here it was not the devil's power that had to be broken so much as God's justifiable anger that had to be satisfied. God the Trinity, like a feudal lord, demanded certain obligations from his subjects in return for his gifts. For subjects to disobey was an insult to God's honour. The 'satisfaction', as in a knightly encounter, might in some circumstances be given by a third party. The disobedience of the whole human race was so great a matter that only God's own Son could take on this burden. So Jesus took over the human duty of obedience to God the Father and created the 'satisfaction' of God's anger for all who acknowledged the new claim of Jesus to their obedience.

The weakness of Anselm's theory was that it could be read as simply a matter of external obedience. A human act of will to submit to God's just claim was enough for salvation. But the Incarnation was also an act of love. Peter Abelard extended atonement theory by stressing again what Augustine had also felt, the greatness of God's seeking love that came in Jesus' decision to go forward even to crucifixion for the sake of lost humanity. Only the experience of being deeply loved can move us to love so much in return. This psychological theory of atonement did not replace the objective theory so much as supplement it by a credible account of why one should move on to Jesus' side of the equation of justice and of power. As F. W. Dillistone remarks, 'In reality Abelard marks the transition from an outlook which saw God dealing with humanity as a *whole*, either through a legal transaction or through a mystical transfusion, to one in which the ethical and psychological qualities of *the individual within the community* began to receive fuller recognition' (1968:325).

The problem with the traditional story is that there is a conflict between the moral judgment of God the Father, that humanity deserves to be punished, and the judgment of God the Son, that it is proper for humanity to be saved. The tension can be seen clearly when we look at one of the best modern attempts to deal with the claim that the action of Jesus was to substitute himself for us.

In *The Atonement and the Modern Mind*, published in 1903, James Denney set out to defend what he took to be the full Biblical doctrine of the atonement, while at the same time taking account of the current understandings of biology, philosophy, history and Biblical studies. He was not concerned to adjust the atonement to the modern mind, but to explain it in terms which would be comprehensible and which would link up with the concepts being developed in other studies. Essentially Denney put forward an ethical view of the atonement. He stated first of all that the atonement is the most important of Christian truths: 'It determines more than anything else our conceptions of God, of man, of history, and even of nature; it determines them for we must bring them all in some way into accord with it' (1903:1).

The definition of the doctrine was simple: 'Christ died for our sins'. The forgiveness came about only through the death. 'The sum of His relation to sin is that He died for it. God forgives, but this is the way in which His forgiveness comes. He forgives freely, but it is at this cost to Himself and to the Son of His love' (1903:11). This is the doctrine of the atonement which Denney wished to defend and his concern was to commend it to the modern mind, not to investigate whether it was a tenable doctrine.

The relation of Christ to us, said Denney, was both personal and ethical. It was personal because it was too intimate to be expressed fully by more formal terms; but it was ethical because it was based on notions of justice and of obligation, and not on mere feeling. The universe had a moral constitution as it had a physical constitution, and this moral constitution had been upset by sin. Denney denied any necessity to account for the origin of sin, though he tended in fact to account for it by a concept of individual evolution and fall. The result of sin was a bad conscience. This was not only an internal sense of guilt, but also a disordering of the relations between the whole of a human being and the whole system of nature in which she or he lived: 'What we have to understand is that when a man sins he does

225

something in which his whole being participates, and that the reaction of God against his sin is a reaction in which he is conscious, or might be conscious, that the whole system of things is in arms against him' (1903:60). Because of this interconnection of spirit and flesh, humanity and nature, the penalties could not be purely spiritual, so the New Testament declared a connection between sin and death. 'Forgiveness is mediated through Christ, but specifically through His death. He died for our sins: if we can be put right with God apart from this, then, St Paul tells us, He died for nothing' (1903:63). The story of Eve and Adam and the serpent (Genesis 3) was not to be interpreted as an explanation of the origin of physical death, but as the work of conscience indicating its own sense of despair. The story was myth, but a myth rooted in a real psychological and physical experience.

Denney summarized his developed doctrine of atonement as being neither 'naturalistic' nor 'sentimental', but as both objective and subjective together.

> The New Testament does not teach, with the naturalistic or the legal mind, that forgiveness is impossible; neither does it teach, with the sentimental or lawless mind, that it may be taken for granted. It teaches that forgiveness is mediated to sinners through Christ, and specifically through His Death . . . . It is possible on these terms, and it becomes actual as sinful men open their hearts in penitence and faith to this marvellous revelation, and abandon their sinful life unreservedly to the love of God in Christ who died for them. (1903:80-81)

The problem of Denney's position was to give a moral content to the experience of substitution. 'The doctrine of Atonement current in the Church in the generation preceding our own answered frankly that in His atoning work Christ is our substitute. He comes in our nature, and He comes into our place' (1903:93). Immediately he saw the problem that this talk of substitution could be read as talk of the transfer of merit and that this would be to treat human nature in the sub-personal category of book-keeping rather than the category of personal relations. 'The credit, so to speak, of one person in the moral sphere cannot become that of another, apart from moral conditions' (1903:95). Without the work of Christ there was no possibility of forgiveness, but even to use the word 'representative' of Jesus was unsatisfactory, because it implied that in Christ the human race died for itself. The gospel was that in the first place we are without Christ: 'the fundamental fact of the situation is that, to begin with, Christ is *not* ours, and we are not one with Him' (1903:98).

Yet it turned out that he had a use for the word 'representative' as describing what happens after human beings have accepted the Atonement. In the first place Jesus was our substitute, 'God's gift to humanity'. But this was not the whole story. 'And when men are won . . . They begin to feel that what He has done for them must not remain outside of them, but be reproduced somehow in their own life' (1903:100). The effectiveness of the atonement lay in its power to motivate human beings to accept that they were forgiven. The action needed to be understood as both objective and subjective, done by Christ objectively, but needing to be accepted in the heart of the believer. This he described as a moral union.

In choosing the concept of a moral union, however, Denney seems to have put himself up against a blank wall — for a moral union, on his terms, could not be more than the following of an example, which was clearly not the sort of atonement that he had in mind. By stopping his concept of substitution short of the concept of incorporation, Denney failed to solve the moral problem. Yet he had a concept of incorporation clearly present, and in the end it was to the possibility of real sharing in love that he appealed.

> The love which can literally go out of itself and make the burden of others its own is the radical principle of all the genuine and victorious morality in the world. And to say that love cannot do any such thing, that the whole formula of morality is, every man shall bear his own burden, is to deny the plainest facts of the moral life. (1903:103)

A hesitation about accepting this point lies at the root of the whole western tradition of theology. For Augustine of Hippo, the first great theologian of the western church, never came fully to see that the unmerited gift of grace from God to sinful human beings was a gift of love to the human being as she or he now is; not to a phantasm to which God gives flesh and blood by the gift of grace, but to an existence which is already in the Spirit by virtue of being created, sinner as he or she may be.

But whatever responsibility Augustine might bear for development of the doctrine of original sin, his primary concern was with the love of God. The aim of human life was communion with the divine, through a reconciliation which came on God's initiative alone, by the action of the Holy Spirit.

> Through that which is common to the Father and the Son, They have willed that we should have communion with one another and with Them, that we should be brought together into one through That one Gift which is of Them Both — the Holy Spirit, God and God's Gift. By that Gift are we reconciled to the Divine and made to delight therein.
> (*Serm.* 71.18, quoted in Burnaby, 1938:117)

Throughout his life this vision of the unity of creation and creator remained a major driving force. He understood the saving power of the incarnate Christ as being in the action of the Incarnation, which by the gift of the Spirit opens the way to our participation in the divine life of the Trinity. Indeed, Augustine saw this love as God's intention towards us from before the Creation:

> The love of God is incomprehensible, but it is unchangeable, He has not begun to love us since we have been reconciled to Him through the blood of His Son. He loved us before the foundation of the world, so that we too might share sonship with the Only-Begotten, before we were anything at all.
> (*In Jo. Ev.* Tr. 110.6, in Burnaby, 1938:170)

This continuing intention of God towards us, even in our present sinfulness, was intelligible only through the paradox of grace:

both faith and right action were gifts of the Spirit, but both were also ours, because of the need for our free consent to the gift. In this sense 'grace' and 'merit' were different words for the same experience. John Burnaby comments:

> But this means that grace and merit are inseparable; for hunger and thirst after righteousness is nothing else than that love of God with all our heart, with all our soul, and with all our mind, which Christ has taught us is the way to inherit eternal life. *This is life eternal, to know Thee the true God.* And that is 'the whole reward in whose promise we rejoice; but the reward cannot precede the deserving of it, nor be given to man before he is worthy' (*De Mor. Eccl.* 47). So Augustine had written shortly after his baptism, and so he believed after all the controversies of the years that followed. It was life more than controversy that taught him to understand how both the faith which makes love possible, and the love which energises faith and 'merits' eternal life, are the gifts of God. (1938:241)

So, finally, it was in the eschatology of love that Augustine found the solution to the paradox of grace. The final work of man was praise: it was not that in heaven there was a reward for a good life lived on earth, but that heaven was praise and that the praise was the reward, and that the praise could be begun now, in this life ('praise' including the action of love towards our fellow human beings). But there was another paradox at the heart of Augustine's thought: that in the foreknowing of God this loving call to praise was set to fail, first for all human beings in the fall of Adam, and then in the failure of many to respond to the gift of grace. For some, the suffering of Christ was indeed in vain. The God in whom there is no wrath, but only sorrow at the separation caused by sin, who calls us to participation, through the Spirit, in the life of the Godhead, was present in Augustine. But the moral problem — how can we be called to such bliss when we are sinners? — was beyond solution in Augustine's terms. The daring of the Greek Fathers, who could speak of a process of 'deification' of humanity, did not enter into the theology of the western church.

The notion of the personal in ethics today requires a return to that Greek tradition, beginning with Paul's teaching on the Second Adam who is the new humanity. 'If it is certain that death reigned over everyone as the consequence of one man's fall, it is even more certain that one man, Jesus Christ, will cause everyone to reign in life who receives the free gift that he does not deserve, of being made righteous' (Rom. 5.17). Paul's theory of the parallel between Christ and Adam was developed by the Greek theologians as the doctrine of 'recapitulation'. J. N. D. Kelly summarizes it as the claim that 'Just as all men were somehow present in Adam, so they are, or can be, present in the second Adam, the man from heaven. Just as they were involved in the former's sin, with all its appalling consequences, so they can participate in the latter's death and ultimate triumph over sin, the forces of evil and death itself' (1958:377).

The problem of the existence of sin then becomes taken up into a theology of a creative process of development for the new humanity. This same theology has been developed more fully in Orthodox thinking. Paulos Gregorios writes of Gregory of Nyssa that already in the fourth century he had a theology which was consonant with the notion of evolution.

> Of course, he could not put forward a scientifically-based theory of the unity of all life and of progression in the character of the species. Nevertheless, he is able to say that organic life is a single whole, that the impulse of life ascended gradually from plants to animals to humanity, and that human nature incorporates the vegetative, the animal and the rational. All elements in the created universe are both directly dependent on God for their very existence, and also totally interlinked with each other. (1978:64-65)

Humanity is created in the image of God in order to represent nature to God and God to nature. 'The universe reveals its full nature only when it brings forth man; and after it has done so, God does not discard it, for it is on the plant of the universe that the human fruit subsists' (1978:64). It is precisely in this that the ethical occurs. To be the conscious power which exists between

God and nature requires freedom; but this also means that the effecting of the good depends on humanity's free choice.

Consequently the work of mediation is understood anew in Christ, as humanity's work, but now assured of its completion. Christ is the *pleroma*, the fullness of creation. 'Christ, together with the new humanity — the "total Christ" — is the true *pleroma* that fills the gap between God's being and the universe, and participates fully in both' (1978:66). The universe is in a process of the unfolding of the fullness of humanity as originally conceived by the creator. 'History, then, is the springtime of the Spirit. It is the time for ploughing by repentance and for sowing seed by heeding the word of God. History is certainly not the final reality, but neither is it meaningless illusion' (1978:67).

So Christian faith is fundamentally an ethical commitment. The cross provides the nature of ethical action, showing a way through the gate of death to new life in the present world. This ethic is not primarily a matter of setting out rules. The 'Kingdom of God' is God's activity of ruling, and the criterion of moral value is the willingness to participate in that action, not a contingent perception of the necessity of particular human actions. It is certainly important to know, contingently, what actions are required, and the next business of Christian ethics is to make suggestions to this end. But first the general principle must be established. As Victor Furnish has written:

> The love Jesus commanded, be it directed towards the 'neighbor' or toward the 'enemy', is understood in just one way: as active good will toward the other, as my affirmation of him as a person who stands or falls quite apart from what I think of him, as my acknowledgement of our common humanity and our common dependence upon One whose judgment and mercy is over all, and as my commitment to serve him in his need. (1973:195)

The context for Christian ethics is not a rule-book, but the eucharistic meal. In the taking and breaking of bread and in the pouring of wine, the Christian community affirms the paradox of death and new life. In the sharing of bread and wine and in the sharing of the peace, it affirms the communal risen life. The communal action affirms that the energy of God permits no limit to the possibilities of the future. It affirms also that forgiveness is both God's business, and its own, and that its task is to share the blessing and the peace, in word and deed, with the whole of creation. The balance of the human and the divine which exists in the eucharist is the balance which should exist in all human dealings with the created order. As Paulos Gregorios says, 'Our mastery of the universe is like the mastery of our bodies; it is not that we may have it for our own use, but that we may give nature, as our extended body, into the hands of the loving God in the great mystery of the eucharistic self-offering'. Only through worship can we know how to deal with ourselves and with the creation. 'The mastery of nature must be held within the mystery of worship. Otherwise we lose both mastery and mystery' (1978:89). Only so can person and community and cosmos become the unity they are intended to be.

(vi) An Ethic for the New Humanity

It has been clear throughout this study that Christian ethics requires a combination of vision and discipline. There is in Proverbs a verse much-quoted in the King James version, 'Where there is no vision, the people perish' (Prov. 29.18). In the Jerusalem Bible the complete verse reads:

> Where there is no vision the people get out of hand;
> blessed are they who keep the Precept.

Vision, or prophecy, is always linked with keeping the Law. Vision is not an absence of discipline, but the basis for it. For vision and discipline are part of the same action, discipline being the means by which a vision is brought to reality and vision being the purpose for which we may be justified in demanding obedience to law.

The balance of vision and discipline in the Christian life is called *ascesis*, originally the training required to learn a craft or to be proficient in athletics. Where the craft worker aims to produce a useful piece of furniture or the athlete to win a competition, Christian *ascesis* aims to bring spirit and body, will and desire into such balance that every human purpose may be directed to one end, which is the fulfilment of the kingdom of God. So the discipline required for the individual person is to be conformed to the vision of Christ for action together with others for the salvation of the whole cosmos.

In every area of Christian ethics this discipline has required reflection upon the vision of what might be possible and upon the steps needed to bring the vision about. Because sexual desire is the most immediate and powerful challenge to the balance of *ascesis*, attention has been concentrated upon it most of all. Yet sexual desire is in itself a positive thing. It requires only direction towards the covenantal love which is expressed in faithfulness and loving-kindness. That this should focus on marriage and procreation was made inevitable by the facts of sexuality and child-upbringing. Now that our civilization has effectively separated sex from the creation of new lives a new criterion has become necessary for the covenantal nature of love: not that it should involve the institution of marriage but that it should renounce exploitation, which is the use of one for another's pleasure without concern for the full humanness of the other. In the sexual revolution of the 1960's, the working party report *Towards a Quaker View of Sex* was one of the first documents to offer the criterion of absence of exploitation as a Christian standard. Today one might wish to put more emphasis on the positive aspect of sexuality as a potential for further growth in relationship, but the basic change from an institutional rule about marriage to a concern for the quality of relationships has set up the vision of what a person may become as the fundamental principle of Christian ethics. The specifics are, of course, another matter. Homosexuality, single parenting and divorce may be treated as questions of pastoral care rather than of immutable principle, and pastoral care is a matter of leading gently forwards, not of coercion through the moral law (Avis, 1989; Coleman, 1989; Woodward, 1990).

The theme of property also directly affects the balance of *ascesis*, even more directly than sexuality, because attention to dead objects leads away from spirit more directly than attention to living persons. Attachment to possessions must be fatal to any attempt at Christian *ascesis*, because it removes the possibility that vision, which comes through Spirit, can make any entry at all. So the traditional monastic practice of poverty, difficult as it was to keep up in practice, was valued not as an achievement for its own sake, but simply as a means of clearing the ground for the vision of what could be done with so much time and energy.

Similarly, the traditional reserve about institutional power, whether in the family, in the state, or intermediate institutions, was a reserve about blocking the sources of vision. The desire for power at any level is a lust which destroys vision and discipline together. It is the most dangerous of all temptations and is the reason why humility, the greatest of the Christian virtues, is also the most under-rated and indeed unknown of the virtues.

Humility is the sense of the self as held in balance by God, not by its own achievement but through the gift of love. Indeed it could be said quite simply to be 'the sense of the self', the only way in which we can know who we are, rather than what we want to be or what we have forced upon us by others. Humility is the centering of the self in a balance held by God, without the props of possessions or conquests, sexual or political. It is initially a painful state because it involves true knowledge of the self in relation to others, but this pain is essential to growth.

To have confidence in the personal task also involves having confidence in a vision of the whole. This is where the problem of Christian ethics for the twenty-first century must lie. In the twentieth century we have taken the enormous step of letting the whole social context become the agenda for Christian action. No ethic is valid today unless it recognizes the centrality of the theme of liberation from oppression. It is a step which has come late in Christian history, as a result of the vast enlargement of practical human possibilities brought about by the scientific and technological revolutions. The sense of hope which has informed both socialism and Christian contextual theology has been based upon a very real human success.

Yet it has now become clear that science and technology are

incapable of producing a lasting moral vision and that this has been true as much under socialism as under capitalism, though socialism at least has the virtue of asking moral questions about the organization of society. For moral vision arises from the intuitive and poetic capability of the human spirit, of which religion is also a part. In the new century there must be a new moral vision, this time for all humanity.

The attempt to place all human experience within a single frame of reference broke down long ago. The problem of the modern experience of the world is no longer that created by the forced imposition of a particular transcendental system. It is rather the problem of the entire absence of a notion of transcendence by which human beings can make sense of what they know. Many Christians would find it tempting to return to an enforced conformity and to the assertion of the ultimacy of one set of values against all others. But the critical spirit of modern human beings is itself the result of the critical heritage of the Jewish and Christian faiths. To go out from the land of one's birth, to question God, to protest, to ask for an answer, all this is the continuing commitment of a pilgrim people. In the New Testament the answer that is given is not a doctrine but a person who joins in our suffering and becomes the source of new life and the sign of the future. Christian practice is defined by the movement from 'This is my beloved son' to 'Why have you forsaken me?' to 'I am the resurrection and the life'. It is a path that needs renewing every day.

To summarize the whole argument, it must be clear that the Christian ethic is a complex of ideas about the cosmos and about human nature. It cannot be put into a single form of 'Do this — do not do that'. But some requirements can be sketched-in as basic principles.

(1) The Christian ethic is about Jesus. In this one human being is united the earliest faith of the Hebrews, that Yahweh works with them for a purpose, and the latest faith of the Gospels, that God is a Trinity of relationship. Only a three-fold imaging, of the resurrection as the promise of life, of the Holy Trinity as the promise of love and of the Kingdom of God as the

promise of the end beginning within history, can create the vision, the power and the purpose for the human action that is now required.

(2) We need to move from biological to moral success. The human race has been a remarkable biological success story. We can live on every part of the planet, from the tops of mountains to the depths of the seas, and even in the airlessness of outer space. But we have now come to the point where the technological extensions of ourselves that enable us to perform these miracles are not enough. Clever and versatile animals as we are, we remain morally and spiritually insecure. Nowhere does this show more clearly than in our inability to recognize ourselves as one people on this earth. Even religious values can block us here.

C. H. Waddington, writing at the end of a life-long career in biology, has suggested that we need to divide our values into three groups. The first group is *universal values*, which promote identification with the whole human race and which put quality of life before the quantity of material goods or the increasing of populations; these values are to be defended at all costs. The second group is *conflicting values*, which disrupt planetary life, such as unrestrained competition and some forms of nationalism; these values are to be rejected, however painful the process. The third group is *free values*, which can be left to individual choice (1978:326). Not even the values of Christianity can be exempt from these criteria.

(3) We have to stop thinking of ourselves simply as reflective minds — as 'believers' — and start thinking of ourselves as doers, and to think of doers as 'persons in relation' in John Macmurray's words. The problem with the word 'faith' is that it tends to make us think of Christianity as a belief rather than as an action. The New Testament is quite clear about this.

> If one of the brothers or one of the sisters is in need of clothes and has not enough food to live on, and one of you says to them, 'I wish you well; keep yourself warm and eat plenty', without giving them these bare necessities of life, then what good is that? Faith is like that: if good works do not go with it, it is quite dead. (James 2.14-17)

(4) Politically it is the task of Christian ethics to question the two great temptations of western society, which are to suppose that success can be attained by pure individualism, and to suppose that the material is the measure of the spiritual. The truth of God is that only by concern for one another's needs can we be human beings and that only by keeping the material in its place as the facilitator of human life, but not the object of it, do we have any chance of learning what the spiritual nature of humanity is.

(5) None of this removes the possibility of tragedy and therefore the need for substitution. We live in the material creation and we live at the hands of one another. As Reinhold Niebuhr has pointed out, our tragedy and our glory are the same thing, that we aim higher than we can attain in history. Patience under adversity, willingness to suffer for the sake of others and the acceptance of contingency constitute the essential ethical training that makes possible the life of Christian action. There is no other promise than this, that the way to life is shown in the way of the crucified.

(6) The whole structure of Christian ethics is therefore built upon the salvation of the individual human being, the just person who lives by faith. This salvation is, and can only be, salvation into responsibility, the responsibility of each human being for the whole of creation. There are thus two aspects to Christian ethics. The first is the aspect within the Christian community which is centered on personal experience of justification by grace through faith, on eucharist and on prayer for the other, especially for the enemy. This is the aspect of preparation. The other is the aspect of action in the world, which is centered on the circumstances in which others, all the others known to us, can arise to the exercise of moral freedom. This is the aspect of final purpose. Both the inner and the outer way come together in the primary image of God as our mother, which is found first in the Book of Hosea.

> When Israel was a child I loved him . . .
> I myself taught Ephraim to walk,

> I took them in my arms,
> yet they have not understood that I was the one looking after
> them...
> I was like someone who lifts an infant against his cheek;
> stooping down to give him his food...
> I am the Holy One in your midst
> and have no wish to destroy. (Hosea 11.1-9)

In the end, ethics is the undertaking of a discipline to change the self and the world. The Christian faith is that only co-operation in the kingdom of God can count as an achievement for the individual. In the kingdom of God we learn to bear one another's burdens, in order that someone else should bear our own. Charles Williams called the ethics of the kingdom of God 'the way of exchange' and argued that the kingdom insists on exchange, or substitution, by prayer, by sharing concern, or compassion, and by every sort of practice, until each and every person is incorporated into the life of the one community (Williams, 1958).

One sin above all, then, stands out as the social sin. It is true that Christianity has no social theory as such, though it inclines towards co-operation rather than coercion and towards the treating of human community with moral seriousness. But one sin stands out as the denial of the kingdom of God in itself, and that is the acceptance of division.

> But now in Christ Jesus, you that used to be so far apart from
> us have been brought very close, by the blood of Christ. For
> he is the peace between us, and has made the two into one
> and broken down the barrier which used to keep them apart,
> actually destroying in his own person the hostility caused by
> the rules and decrees of the Law. (Eph. 2.13, 14)

What Jesus has done between the Jews and the Gentiles he has done, by the same love, between every people on earth. The most basic social creativity of Christianity has been the recognition that there is only one kingdom, stretching from the creation to the eschaton, encompassing every created existence.

Sigmund Freud claimed that the ethics of civilization, in particular the injunction 'Love thy neighbour as thyself', created an impossible burden. 'The commandment is impossible to fulfil; such an enormous inflation of love can only lower its value, not get rid of the difficulty' (1982:80). But it is not a question of 'civilization' making this claim; most of the effort of modern civilization has been put into rejecting it, as was clear in Freud's own time. This is a demand of religion; specifically, of the Christian religion and more specifically of Jesus Christ himself. It is the meaning of the cross. That the demand is made is a measure of how far we have come from our biological origins; that we still find it so difficult is the measure of how far we have to go.

References

Chapter 1
Setting the Scene

BARTH, Karl, 1933. *The Epistle to the Romans*, Oxford University Press.

BARTH, Karl, 1960. 'The Humanity of God' and 'The Gift of Freedom', in *The Humanity of God*, Atlanta, Ga, John Knox Press.

BARTH, Karl, 1981. *Ethics*, T. and T. Clark.

BENTLEY, James, 1982. *Between Marx and Christ: The Dialogue in German-Speaking Europe 1870-1970*, N.L.B.

BIKO, Steve, 1973. 'Black Consciousness and the Quest for a True Humanity', in Basil Moore, editor, *Black Theology: The South African Voice*, C. Hurst.

BOESAK, Allan Aubrey, 1976. *Black Theology, Black Power*, Mowbrays.

BONHOEFFER, Dietrich, 1954. *Life Together*, SCM Press.

BONHOEFFER, Dietrich, 1959. *The Cost of Discipleship*, SCM Press.

BONHOEFFER, Dietrich, 1963. *Ethics*, SCM Press.

BONHOEFFER, Dietrich, 1971. *Letters and Papers from Prison*, SCM Press.

BRUNNER, Emil, 1937. *The Divine Imperative: A Study in Christian Ethics*, Lutterworth Press.

CAMARA, Helder, 1971. *Spiral of Violence*, Sheed and Ward.

GOLLWITZER, Helmut, Käthe Kuhn, and Reinhold Schneider, editors, 1958. *Dying We Live*, Fontana.

GUTIERREZ, Gustavo, 1974. *A Theology of Liberation: History, Politics and Salvation*, SCM Press.

MACKIE, Steven G., 1989. 'God's People in Asia: A Key Concept in Asian Theology', in *Scottish Journal of Theology*, Vol. 42.

MOLTMANN, Jürgen, 1967. *Theology of Hope: On the Ground and the Implications of a Christian Eschatology*, SCM Press.

NIEBUHR, Reinhold, 1932. *Moral Man and Immoral Society: A Study in Ethics and Politics*, New York, Charles Scribner's Sons.

NIEBUHR, Reinhold, 1941/43. *The Nature and Destiny of Man: A*

Christian Interpretation., 2 Vols., New York, Charles Scribner's Sons.

PRESTON, Ronald, H., 1987. *The Future of Christian Ethics*, SCM Press.

RAUSCHENBUSCH, Walter, 1918. *A Theology for the Social Gospel*, New York, Macmillan.

RUETHER, Rosemary Radford, 1983. *Sexism and God-Talk*, SCM Press.

SONG, C. S., 1988. *Theology from the Womb of Asia*, SCM Press.

VATICAN COUNCIL II, 1966. *Gaudium et Spes: The Pastoral Constitution on the Church in the World of Today*, The Catholic Truth Society.

VORGRIMLER, Herbert, editor, 1969. *Commentary on the Documents of Vatican II: Vol. V, Pastoral Constitution on the Church in the Modern World*, Burns and Oates.

WHITE, Ronald C., Jr, 1978. 'Social Reform and the Social Gospel in America', in Julio de Santa Ana, editor, *Separation Without Hope?: Essays on the Relation between the Church and the Poor during the Industrial Revolution and the Western Colonial Expansion*, Geneva, World Council of Churches.

WORLD COUNCIL OF CHURCHES, 1967. *World Conference on Church and Society*, Geneva, July 12-26, 1966: *Christians in the technical and social revolutions of our time*, Geneva, World Council of Churches.

WORLD COUNCIL OF CHURCHES, 1968. *The Uppsala Report 1968, Official Report of the Fourth Assembly of the World Council of Churches*, Uppsala, July 4-20, 1968, Geneva, World Council of Churches.

WORLD COUNCIL OF CHURCHES, 1970. *Fetters of Injustice, Report of an Ecumenical Consultation on Ecumenical Assistance to Development Projects*, 26-31 January, 1970, Montreux, Switzerland, edited by Pamela H. Gruber, Geneva, World Council of Churches.

WORLD COUNCIL OF CHURCHES, 1976. *Breaking Barriers Nairobi 1975, The Official Report of the Fifth Assembly of the World Council of Churches*, Nairobi 23 November — 10 December, 1975, Geneva, World Council of Churches.

WORLD COUNCIL OF CHURCHES, 1980. *Faith and Science in an Unjust World, Report of the World Council of Churches' Conference on Faith, Science and the Future,* Massachusetts Institute of Technology, USA, 12-24 July, 1979, 2 Vols., Geneva, World Council of Churches.

Chapter 2
The Bible as the Source of Authority in Ethics

(Biblical quotations here and throughout are from *The Jerusalem Bible,* by kind permission of Darton, Longman and Todd.)

BIRCH, Bruce C. and Larry L. Rasmussen, 1989. *Bible and Ethics in the Christian Life,* Augsburg, Minn., Augsburg Publishing House.

BRIGHT, John, 1977. *Covenant and Promise,* SCM Press.

CAIRNS, David, 1973. *The Image of God in Man,* Fontana.

CHILDS, Brevard S., 1979. *Introduction to the Old Testament as Scripture,* SCM Press.

DOUGLAS, MARY, 1984. *Purity and Danger: An Analysis of the Concepts of Pollution and Taboo,* Ark Paperbacks.

GASTON, Lloyd, 1979. 'Paul and Torah', in Alan T. Davies, editor, *Anti-Semitism and the Foundations of Christianity,* New York, Paulist Press.

HENGEL, Martin, 1974. *Property and Riches in the Early Church: Aspects of a Social History of Early Christianity,* SCM Press.

HENGEL, Martin, 1975. *Victory over Violence,* SPCK.

HENGEL, Martin, 1977. *Christ and Power,* Christian Journals.

HESCHEL, Abraham I., 1956. 'A Hebrew Evaluation of Reinhold Niebuhr', in Charles W, Kegley and Robert W. Bretall, editors, *Reinhold Niebuhr: His Religious, Social and Political Thought,* New York, Macmillan.

KELSEY, David H., 1975. *The Uses of Scripture in Recent Theology,* SCM Press.

KOSNIK, Anthony, *et. al.,* 1977. *Human Sexuality: New Directions in Catholic Thought,* Search Press.

MARTIN, James D., 1989. 'Israel as a tribal society' in R. E. Clements, editor, *The World of Ancient Israel,* Cambridge University Press.

McDONALD, J. I. H., 1989. *The Resurrection: Narrative and Belief,* SPCK.

MEALAND, David L., 1980. *Poverty and Expectation in the Gospels,* SPCK.

MEEKS, Wayne A., 1983. *The First Urban Christians: The Social World of the Apostle Paul,* Yale University Press.

MEEKS, Wayne A., 1987. *The Moral World of the First Christians,* SPCK.

MOULE, C. F. D., *The Birth of the New Testament,* A. and C. Black.

PERRIN, Norman, 1963. *The Kingdom of God in the Teaching of Jesus,* SCM Press.

PERRIN, Norman, 1976. *Jesus and the Language of the Kingdom,* SCM Press.

ROWLAND, Christopher, 1988. *Radical Christianity: A Reading of Recovery,* Polity Press.

SANDERS, E. P., 1977. *Paul and Palestinian Judaism: A Comparison of Patterns of Religion,* SCM Press.

SANDERS, E. P., 1985. *Jesus and Judaism,* SCM Press.

SCHRAGE, Wolfgang, 1988. *The Ethics of the New Testament,* T. and T. Clark.

SEGAL, Phillip, 1980. *The Emergence of Contemporary Judaism,* Vol. I, *The Foundations of Judaism from Biblical Origins to the Sixth Century A.D., Part One,, From the Origins to the Separation of Christianity,* T. and T. Clark.

SØE, Norman H., 1968. 'The Three "Uses" of the Law', in Gene H. Outka and Paul Ramsey, editors, *Norm and Context in Christian Ethics,* SCM Press.

DE VAUX, Roland, 1961. *Ancient Israel,* Darton, Longman and Todd.

WEBER, Hans-Ruedi, 1989. *Power: Focus for a Biblical Theology,* Geneva, World Council of Churches.

WEDDERBURN, A. J. M., 1978. 'The New Testament as the Church's Book?', in *Scottish Journal of Theology,* Vol. 31, 1978.

WOLFF, Hans Walter, 1974. *Anthropology of the Old Testament*, SCM Press.

Chapter 3
Ethics in the Church

ALLEN, Walter, 1958. *The English Novel*, Penguin Books.

ANON., 1980. *The Theologia Germanica of Martin Luther*, SPCK.

ANON., 1981. *The Cloud of Unknowing*, SPCK.

ATHANASIUS, 1980. *Athanasius: The Life of Antony and the Letter to Marcellinus*, SPCK.

AUGUSTINE OF HIPPO, 1945. *The City of God*, J. M. Dent and Sons.

AUGUSTINE OF HIPPO, 1961. *Confessions*, Penguin Books.

AVILA, Charles, 1983. *Ownership: Early Christian Teaching*, Sheed and Ward.

BAILEY, Derrick Sherwin, 1952. *The Mystery of Love and Marriage*, SCM Press.

BAINTON, Roland H., 1950. *Here I Stand: A Life of Martin Luther*, New York, Mentor Books.

BERNARD, Jacques, 1972. 'Trade and Finance in the Middle Ages 900-1500', in Carlo M. Cipolla, *The Fontana Economic History of Europe*, Vol. 1, *The Middle Ages*, Fontana.

BOSWELL, John, 1980. *Christianity, Social Tolerance and Homosexuality*, University of Chicago Press.

BRONOWSKI, Jacob, 1973. *The Ascent of Man*, BBC Publications.

BROOKE, Christopher N. L., 1978. *Marriage in Christian History*, Cambridge University Press.

BROWN, Peter, 1967. *Augustine of Hippo: A Biography*, Faber and Faber.

BRUNDAGE, James A., 1987. *Law, Sex and Christian Society in Medieval Europe*, University of Chicago Press.

BURNABY, John, 1938. *Amor Dei: A Study of the Religion of St Augustine*, Hodder and Stoughton.

CALVIN, John, 1960. *Institutes of the Christian Religion*, 2 Vols., Philadelphia, The Westminster Press.

CHADWICK, Henry, 1966. *Early Christian Thought and the Classical Tradition: Studies in Justin, Clement and Origen*, Oxford University Press.

CHADWICK, Henry, 1967. *The Early Church*, Penguin Books.

CHRYSSAVIGIS, John, 1989. 'The Sacrament of Marriage: an Orthodox Perspective', in *Studia Liturgica*, Vol. 19, No. 1, 1989.

CIPOLLA, Carlo M., 1972. 'The origins' in Carlo M. Cipolla, editor, *The Fontana Economic History of the Middle Ages*, Vol. 1, *The Middle Ages*, Fontana.

COPLESTONE, F. C., 1955. *Aquinas*, Penguin Books.

D'ENTREVES, A. P., editor, 1948. *Aquinas: Selected Political Writings*, Basil Blackwell.

DILLENBERGER, John, editor, 1961. *Martin Luther: Selections from his Writings*, Garden City, N.Y., Anchor Books.

DUBY, Georges, 1981. *The Age of the Cathedrals: Art and Society, 980-1420*, Croom Helm.

ECKHART, Meister, 1981. *Meister Eckhart: The Essential Sermons, Commentaries, Treatises and Defense*, SPCK.

EVDOKIMOV, Paul, 1985. *The Sacrament of Love: the nuptial mystery in the light of the Orthodox tradition*, St. Vladimir's Seminary Press.

FORELL, George, editor, 1971. *Christian Social Teaching from the Bible to the Present*, Minneapolis, Minn., Augsburg Publishing House.

FOUCAULT, Michel, 1984. *L'Usage des Plaisirs, Histoire de la Sexualité 2*, Paris, Gallimard.

FOUCAULT, Michel, 1985. 'The battle for chastity', in Philippe Ariès and André Béjin, editors, *Western Sexuality*, Basil Blackwell. (This article is excerpted from *The History of Sexuality*, Volume 3.)

FRANCIS OF ASSISI, 1982. *Francis and Clare: The Complete Works*, SPCK.

FREND, W. H. C., 1982. *The Early Church: From the beginnings to 461*, SCM Press.

FREND, W. H. C., 1984. *The Rise of Christianity*, Darton, Longman and Todd.

GILSON, Etienne, 1936. *The Spirit of Mediaeval Philosophy*, Sheed and Ward.

GILSON, Etienne, 1955. *History of Christian Philosophy in the Middle Ages*, Sheed and Ward.

GRANT, Robert M., 1978. *Early Christianity and Society*, Collins.

GREGORY OF NYSSA, 1978. *Gregory of Nyssa: The Life of Moses*, SPCK.

GUSTAFSON, James M., 1978. *Protestant and Roman Catholic Ethics: Prospects for Rapprochement*, SCM Press.

HADEWIJCH, 1980. *Hadewijch: The Complete Works*, SPCK.

HELGELAND, John, Robert J. Daly & J. Patout Burns, 1985. *Christians and the Military: The Early Experience*, SCM Press.

HENGEL, Martin, 1974. *Property and Riches in the Early Church: Aspects of a Social History of Early Christianity*, SCM Press.

HENGEL, Martin, 1977. *Christ and Power*, Christian Journals.

HILDEBRANDT, Franz, 1946. *Melancthon: Alien or Ally?*, Cambridge University Press.

HUYGHE, René, 1962. *Art and the Spirit of Man*, Thames and Hudson.

JANTZEN, Grace M., 1987. *Julian of Norwich: Mystic and Theologian*, SPCK.

JOHN OF THE CROSS, 1935. *The Complete Works of Saint John of the Cross*, Anthony Clarke.

JULIAN OF NORWICH, 1978. *Showings*, SPCK. (Known in other editions as *The Revelations of Divine Love.*)

LANGLAND, William, 1959. *Piers the Plowman*, Penguin Books.

LARNER, Christina, 1984. *Witchcraft and Religion: The politics of popular belief*, Basil Blackwell.

LOHSE, Bernhard, 1986. *Martin Luther: An Introduction to his Life and Work*, T. and T. Clark.

LOSSKY, Vladimir, 1957. *The Mystical Theology of the Eastern Church*, James Clarke.

LOUTH, Andrew, 1981. *The Origins of the Christian Mystical Tradition from Plato to Denys*, Oxford University Press.

MACQUARRIE, John, 1984. *In Search of Deity*, SCM Press.

MAHONEY, John, 1987. *The Making of Moral Theology*, Oxford University Press.

MEALAND, David L., 1980. *Poverty and Expectation in the Gospels*, SPCK.

MEEKS, Wayne A., 1983. *The First Urban Christians: The Social World of the Apostle Paul*, Yale University Press.

MERTON, Thomas, 1974. *The Wisdom of the Desert: Sayings from the Desert Fathers of the Fourth Century*, Sheldon Press.

MOLINARI, Paul, S.J., 1958. *Julian of Norwich: The Teaching of a 14th Century English Mystic*, Longmans, Green.

OSBORNE, Eric, 1976. *Ethical Patterns in Early Christian Thought*, Cambridge University Press.

PAGELS, Elaine, 1988. *Adam, Eve and the Serpent*, Weidenfeld and Nicolson.

PEERS, E. Allison, 1943. *Spirit of Flame: A Study of St John of the Cross*, SCM Press.

ROWLAND, Christopher, 1988. *Radical Christianity : A Reading of Recovery*, Polity Press.

RUPP, Gordon, and Benjamin Drewery, editors, 1970. *Martin Luther*, Edward Arnold.

SANTA ANA, Julio de, 1978. *Good News for the Poor*, Geneva, World Council of Churches.

SOUTHERN, R. W., 1953. *The Making of the Middle Ages*, Hutchinson.

SOUTHERN, R. W., 1970. *Western Society and the Church in the Middle Ages*, Penguin Books.

TAWNEY, R. H., 1938. *Religion and the Rise of Capitalism*, Penguin Books.

TERESA OF AVILA, 1979. *The Interior Castle*, SPCK.

TESELLE, Eugene, 1970. *Augustine the Theologian*, Burns and Oates.

THOMAS à KEMPIS, no date. *The Imitation of Christ*, Thomas Nelson and Sons.

TROELTSCH, Ernst, 1931. *The Social Teaching of the Christian Churches*, George Allen and Unwin.

WEBER, Max, 1930. *The Protestant Ethic and the Spirit of Capitalism*, George Allen and Unwin.

WENDEL, François, 1965. *Calvin: The Origins and Development of his Religious Thought*, Fontana.

WILES, Maurice, 1967. *The Making of Christian Doctrine: A Study in the Principles of Early Doctrinal Development*, Cambridge University Press.

WILES, Maurice, and Mark Santer, editors, 1975. *Documents in Early Christian Thought*, Cambridge University Press.

WILLIAMS, Rowan, 1979. *The Wound of the Spirit: Christian Spirituality from the New Testament to St John of the Cross*, Darton, Longman and Todd.

WOMER, Jan L., editor, 1987. *Morality and Ethics in Early Christianity*, Philadelphia, Fortress Press.

ZIZIOULAS, John D., 1985 *Being as Communion: Studies in Personhood and the Church*, Darton, Longman and Todd.

Chapter 4
The Challenge from the Modern World

ALLISON, C. F., 1966. *The Rise of Moralism*, SPCK.

ARBLASTER, Anthony, 1984. *The Rise and Decline of Western Liberalism*, Basil Blackwell.

ARNOLD, Matthew, 1939. *Arnold: Poetry and Prose*, Oxford University Press.

BARNETT, S. A., 1958. *A Century of Darwin*, Heinemann.

BARTHOLOMEW, D. J., 1984. *God of Chance*, SCM Press.

BLAKE, William, 1974. *Blake: Complete Writings*, ed. Geoffrey Keynes, Oxford University Press.

BLURTON JONES, N. G., 1976. 'Growing Points in human ethology: another link between ethology and the social sciences?' in P. P. G. Bateson and R. A. Hinde, editors, *Growing Points in Ethology*, Cambridge University Press.

BRONOWSKI, Jacob, 1972. *William Blake and the Age of Revolution*, Routledge and Kegan Paul.

BUTLER, Joseph, 1953. *Fifteen Sermons Preached at the Rolls Chapel and a Dissertation upon the Nature of Virtue*, G. Bell and Sons.

CASSIRER, Ernst, 1980. *Kant's Life and Thought*, Yale University Press.

DARWIN, Charles, 1968. *The Origin of Species by Means of Natural Selection or The Preservation of Favoured Races in the Struggle for Life*, Penguin Books.

DAWKINS, Richard, 1986. *The Blind Watchmaker*, Penguin Books.

DESCARTES, René, 1968. *Discourse on Method and the Meditations*, Penguin Books.

DOBZHANSKY, Theodosius, 1958. 'Species after Darwin' in S. A. Barnett, editor, *A Century of Darwin*, Heinemann.

DOUGLAS, Mary, 1984. *Purity and Danger: An Analysis of the Concepts of Pollution and Taboo*, Ark Paperbacks.

DURANT, John, editor, 1985. *Darwinism and Divinity: Essays on Evolution and Religious Belief*, Basil Blackwell.

FORELL, George, editor, 1971. *Christian Social Teaching: A Reader on Christian Social Ethics from the Bible to the Present*, Minneapolis, Augsburg Publishing House.

FRANKLIN, Benjamin, 1961. 'Advice to a Young Tradesman, written by an Old One' in *The Papers of Benjamin Franklin*, Vol. 3, Yale University Press.

GUSTAFSON, James M., 1981. *Theology and Ethics*, Basil Blackwell.

HARRISON, J. F. C., 1984. *The Common People: A History from the Norman Conquest to the Present*, Fontana.

HAWKING, Stephen W., 1988. *A Brief History of Time: From the Big Bang to Black Holes*, New York, Bantam Press.

HAWTHORN, Geoffrey, 1987. *Enlightenment and Despair: A History of Social Theory*, Cambridge University Press.

HUME, David, 1975. *Enquiries Concerning Human Understanding and Concerning the Principles of Morals*, Oxford University Press.

HUME, David, 1978. *A Treatise of Human Nature*, Oxford University Press.

JAMES, Patricia, 1979. *Population Malthus: His Life and Times*, Routledge and Kegan Paul.

KANT, Immanuel, 1934. *Critique of Pure Reason*, Dent.

KANT, Immanuel, 1953. *The Moral Law or Kant's Groundwork of the Metaphysic of Morals*, Hutchinson.

KITCHER, Philip, 1985. *Vaulting Ambition: Sociobiology and the Quest for Human Nature*, Cambridge, Mass., The M.I.T. Press.

LANGLAND, William, 1959. *Piers the Plowman*, Penguin Books.

LOVELL, Bernard, 1979. *In the Centre of Immensities*, Hutchinson.

LUCAS, J. R., 1984. *Space, Time and Causality: An Essay in Natural Philosophy*, Oxford University Press.

LYELL, Sir Charles, 1830-1833. *Principles of Geology, Being an Attempt to Explain the Former Changes of the Earth's Surface by Reference to Causes now in Operation*, John Murray.

McADOO, H. R., 1965. *The Spirit of Anglicanism*, A. and C. Black.

MacINTYRE, Alasdair, 1967. *A Short History of Ethics*, Routledge and Kegan Paul.

MacINTYRE, Alasdair, 1981. *After Virtue: A Study in Moral Theory*, Duckworth.

MARX, Karl, 1983. *The Portable Karl Marx*, edited by Eugene Kamenka, Penguin Books.

MOLTMANN, Jürgen, 1985. *God in Creation: An ecological doctrine of creation*. SCM Press.

MOORE, James R. *The Post-Darwinian Controversies: A study of the Protestant struggle to come to terms with Darwin in Great Britain and America 1870-1900*, Cambridge University Press.

POLKINGHORNE, John, 1988. *Science and Creation: the search for understanding*, SPCK.

RAINE, Kathleen, 1970. *William Blake*, Thames and Hudson.

SALTER, K. W., 1964. *Thomas Traherne: Mystic and Poet*, Edward Arnold.

SANTA ANA, Julio de, 1978. *Separation Without Hope? Essays on the Relation between the Church and the Poor during the Industrial Revolution and the Western Colonial Expansion*, Geneva, World Council of Churches.

SELLA, Dominico, 1974. 'European Industries 1500-1700' in Carlo M. Cippola, editor, *The Fontana Economic History of Europe*, Vol. 2, *The Sixteenth and Seventeenth Centuries*, Fontana.

SKINNER, Andrew, 1975. 'Adam Smith: An Economic Interpretation of History' in Andrew Skinner and Thomas Wilson, editors, *Essays on Adam Smith*, Oxford University Press.

SMITH, Adam, 1950. *An Inquiry into the Nature and Causes of the Wealth of Nations*, 2 Vols., J. M. Dent and Sons.

SMITH, John Maynard, 1975. *The Theory of Evolution*, Pen-

guin Books.

SMITH, Norman Kemp, 1941. *The Philosophy of David Hume: A Critical Study of Its Origins and Central Doctrines*, Macmillan.

STEPHEN, Leslie, 1873. *Essays in Free Thinking and Plain Speaking*, Longmans, Green.

TENNANT, F. R., 1902. *The Origin and Propagation of Sin*, Cambridge University Press.

TENNANT, F. R., 1903. *The Sources of the Doctrines of the Fall and of Original Sin*, Cambridge University Press.

THODAY, J. M., 1958. 'Natural Selection and Biological Progress' in S. A. Barnett, editor, *A Century of Darwin*, Heinemann.

TRAHERNE, Thomas, 1963. *Centuries*, The Faith Press.

WICKHAM, E. R., 1957. *Church and People in an Industrial City*, Lutterworth Press.

WILLIAMS, Bernard, 1978. *Descartes: The Project of Pure Enquiry*, Penguin Books.

WINSTANLEY, Gerrard, 1973. *Winstanley: The Law of Freedom and Other Writings*, Penguin Books.

Chapter 5
Vision and Discipline

AKHMATOVA, Anna, 1976. *Requiem and Poem without a Hero*, translated by D. M. Thomas, Paul Elek.

ANSELM OF CANTERBURY, 1977. *Cur Deus Homo?* Open Court Publishing.

AVIS, Paul, 1989. *Eros and the Sacred*, SPCK.

BAILLIE, D. M., 1956. *God Was in Christ: An Essay on Incarnation and Atonement*, Faber and Faber.

BERGSON, Henri, 1911. *Creative Evolution*, Macmillan.

BETTELHEIM, Bruno, 1986. *The Informed Heart: A study of the psychological consequences of living under extreme fear and terror*, Penguin Books.

BIKO, Steve, 1973. 'Black Consciousness and the Quest for a True Humanity' in Basil Moore, editor, *Black Theology: The South African Voice*, C. Hurst.

BOEHME, Jacob, 1978. *The Way to Christ*, New York, Paulist Press.

BRADLEY, Ian, 1990. *God is Green*, Darton, Longman and Todd.

BRUNER, Jerome, 1986. *Actual Minds, Possible Worlds*, Harvard University Press.

BUBER, Martin, 1959. *I and Thou*, T. and T. Clark.

BUBER, Martin, 1961. 'Dialogue' in *Between Man and Man*, Fontana.

BUNYAN, John, 1985. *The Pilgrim's Progress*, Dent.

BURNABY, John, 1938. *Amor Dei: A Study of the Religion of St Augustine*, Hodder and Stoughton.

COLEMAN, Peter, 1989. *Gay Christians: A Moral Dilemma*, SCM Press.

CROOK, J. H., 1980. *The Evolution of Human Consciousness*, Oxford University Press.

DENNEY, James, 1903. *The Atonement and the Modern Mind*, Hodder and Stoughton.

DILLISTONE, F. W., 1968. *The Christian Understanding of Atonement*, James Nisbet.

DOMINIAN, Jack, 1977. *Proposals for a New Christian Ethic*, Darton, Longman and Todd.

FREUD, Sigmund, 1982. *Civilization and Its Discontents*, The Hogarth Press.

GILSON, Etienne, 1955. *History of Christian Philosophy in the Middle Ages*, Sheed and Ward.

GOLLWITZER, Helmut, Käthe Kuhn and Reinhold, Schneider, editors, 1958. *Dying We Live*, Fontana.

HSU, Francis L. K., 1985. 'The Self in Cross-Cultural Perspective' in Marsella, Anthony J., DeVos, George and Hsu, Francis L. K., editors, *Culture and Self: Asian and Western Perspectives*, Tavistock Publications.

JOHNSON, Frank, 1985. 'The Western Concept of the Self' in Marsella, Anthony J., George De Vos and Francis L. K. Hsu, editors, *Culture and Self*, Tavistock Publications.

KELLY, J. N. D., 1958. *Early Christian Doctrines*, A. and C. Black.

LAW, William, 1969. *The Spirit of Prayer and The Spirit of Love*, James Clarke.

LOCKWOOD, Michael, 1985. 'When does a life begin?' in

Michael Lockwood, editor, *Moral Dilemmas in Modern Medicine,* Oxford University Press.

LUTHER, Martin, editor, 1980. *The Theologia Germanica* (also known as the *Theologia deutsch*), SPCK.

MACMURRAY, John, 1957. *The Self as Agent,* Faber and Faber.

MACMURRAY, John, 1961. *Persons in Relation,* Faber and Faber.

MACQUARRIE, John, 1973. *Existentialism,* SCM Press

MAUSS, Marcel, 1985. 'A Category of the human mind: the notion of self' in Michael Carrithers, Steve Collins and Steven Lukes, editors, *The Category of the Person: Anthropology, philosophy, history,* Cambridge University Press.

MERTON, Thomas, 1977. *Conjectures of a Guilty Bystander,* SPCK.

NIEBUHR, Reinhold, 1941/1943, *The Nature and Destiny of Man: A Christian Interpretation,* 2 Vols. New York, Charles Scribner's Sons.

OVERTON, J. H., 1881. *William Law, Nonjuror and Mystic,* Longmans, Green.

OZMENT, Steven, 1973. *Mysticism and Dissent: Religious Ideology and Social Protest in the Sixteenth Century,* Yale University Press.

PANNENBERG, Wolfhart, 1983. *Christian Spirituality,* Philadelphia, Pa., Westminster Press.

PAULOS GREGORIOS, 1978. *The Human Presence : An Orthodox View of Nature,* Geneva, World Council of Churches.

RADCLIFFE-BROWN, A. R., 1952. 'On Social Structure' in *Structure and Function in Primitive Society: Essays and Addresses,* Routledge and Kegan Paul.

SCHILLEBEECKX, Edward, 1979. *Jesus: An Experiment in Christology,* Collins.

SCHILLER, Friedrich, 1967. *On the Aesthetic Education of Man,* Oxford University Press.

STEINER, George, 1979. 'A kind of Survivor: for Elie Wiesel' and 'Postscript' in *Language and Silence: Essays 1958-1966,* Faber and Faber.

TILLICH, Paul, 1952. *The Courage to Be,* Nisbet.

Towards a Quaker View of Sex: An essay by a group of Friends, 1963, Friends Home Service Committee.

WADDINGTON, C. H., 1978. *The Man-Made Future,* Croom Helm.

WARE, Kallistos, 1987. 'The Unity of the Human Person According to the Greek Fathers' in Arthur Peacocke and Grant Gillett, editors, *Persons and Personality*, Basil Blackwell.

WILES, Maurice, and Mark Santer, editors, 1975. *Documents in Early Christian Thought*, Cambridge University Press.

WILLIAMS, Charles, 1938. *He Came Down From Heaven*, Heinemann.

WILLIAMS, Charles, 1958. *The Image of the City and Other Essays*, Oxford University Press.

WOODWARD, James, 1990. *Embracing the Chaos: Theological Responses to AIDS*, SPCK.

INDEX

à Kempis, Thomas, 114
Abelard, Peter, 224
abortion, 91, 209
abstinence, sexual, 88
accumulation,
    of capital, 115, 167
    of material things, 50-51, 70, 94, 97,
        136
action, 236, 237
Adam, 46, 63, 93, 134, 189, 223, 226
    and Christ, 120, 230
    fall of, 120, 194-195, 229
Adam, Second, 230
Adeodatus, 92
adultery, 44, 91
Aelred of Rievaulx, St, 94
aesthetic education, 203
affirmation of individual and
    humanity, 220-221
*Against the Robbing and Murdering
    Hordes of Peasants* (Luther), 129
agape, 75
agricultural life, 166
agriculture, revolution in, 164-165
Akhmatova, Anna, 215-216
Alaric the Goth, 102
alienation, 23
Allen, Walter, 91
Alypius, 92
Ambrose of Milan, St, 90, 94-95, 97,
    100, 101
Ananias and Sapphira, 73
anger, 26
Anselm of Canterbury, St, 224
anti-Semitism, 58, 214
Antonino, St, 140
Antony of Egypt, St, 84, 85
Apolinaris, Sidonius, 94
Apology (Tertullian), 83-84, 98
Aquinas, Thomas, St, 107-113, 129,
    138, 139, 140, 144, 145, 149, 172
Archimides, 126
architecture, 126
Arians, 85
Ariès, Philippe, 137
Aristotle, 108, 139, 149
Armenians, massacre of, 214-215

Arnold, Matthew, 188
Ascent of Mount Carmel (John of the
    Cross), 121-122
ascesis, 232-233, 234
Asia, theology in, 24
Athanasius, St, 84, 85
atonement, 55, 194-195, 220, 221, 222-
    224
    theories of, 223-227
Atonement and the Modern Mind
    (Denney), 225-227
attachment, 95
Augustine of Hippo, St, 82, 90-93,
    101, 102-104, 129, 145, 189, 223,
    224, 228, 229
    Confessions, 91-92
    On the Trinity, 223
    The City of God, 102-103
Augustinianism, 190
Aurora (Boehme), 218
Ausonius, 94
authority, challenge to, 217
avarice, 98
Avila, Charles, 96, 97
Avis, Paul, 233

Bacon, Roger, 125
Bailey, Derrick S., 94
Bainton, Roland, 128
Ball, John, 170
baptism, 71, 130
Barker, Ernest, 103
Barnabas, 73
Barth, Karl, 6-8, 12-13
    Ethics, 7
    The Epistle to the Romans, 6-7
Bartholomew, D. J., 197-198
Basil the Great, St, 86, 97
Beguine movement, 114
being, nature of, 150
Benedict of Nursia, St, 86
Benedictines, 115
benevolence, 177, 178
Bergson, Henri, 204
Bernard, Jacques, 127

255